INVISIBLE WINGS

INVISIBLE WINGS

An Annotated Bibliography on Blacks in Aviation, 1916–1993

COMPILED BY
BETTY KAPLAN GUBERT

Bibliographies and Indexes in Afro-American
and African Studies, Number 32

GREENWOOD PRESS
Westport, Connecticut • London

Library of Congress Cataloging-in-Publication Data

Gubert, Betty Kaplan.
   Invisible wings : an annotated bibliography on Blacks in aviation,
1916-1993 / compiled by Betty Kaplan Gubert.
      p.   cm.—(Bibliographies and indexes in Afro-American and
African studies, ISSN 0742-6925 ; no. 32)
   Includes index.
   ISBN 0-313-28553-5 (alk. paper)
   1. Afro-Americans in aeronautics—United States—Bibliography.
2. Afro-Americans in aeronautics—United States—History.
I. Title. II. Series.
Z5065.U5G83   1994 TL521
016.6291'08996073 — dc20   93-37180

British Library Cataloguing in Publication Data is available.

Library of Congress Catalog Card Number: 93-37180
ISBN: 0-313-28553-5
ISSN: 0742-6925

First published in 1994

Greenwood Press, 88 Post Road West, Westport, CT 06881
An imprint of Greenwood Publishing Group, Inc.

Printed in the United States of America

The paper used in this book complies with the
Permanent Paper Standard issued by the National
Information Standards Organization (Z39.48-1984).

10 9 8 7 6 5 4 3 2 1

To my grandson
Daniel Robert Gubert:

Let your imagination and courage take you far
and
let these stories of brave men and women
be the wind under your wings.

Contents

Photo essay follows p. 156.

Acknowledgments

There are many people I want to thank for their assistance, which took so many forms. Friends both old and new, colleagues, family, and strangers all gave me willing support. Some found books and articles or gave me the names of important sources of information. Others proofread the manuscript, listened to endless stories, and did the unusual. My daughter Emily drove me to Hubert Julian's grave site, almost inaccessible without a car. My son and daughter-in-law, George and Karen, were wonderful hosts when I did research in Los Angeles.

Special thanks are due to the pilots who made black aviation history, and who replied to a stranger's requests with lively wit, charm, and abundance. It was a privilege to know them through letters and by telephone. They are Chauncey E. Spencer of Lynchburg, Virginia, James L.H. Peck of San Diego, California, and Dorothy A. Layne McIntyre of Cleveland, Ohio. Among the Tuskegee Airmen I would like to thank for books and other information and kindnesses, George Watson Sr. stands out. Others I was honored to know are Jason C. Arrington, Jean R. Esquerre, William C. Ferguson, and Charles E. Washington. Two pilots who are historians and who are flying now, were wonderfully generous with their time, books, articles, and encouraging friendship. I thank George F. Bailey and Joseph H. Haynes for their exceptional assistance. Thanks, too, to Joe for his suggestion of the title. Rufus A. Hunt, a pilot-historian in Chicago, was also generous. Pilot Ida Van Smith-Dunn was interested and helpful.

Appreciative thanks go to my friends and colleagues in libraries: Alice Adamczyk, Paul Bunten, Pamela Cash-Menzies, George

Cholewczynski, Timothy J. Cronen, Betty Culpepper, Johnnie Dent, Rosalind K. Goddard, Dorothy Gray, Sharon M. Howard, Glenderlyn Johnson, Melissa Keiser, Diana Lachatanere, Danny Luce, Chris McKay, Archie Motley, Otillia Pearson, Miriam Sawyer, and Larry Wilson. Other colleagues and friends whose help greatly enriched the bibliography are: June Jackson Christmas, Paula Diamond, Margaret L. Dwight, Michel Fabre, Von Hardesty, Marc T. Henderson, Dale C. Hopper, Julia Hotton, Daniel M. Johnson, Marc Anthony Bernard Julian, Anita King, Barbara Lawrence, Craig Lloyd, Antonia Martin, Berkely McCollum, Bill Miles, Patrick Miller, Lisa Mincey, Brenda Mitchell-Powell, Richard Newman (for many citations, important editorial assistance, and for his activation of the Skeel Fund of the New York Public Library, which provided financial assistance), Doris L. Rich, Theodore W. Robinson, Fay Stetner, Harriet A. Towns, Gloria Vanterpool, and Wilhelmina Wynn.

And last, but most, a grateful thank you to my husband Erminio. Without his knowledge of computers and his patience at my lack thereof, this bibliography would have needed years longer to be published.

Introduction

The idea of flight has been a powerful metaphor for freedom ever since Daedalus and Icarus escaped from prison with wings of feathers and wax. Theirs was a literal prison, but the wish to surmount ordinary life on earth and enter a purer realm, the air, has appealed to and appeared in daring minds in all times and in all countries. Ancient Egypt, medieval England, Renaissance Italy, and European countries in the eighteenth and nineteenth centuries, produced models, writings, and drawings of flying devices. They reveal the hold that soaring flight has had on the human imagination.

It was Wilbur and Orville Wright, brothers who owned a bicycle shop in Dayton, Ohio, who began the modern age of aviation near Kitty Hawk, North Carolina. On December 17, 1903 Orville, lying on the lower wing of a machine he and Wilbur had built, flew the first heavier-than-air, engine-driven airplane. It was airborne for twelve seconds. The distance he traveled was 120 feet. Little notice was taken of the flight, nor of the other three the Wrights made that day. But by 1908, after the French lionized the Wright brothers and the U.S. Army began exploring the military possibilities of the new invention, the world began its infatuation with aviation. Private air shows and the Army's public demonstrations were well-attended popular entertainments.

Flying captured the imagination of the young, the brave, and the daring of all races. Hubert F. Julian (1897-1983), as a boy of twelve in Trinidad, attended an air show. That he saw the pilot crash and die did not deter him from making and following aviation as his dream. Julian's daring exploits made him famous as the "Black Eagle" in the 1920s and

'30s. In 1917 nine-year-old Thomas C. Allen (1907-1989) was sent to guard a downed plane from cows on his family's farm in Texas. He knew then that he would fly. Allen accompanied James Herman Banning (1900-1933) on the first cross-continental flight made by African Americans. They flew from Los Angeles to New York in 1932 in a ramshackle plane and with frequent stops for repairs, and to raise money to keep going. They called themselves "The Flying Hobos." In 1927 Banning became one of the first licensed pilots in the United States.

These certainly were the pioneer black aviators. But they were not the first. There is substantial documentation that Eugene J. Bullard (1894-1961) was the first black man to fly an airplane. He was a pilot in the French Flying Corps in 1917. Two other names have been mentioned as "firsts": Lucian Arthur Hayden (with variant spellings), and Charles Wesley Peters. See bibliography entries for Jakeman, Robert, p. 331, n. 14 and Barbour, George, p.97. Bullard, born into a poor family in Georgia, was inspired by his father's stories of far-away France, a country where color prejudice was little known. As a boy, Bullard stowed away on a ship, was put ashore in Scotland, reached France, became a prize fighter, and finally joined the French Foreign Legion. After he recuperated from serious wounds received in the World War I battle of Verdun, Bullard transferred to the flying corps, where he became known as the "Black Swallow of Death." Because of race he was not accepted for active duty by the U.S. Air Corps when America entered World War I. He then remained in Paris until 1940 . Bullard operated two nightclubs and a gym, and spied for the French in World War II. France awarded him fifteen medals but he received no recognition from his own country.

The first black woman to become a pilot was Bessie Coleman (1892-1926), who earned her license in France in 1921. Coleman, the twelfth of thirteenth children, was born in Texas, also to a poor family. Reports of aerial combat in World War I inspired her to learn to fly. Her aim was not to become a fighter pilot, but believing that aviation would develop rapidly, she wanted members of her race to be part of it. Coleman was refused admission to American flying schools because she was black and a woman. She moved to Chicago, where an older brother lived. She ran a chili parlor and worked as a manicurist until she was able, with the assistance of Robert S. Abbott, to enroll in a school in France. Abbott, the founder and publisher of the *Chicago Defender*, had an interest in aviation and in the advancement of African Americans. Coleman's death in a crash while rehearsing for an air show in 1926 stunned blacks whose dreams were personified by "Brave Bessie." She was never able to realize her ambition as she said to " turn Uncle Tom's Cabin into an airplane hangar." But her own example of determination and achievement inspired and galvanized numerous African Americans to learn to fly.

Other early black aviators were William J. Powell (1899-1942), who organized the Bessie Coleman Aero Club in Los Angeles in 1929, and who wrote *Black Wings* in 1934, to interest African Americans in flying careers; and John C. Robinson (1903-1954) who organized the Challenger Air Pilots Association in Chicago in 1931. In 1935, Robinson became aviation advisor to Emperor Haile Selassie of Ethiopia. Other pilots of the Chicago group included Janet H. Waterford Bragg (1907-1993), who bought a plane for their use, Harold Hurd, Cornelius R. Coffey (1903-), and Willa B. Brown (1906-1992). Coffey and Brown established and operated the Coffey School of Aeronautics.

These are remarkable accomplishments, particularly when one considers the economic and racial climate of the 1930s. The country was paralyzed by the Great Depression, and every aspect of life was rigorously segregated. Aviation enthusiasts had to, in some cases, buy their own planes, build their own airports, and search for an instructor, or a school that would admit them. Robinson and Coffey threatened legal action to enter the Curtiss-Wright Aeronautical School in Chicago. After their success the School was then opened to other blacks. Every one of these pilots had to overcome the obstacles of limited finances and the pervasive racism of the time, which denied them the chance to learn, and then ridiculed them for incompetence. In fact, a study conducted by the Army Central Staff College in 1925 concluded that the American Negro had not developed leadership qualities, was mentally inferior, and had inherent weakness of character. He was also lazy and not physically active, according to the 1925 report.

These opinions were general in white America, but African Americans knew that if given the opportunity they could become aviators, or, for that matter, anything else. And success would decrease the most virulent forms of racism by undermining its claims of black inferiority. Members of the black aviation community were always aware that they worked not only for their own personal freedom in the skies, but also with the expectation that their accomplishment would improve life on the ground. To this end, C. Alfred Anderson (1907-   ) and Dr. Albert E. Forsythe (1898-1986) undertook their Good Will Flights in 1934, in a plane they named the "Spirit of Booker T. Washington." Anderson was the first black airline transport pilot in the U.S., and later became the chief instructor at the Tuskegee Air School. Chauncey E. Spencer (1906-   ), whose personal papers are at the Bentley Library of the University of Michigan at Ann Arbor, and Dale L. White, founding members of the National Airmen's Association of America in 1939, flew to Washington, D.C. that year. They little realized the far-reaching effect their flight would have. They wanted blacks to be included in the new Civilian Pilot Training Program (CPTP), which was being formed to provide a reserve group of pilots in case of war. In a chance meeting with Senator Harry S. Truman of Missouri the fliers stated their case, surprising him with the news that blacks were not included. Legislation was later passed, and separate training programs were established. Nine years later, as President, Truman boldly desegregated the Armed Forces with Executive Order 9981. The performance of the separate African-American air force undoubtedly was a factor in Truman's decision. And that decision stands as a landmark event in the long struggle for civil rights.

The CPTP was responsible for training 400,000 pilots. Of these, 2,700 were African Americans. Primary training took place at six black colleges (Delaware State College, Hampton Institute, Howard

University, North Carolina Agricultural and Technical State University, Tuskegee Institute, and West Virginia State College), and at the Coffey School of Aeronautics in Chicago run by Willa Brown. Tuskegee became the main training center and offered secondary training. The 99th Pursuit Squadron was formed in March 1941, and in June 1942, the first five black pilots, out of an original class of twelve, received their wings. They were Benjamin O. Davis Jr. (1912-), George Spencer Roberts, Mac Ross, Charles DeBow, and Lemuel R. Custis. It was not until April 1943, however, that the 99th, as part of the 332nd Fighter Group, was permitted to go into combat. Other components of the group were the 100th, 301st, and 302nd divisions. Their record was outstanding. By the end of the war in Europe in April 1945, 450 pilots had flown 1,578 missions and 15, 533 sorties with the 12th and 15th Air Forces. They destroyed or damaged 409 enemy aircraft. They won 150 Distinguished Flying Crosses, fourteen Bronze Stars, and one Silver Star. Davis, their commander, became in 1965 the first black three-star general. He retired in 1970.

Some of the heroes of World War II are Lee A. Archer, Charles Hall, Clarence D. Lester, and Louis R. Purnell. Daniel "Chappie" James Jr. (1920-1978) was a Tuskegee Airman who did not see combat in World War II, but he did fly in the Korean and Vietnam wars. He later, in 1975, became the Air Force's first black four-star general, and then commander of the North Atlantic Air Defense Command (NORAD). Many other Tuskegee Airmen achieved prominence outside the field of aviation. Some of the best known are Roscoe C. Brown, president of Bronx Community College; William T. Coleman, Secretary of Transportation during the Ford Administration; Albert Murray, author and professor; Lloyd Richards, retired dean of the Yale School of Drama; Percy Sutton, former Borough President of Manhattan; and Coleman Young, Mayor of Detroit. Among those who served in the Air Force, during the war and after, may be counted artists Ed Clark, Houston Conwill, Tom Feelings, James Hampton, and Ronald Joseph. Derrick A. Bell, the civil rights lawyer and professor, was in the Air Force from

1952-1954. The first black pilot in the Marine Corps was Frank E. Petersen Jr., who was commissioned in 1952. Twenty-seven years later he became the first black general in the Marine Corps.

A pilot who flew during the Spanish Civil War in 1937 was James Lincoln Holt Peck (1912-   ). Peck, however, was not accepted by the U.S. Army Air Corps. He has written extensively on aviation and scientific subjects for 56 years, and he is completing his third book now. After holding various editorial positions for *Aviation News*, *Argosy*, and *Popular Science*, Peck worked in the aerospace industry from 1959 to 1981, writing scientific documents and manuals for the Mercury and Gemini space programs.

When the war ended, African-Americans believed, as they had after all other wars, that their participation would help open up economic and other opportunities at home in the United States. Although they had proven themselves patriotic, competent, and heroic, they still encountered racism. The skills of this large pool of trained pilots and mechanics were not wanted. An African American who wanted to become a pilot or a stewardess (as flight attendants were then called) often had to face years of litigation. Perry H. Young Jr. (1920-) tried from 1945 to fly for an American airline. In December 1956 he became the first black to break aviation's color barrier when he became a helicopter pilot for New York Airways, the world's first regularly-scheduled helicopter line.

Marlon D. Green (1930-) went to work for Continental in 1965, after his case had been in the courts for seven years. Green had been a captain in the Air Force for nine years. Ruth C. Taylor became in December 1957 the first black stewardess, hired by Mohawk, a domestic airline. She was assisted by the New York State Commission Against Discrimination (SCAD). Around the same time, Margaret Grant became the first black hostess on an international line, TWA. She was hired after a suit was brought against TWA by Dorothy Franklin, who dropped the suit after TWA agreed to hire "a Negro girl," but not necessarily Franklin. By 1958 Grant was discovered to have " a rare disability," and Taylor had left to marry, so Perry Young remained the only African American in commercial aviation. In 1992 the Organization of Black Airline Pilots noted that only 600 of the 72,000 commercial pilots are black.

Some airports continued to segregate restaurants, waiting rooms, and washrooms despite a U.S. ban. Montgomery, Alabama's airport, in 1962, threatened to close these facilities if they had to integrate them. In 1961 African-American diners were still sometimes required to eat behind a screen at southern airports.

After the Russians succeeded in sending a man into space in 1957 the United States stepped up its own aerospace program. Edward Dwight was the first black astronaut candidate, from 1962 until his resignation in 1966. Many theories have been advanced to account for his stormy time with NASA. The next black astronaut candidate was Robert H. Lawrence (1935-1967), a pilot with a Ph.D. in physical chemistry. His death in a plane accident in 1967 left the space program without an African American astronaut candidate until 1978, when three were chosen: Guion S. Bluford Jr., Frederick D. Gregory, and Ronald E. McNair. All three have doctorates and Bluford and Gregory are pilots. In 1983 Bluford became the first African American to explore space. The first black man in space, however, was a Cuban, Arnaldo Tamayo Mendez who participated in the Soviet Union's Soyez 8 launch in 1980. Other current black American astronauts are Charles F. Bolden, Mae C. Jemison, and Bernard A. Harris Jr. In September 1992 Jemison became the first black woman to go into space.

It is evident that there are still enormous barriers to overcome if one is black and wants a career in aviation. This brief overview of the role African Americans have played in aeronautics, and the following bibliography itself, is designed to interest and stimulate students, researchers, and scholars. My hope is that the bibliography will be a beginning, an incentive that will lead to both scholarly and popular works that will reveal the mainly invisible achievements of these men and women who made their dream of flying come true, against powerful odds.

Notes to the User

This bibliography is arranged by broad chronological sections beginning with "The Pioneers" of African-American aviation. Entries within these large units are then arranged by major figures such as Eugene J. Bullard. The citations under Bullard are listed alphabetically by author, or by title, if the article is unsigned. In addition to these chronological periods, other chapters cover such topics as "Women" and "Discrimination." Here, too, entries are arranged alphabetically by author, or by title if there is no author.

Because some articles may cover numerous subjects, the index must be consulted for more finely-tuned access. Articles where Bullard is only mentioned instead of being the primary subject will be found under his name here in the index. It includes names of persons, places, organizations, and events. The name of some individuals listed in the index may not be mentioned in the corresponding annotation. But these persons are indeed cited in the article, and the reader may refer to it to find information about them.

Subjects such as "Art," "Statistics," and "Prisoners of War" are included. Chicago is the only city with its own heading because of its role in the history of black aviation. Articles which discuss other cities can be found under the name of the state where they are located. The women who have their own sections - Willa B. Brown, Bessie Coleman, and Mae C. Jemison - are not listed under "Women." Women should be checked under all the names they used: Pearl Marshall Beard, Janet Harmon Waterford Bragg, and Dorothy Layne McIntyre.

I would like to think that this bibliography is complete, but I know it is not: none is. I have been unable, for example, to locate any substantive article on Dr. Bernard A. Harris Jr., who became an astronaut in

1990. For further information the reader should consult the *Kaiser Index to Black Resources 1948-1986* (Carlson Publishing, 1992), and the Black Military Oral History Project at the Moorland-Spingarn Research Center at Howard University. To see the actual articles, especially those with incomplete bibliographic citations, the reader is referred to the clipping files at the Schomburg Center for Research in Black Culture, New York Public Library, the Claude A. Barnett Papers at the Chicago Historical Society, the Alexander Gumby Scrapbooks at Columbia University, and the library and archives of the National Air and Space Museum of the Smithsonian Institution. Schomburg's clipping files are available on microfiche; the Gumby Scrapbooks and the Barnett Papers are available on microfilm. Black newspapers (1940-1945) were filled with war news as it affected African Americans. The names of pilots or ground crewmen that may be found reflect the pride of home towns, and provide additional hard-to-find information.

The Pioneers

Eugene J. Bullard

1. Allen, Stookie. "Above the Crowd." [No source, no date. Stookie Allen worked for the *New York Mirror*, but this is probably from a black newspaper]. Cartoon depicting Eugene J. Bullard's exploits and giving biographical information.

2. Apple, Nick. "Flying High in AF Museum." *Columbus Ledger-Enquirer* (February 13, 1990): C-1. The Air Force Museum near Dayton, Ohio, has mounted an exhibition about the accomplishments of American black aviators. The fifteen medals Eugene J. Bullard earned from France are on display, as are photographs. Biographical information about Bullard and Mac Ross, Charles B. Hall, and John L. Hamilton.

3. "Art Focus: Eddie Dixon." *Black Ethnic Collectibles* 5:3 (Fall 1992): 33-34. Eddie Dixon has sculpted two bronze figures of Eugene J. Bullard. No information is given about these figures, but the two photographs on p. 34 are detailed and clear.

4. "Artifacts." *Air & Space* (December 1992/January 1993): 21. A photograph, in color, shows the bust of Eugene Jacques Bullard that was unveiled in October at the Museum. The sculptor is Eddie Dixon, the donor was the McDonnell Douglas Foundation, and the sculpture may be seen in the World War I gallery.

5. Bechet, Sidney. *Treat it Gentle*. New York: Hill and Wang, 1960. The memoirs of the jazz clarinetist, told in his own words. He tells how he became involved in a gun fight in Paris and went to jail for 11 months. He describes the help of Gene Bullard, here spelled Boulard, on pp. 153-154, 156, as both financial and psychological. "Gene was a real man about

Paris; he had a way... Gene had no meaness in him. He'd make himself the kind of man people around Paris had a need for. The cabarets, the clubs, the musicianers - when there was some trouble they couldn't straighten out by themselves, they called on Gene. He was a man you could count on."

6. Benham, Liza. "From Columbus to French Army, Air Corps." *Columbus Ledger-Enquirer* (June 11, 1982): A-6. Biographical information on Eugene J. Bullard from articles by Will Irwin and Herbert M. Mason (see bibliography entries).

7. Benham, Liza. "World's First Black Aviator Remembered as Trailblazer." *Columbus Ledger-Enquirer* (November 19, 1988): A-3. Ceremonies were held at Gunter AFB in Montgomery, Alabama to honor Eugene J. Bullard. A dormitory at the base was named for him. Later there was a luncheon at Columbus College, sponsored by Craig Lloyd, who is writing a biography of Bullard. There are quotations by Lloyd and by Bullard's daughter and grandson, Richard Reid. A great-grandson, Kenneth Reid, is also mentioned.

8. "Bullard, Former U.S.A. Subject, Weds Paris Girl." *Chicago Defender* (September 1, 1923): 1. [Part Two]. Eugene Bullard married Marcelle Straumann on July 17, 1923 at the mayoralty of the 10th arrondissement.

9. Burke, James Wakefield. "The Black Eagle." *Retired Officer* (May 1984): 28-31. Biographical information about Eugene Bullard, much of it taken from his journal, and describes battles he fought in during World War I. Describes his death.

10. Burson, Pat. "State Inducting Seven into Aviation Hall of Fame." *Atlanta Journal and Constitution* (August 27, 1989): B 5. In April the governor signed a bill to establish the Georgia Aviation Hall of Fame at the Museum of Aviation at Robins AFB. Eugene Jacques Bullard, born in Georgia and the world's first black military pilot, is one of the seven to be honored.

11. Byrne, Mary Margaret. "Following the Legend of Eugene Bullard." *Columbus Ledger-Enquirer* (February 5, 1989): A-9. The article reports on the efforts to assemble information on the life of Eugene J. Bullard, a native of Columbus, Georgia. The man most responsible for the effort is

Craig Lloyd, professor of history and director of archives at Columbus College.

12. Carisella, P. J., and James W. Ryan. *The Black Swallow of Death: The Incredible Story of Eugene Jacques Bullard, The World's First Black Combat Aviator*. Boston: Marlborough House; dist. by Van Nostrand Reinhold, 1972. This biography quotes profusely from Bullard's journal which was placed at the authors' disposal.

13. Chilton, John. *Sidney Bechet: The Wizard of Jazz*. New York: Oxford, 1987. Biographical information on Eugene Bullard when he was in Paris. Bullard was Bechet's friend and testified at his trial. Bullard is described as brave, reckless, and flamboyant, pp. 82, 84.

14. Curtis, Albert. "Bullard, French Ace, Wins 'Truth' Fight." *Chicago Defender* (June 16, 1923): 1, 3. Eugene Bullard won his case against the *Chicago Daily Tribune* and the *New York Daily News* (Paris editions). French law required the *Tribune* in Paris to publish Bullard's own account in the same length as the incorrect article. It appeared on p.1, and it is reprinted here in its entirety. Information about his war service with quotations from his military dossier. Bullard was, according to French law, a French citizen because his father was from Martinique.

15. Curtis, Albert. "French Hero, Georgia Born, Whips White Bully in Paris." *Chicago Defender* (January 26, 1923): 1. Curtis corrects the story in an American newspaper that Eugene Bullard had assaulted two white Americans and the wife of one of them outside a restaurant. "The entire story is a lie." Bullard was defending himself, and was released by the police, while the others were held. There is biographical information, and there are references to his war record. The article further states he is interested in starting an aviation school in France for members of his race, and he is acquainted with Bessie Coleman.

16. Driggs, Frank. *Black Beauty, White Heat: A Pictorial History of Classic Jazz 1920-1950*. New York: William Morrow and Company, 1982. Bullard is pictured on p. 210 with others in the house band at Joe Zelli's Royal Box. Bullard played the drums. "Few Montmartre nightclubs were better known... "

17. "Eugene Bullard, Ex-Pilot, Dead; American Flew for French in '18." *New York Times* (October 21, 1961): 23. Obituary.

18. "Eugene J. Bullard." *Jet* (November 5, 1959): 17. Member of the French Underground in World War II, Bullard is awarded France's highest civilian decoration, Chevalier of the Legion of Honor.

19. "French Air Chief Has Negro Pilot." *New York Amsterdam News* (January 7, 1956): 1, 27. General Martial Valin of the French Air Force has a black aide-de-camp and pilot, Hubert Cournal, who was born in Martinique. They stopped in New York en route to Ciudad Trujillo, and attended a champagne party at the home of Eugene Bullard.

20. "French Hero, a Man with 2 Countries, Dies." *Jet* (November 2, 1961): 7. Biographical information about Eugene Bullard, including "leaving a manuscript of his autobiography, which he hoped poet [Langston] Hughes would proofread."

21. "Gene Bullard, French War Hero, is Dead." *New York Amsterdam News* (October 21, 1961): 1, 13. Obituary.

22. Genet, Edmond Charles Clinton. *An American for Lafayette: The Diaries of E.C.C. Genet Lafayette Escadrille*. Charlottesville, VA: University Press of Virginia, 1981. [Edited by Walt Brown Jr.] In the entry dated October 5, 1916 Genet writes, "Bullard the American niger [sic] came here today to learn mitrailleuse." The editor notes Bullard was in the Foreign Legion then, and was transferred to the French Aviation Service on November 30, 1916.

23. Gerdes, Carol. "Mr. Eugene Bullard Finally Receives Overdue Recognition." *Columbus Times (Georgia)* (December 30, 1988): A-1, A-4. Eugene J. Bullard was honored at Gunter Air Force Base in Montgomery, Alabama, with the dedication of a life-size portrait in Heritage Hall. He was also honored at the Columbus Museum. Attendees at the ceremonies included his daughter Jacqueline O'Garro and his grandsons, Richard and Keith Reid.

24. Gierer, Larry. "'Black Swallow': Dendy Wants Recognition for Columbus War Hero." *Columbus Ledger-Enquirer* (September 6, 1992): E-1, E-3. Edmond Dendy has completed a manuscript about the life of Eugene J. Bullard, which he calls *Chameleon*, because Bullard was a pilot, boxer, drummer, entrepreneur, and spy. He hopes to have it published. He has commissioned a full length portrait of Bullard. Biographical information about both Bullard and Dendy.

25. Goffin, Robert. *Horn of Plenty: The Story of Louis Armstrong*. New York: Allen, Towne and Heath, 1947. In 1933 Louis Armstrong returned to his flat in Paris after triumphs in major European cities, except for those in Germany. Author states he took his "daily dozen" at [Eugene] Bullard's Gym.

26. Hall, James Norman, and Charles Bernard Nordhoff. *The Lafayette Flying Corps*. Port Washington, NY: Kennikat Press, 1964. [Reprint of the 1920 edition]. In volume I, on p. 151 is the service record of Eugene J. Bullard, a photograph and a personal memoir: "... a vision of military splendor such as one does not see twice in a lifetime. ... There was scarcely an American at Avord [the location of an aviation school] who did not know and like Bullard." In volume II, composed of letters, on p. 21, there is a description of a colored boxer, a corporal, who is clearly Bullard. Comments on his medals, wounds, bravery, knowledge of French, and considerable personal charm. The letter is dated Avord, July 22, 1917.

27. Haskins, James. *Bricktop*. New York: Atheneum, 1983. Information on Eugene Bullard: pp.82, 84-88, 118-119, 145, 167, 203.

28. Hodges, R. H. "The Lafayette Escadrille and Its 'Ringers'." *New York Times* (September 7, 1983). [Letter to the Editor]. Hodges writes Bullard was not a member of the official Nieuport 124 L'Escadrille Lafayette de Chasse, but he was listed in the roster of the Lafayette Flying Corps. He gives authors and titles to prove his point.

29. Irwin, Will. "Flashes from the War Zone." *Saturday Evening Post* (July 15, 1916): 12-13. Author reports from a French hospital during World War I. Recounts conversation between the U.S. Consul and the " wounded American Pvt. Eugene So-and-So of the this-or-that infantry regiment." At first he has Pvt. Gene speak in broad dialect but then he quotes his description in standard English of the terrible battles at Verdun, Arras, and Champagne. He then describes him: "He wasn't at all the negro [*sic*] we know at home. War and heroism had given him an air of authority. He was a young black Hercules, a monument of trained muscle. The democracy of the French army had brushed off onto him." He goes on to quote Bullard as he expresses sympathy for the men they killed.

30. Julian, Bea. "Codes and Ciphers: Secret Keys in Sharing Messages." *Ebony, Jr!* 10:8 (February 1983): 8-11, 44. An article for children about

codes. There is coded information on Hubert F. Julian and Eugene J. Bullard, with answers on p. 44.

31. Mason, Herbert Molloy. *High Flew the Falcons: The French Aces of World War I.* Philadelphia: Lippincott, 1965. Molloy has used many sources to retell the details of Eugene Bullard's life from childhood to his death. He terms him the planet's first pure-black aviator and the only American Negro to fly in combat in World War I. He concludes, "He died as he had lived - just game as hell," pp.152-167.

32. "Museum to Honor Pioneering Pilot." *Columbus Ledger-Enquirer* (October 12, 1992): B-1. The Smithsonian Institution will hold ceremonies to honor the achievements of Eugene J. Bullard. Interview with Dom Pisano, deputy chairman of the National Air and Space Museum's Aeronautics Department, about Bullard.

33. "National Air and Space Museum Unveils Bust of First Black Combat Pilot." *New York Voice* (October 15-21, 1992): 11. In a private ceremony on October 14, a portrait bust of Eugene Jacques Bullard was unveiled at the Museum. Gen. Benjamin O. Davis Jr. participated in the program. The sculpture will be displayed in the World War I gallery. The sculptor is Eddie Dixon. Biographical information.

34. Perry, Kimball. "Columbus War Hero who Battled Racial Woes to be Inducted in Georgia Hall of Fame." *Columbus Ledger-Enquirer* (August 26, 1989): A-3. Eugene J. Bullard will be in the first group of flyers inducted into the Georgia Aviation Hall of Fame at Warner Robins AFB.

35. Rampersad, Arnold. *The Life of Langston Hughes.* New York: Oxford, 1986. Vol.I; 1902-1941 *I, Too, Sing America* contains references to Eugene Bullard on pp.85, 341.

36. Robeson, Susan. *The Whole World in His Hands: A Pictorial Biography of Paul Robeson.* Secaucus, NJ: Citadel Press, 1981. There are four photographs of Eugene J. Bullard, here spelled Ballard, being beaten by policemen at Robeson's concert at Peekskill, NY, on September 4, 1949, pp.182-183.

37. Roosevelt, Eleanor. "My Day." *New York Post* (November 1, 1959). Report of "a very interesting little ceremony" which took place on October 9, at the Consulate General of France in New York. Eugene J. Bullard, the

grandson of a slave, became a Chevalier of the Legion of Honor of France.

38. Rose, Phyllis. *Jazz Cleopatra: Josephine Baker in Her Time*. New York: Doubleday, 1989. Eugene Bullard in Paris as a nightclub manager, p. 69.

39. Ryan, James W. "America's Neglected Knight." *Newsday* (February 18, 1984): 1-3. [Part II]. A lengthy account of the life of Eugene Bullard, by one of his biographers.

40. Shannon, Anthony. *New York World Telegram* (October 10, 1959). [This article is reprinted in Carisella and Ryan, *The Black Swallow of Death*, pp. 255-257]. Report of Eugene J. Bullard's installation as a Knight of the Legion of Honor, his fifteenth French decoration. The ceremony took place at the Consulate General of France at 934 Fifth Avenue. Biographical information with comments by Bullard.

41. Smith, Mary H. "The Incredible Life of Monsieur Bullard." *Ebony* (December 1967): 120-122, 124-126, 128. Details the many activities of Eugene Jacques Bullard, the first black aviator in the world. He got his license in France in 1917, served in both world wars for the French, owned night clubs and a gym in Paris. He received 15 French medals. "On or off the battlefield, nothing but death could stop this red-hot swinger."

42. Teasley, Luke. "J. Bullard, Negro Hero Identified." *Columbus Ledger-Enquirer* [after December 12, 1961]: In response to the earlier column, Teasley was contacted by Henry Walker, who knew Eugene J. Bullard as a child. Biographical information.

43. Teasley, Luke. "Who Knows J. Bullard, Negro Hero?" *Columbus Ledger-Enquirer* (December 12, 1961). A story from UPI and a clipping sent from New York inpired the author to ask the question about Eugene J. Bullard, a native of Columbus, Georgia. He retells the biographical facts from the obituaries.

44. Vecsey, George, and George C. Dade. *Getting Off the Ground: The Pioneers of Aviation Speak For Themselves*. New York: Dutton, 1979. James H. McMillen, in Chapter 7, pp.65-66, describes "his buddy" Eugene Bullard.

45. Wallace, Irving, David Wallechinsky, and Amy Wallace. "The Black Swallow." *Boston Globe* (September 26, 1982). Biographical information about Eugene Bullard.

Bessie Coleman

46. Allison, Madeline G. "The Horizon." *Crisis* (December 1922): 74-75. "Among those present at the Paris session of the Second Pan-African Congress was a colored girl, Bessie Coleman." The article claims Coleman went to France as a nurse during the war, and later received instruction in flying. She received a French pilot's license, and according to the article, one in Germany. She flew planes in Holland and America.

47. "Aviatrix Must Sign Away Life to Learn Trade." *Chicago Defender* (October 8, 1921). A lengthy interview of Bessie Coleman by an unnamed reporter. Coleman describes her training in France, the kinds of planes she has flown and those she plans to fly, and gives her opinions on the need for "men and women of the Race" to be represented in this most important line.

48. Bergman, Peter. *The Chronological History of the Negro in America*. New York: Harper & Row, 1969. Notes the death of Bessie Coleman in 1926, p. 426.

49. "Bessie Coleman and White Pilot in 2,000 Ft. Crash." *New York Amsterdam News* (May 6, 1926). Bessie Coleman and William D. Wills died in a plane crash on April 30, in Jacksonville, Florida. Lengthy description of the accident, and speculation as to its cause.

50. "Bessie Coleman, Aviatrix, Killed." *Chicago Defender* (May 8, 1926). A long detailed article of the crash and its aftermath, including the funeral service and biographical information.

51. "Bessie Coleman Back in the U.S." *Hotel Tattler [New York]* (August 20, 1922). "...the only person of our race to complete a course of aviation in the world..." Describes her stay in Europe (France, Belgium, Holland, and Germany) and her plans for travel in the United States.

52. "Bessie Coleman Leaves New York for France." *Chicago Defender* (February 25, 1922). Miss Coleman will purchase planes in France for

her school of aviation. While in New York she stayed with her aunt on 136th Street, and spoke at the Metropolitan Baptist Church.

53. "Bessie Gets Away, Does Her Stuff." *Chicago Defender* (September 9, 1922). After Miss Coleman's performance, Dr. Herbert [*sic*] Julian, who was connected with the Canadian Aviation Corps during the war, thrilled the spectators with a parachute jump from a Curtis plane from over 2,000 feet and landed without injury.

54. "Bessie in Booster Role." *Chicago Defender* (June 23, 1923). Photograph of Bessie Coleman advertising the Coast Tire & Rubber Company of Oakland, California. "Miss Coleman has the distinction of being the only American flyer who has ever flown over the ex-kaiser's palace in Berlin."

55. "Bessie to Fly Over Gotham." *Chicago Defender* (August 26, 1922). "Chicago aviatrix to show New Yorkers how she does her stuff." Bessie Coleman will give an exhibition in her own plane at Curtiss Field in New York on August 27. This will be her first flight in America. She has just returned from seven months abroad. Information about the experiences abroad.

56. Brown, Ross D. *Afro-American World Almanac.* Chicago: The author, 1948. Bessie Coleman, pp.85-86. Brown provides short alliterative paragraphs to tell the story of Bessie Coleman. "She believed in service rather than sentiments, she loved performance better than pleasure, she gave exhibitions and not excuses."

57. Calloway, Earl. "CAP Association to Honor Pilot Bessie Coleman." *Chicago Defender* (April 25, 1991): 29. Chicago American Pilots Association, Inc. will honor Bessie Coleman on Saturday April 27 by flying over her grave to drop flowers on the site. Mayor Daley will proclaim that day "Bessie Coleman Day." Photo of Sylvia Stallworth, Coleman's grand niece and of Juan C.Haygood, flight leader.

58. "Chicago Girl is a Full-Fledged Aviatrix Now." *Chicago Defender* (October 1, 1921). [Another article in the *New York Age* (October 1, 1921), p. 1]. Bessie Coleman returned to the United States after ten months in France. She completed her courses at the Condrau School of Aviation in Somme. "With the exception of Miss Coleman and a Chinese woman, all aviatrix are white."

59. "Chicago Pays Parting Tribute to 'Brave Bessie' Coleman." *Chicago Defender* (May 15, 1926). A long description of Coleman's last rites at Pilgrim Baptist Church in Chicago. Ida B. Wells Barnett was the mistress of ceremonies, and it was estimated that 10, 000 people viewed the body.

60. "Colored Aviatrix Bobs Up Again." *Air Service News Letter* 7 (February 20, 1923). "Our correspondent from Rockwell Field, Coronado, California, informs us that Miss Coleman recently purchased three Curtiss airplanes...and is supervising the testing of these ships which will be sent to San Francisco." The correspondent further reports on her clothes (O.D. breeches instead of short skirts) and quotes her saying she went to France to drink wine and learn to fly. He comments she has been successful in the latter aim, but cannot comment on the former.

61. "Colored Girl Learns to Fly Abroad." *Aerial Age Weekly* (October 17, 1921): 125. [This article also apears in *New York Tribune* (September 26, 1921)]. Bessie Coleman arrived in New York on the Manchuria, after studying aviation in France for ten months. She brought with her credentials certifying she had qualified as an aviatrix.She is having a special Nieuport scout plane built for her in France, and she hopes to inspire people of her race to take up aviation.

62. "Detroit Council Votes to Name Building for Pilot Bessie Coleman." *Michigan Chronicle* (November 7, 1981): A9.

63. Eliot, Ralph. "Bessie Coleman Says Good Will Come From Hurt." *Chicago Defender* (March 10, 1923). Interviewed from her hospital bed in Santa Monica, California, Bessie Coleman is still full of plans to fly again and to open a school that Negroes may attend. She is fearful that her people will not grasp the opportunity to get in on something that will be of value to them later. Coleman broke her leg in a plane accident. Numerous experiences recounted, as are her opinions.

64. "Entertainment." *Chicago Defender* (April 28, 1990): 35. The Chicago American Pilots Association, along with affiliates of the Detroit and New York Negro Airmen International, will once again pay tribute to Bessie Coleman by dropping flowers on her grave. Rufus Hunt, aviation historian, will participate and the lead pilot will be Juan C. Haygood. A service road to O'Hare Airport will be renamed Bessie Coleman Drive. Photograph of nineteen people, but none is identified.

65. "First Black Aviatrix Honored." *Chicago Defender* (April 30, 1984): 16. Chicago American Pilots Association observed its annual memorial to Bessie Coleman by dropping a wreath on her grave from a plane. The lead aircraft was piloted by Ann Baker and Rufus Hunt.

66. "The 1st Black Woman Flyer." *Chicago Tribune* (May 8, 1980). Rufus Hunt, technician at the Aurora air traffic control center, brought his light plane low over the cemetery, and aimed a wreath at the white sheet spread by Bessie Coleman's nieces and nephews near her marble marker. She is buried in Lincoln Cemetery at 123rd Street and Kedzie. Inscription on tombstone is included in the article.

67. Freydberg, Elizabeth Hadley. *Bessie Coleman: The Brownskin Lady Bird.* : Indiana University, 1990. This dissertation will be published by Garland Publishing, 1994.

68. Goodrich, James. "Salute to Bessie Coleman." *Negro Digest* (May 1950): 82-83. On Memorial Day over 25 Negro-manned planes will fly over Lincoln Cemetery to allow women passengers to drop flowers on Coleman's grave. Cornelius Coffey started this tribute in 1937 with one plane. Today only 50 Negro women hold commercial pilots licenses.

69. "Harlem's Newest Apartments Named after Black 'Joan of Arc'." *New York News* (July 23, 1927). [An advertisement for Coleman Manor appears in *Opportunity* (November 1927). The location is 140th Street and Edgecombe Avenue, and is described as exclusive and luxurious, with parquet and oak floors and other amenities]. The apartment building, named for Bessie Coleman, is called Coleman Manor and is at St. Nicholas Avenue and 140th Street.

70. Hodgman, Ann, and Rudy Djabbaroff. *Skystars: The History of Women in Aviation.* New York: Atheneum, 1981. Bessie Coleman, pp.35-37. A book for young adults.

71. Holden, Henry M. "Brave Bessie the Barnstormer." *Sisters* 2:4 (Spring 1989): 6-8. Biographical information, with many quotations from Coleman.

72. Hunt, Rufus A. "First Pilot Was a Woman." *Afro-American (Baltimore)* (August 8, 1981): 5. [Dawn Magazine, a supplement to various black newspapers]. Biographical information, and mention of relatives in the

Chicago area: Marion Coleman, Gigi Coleman, Vera Ramey, Carol Ramey, and Arthur Freeman. A special memorial program for Coleman was held on April 27, 1979 at the Du Sable Museum of Afro-American History.

73. Hunt, Rufus. "A Page from Chicago's Aviation History." *Chicago Defender* (May 2, 1981): 10. Mostly about Bessie Coleman, although other pilots are mentioned. Photograph of pilot/author Rufus A. Hunt and Janet Harmon Waterford Bragg.

74. Johnson, Laverne C. *Bessie Coleman*. Chicago: Empak Publishing Company, 1992. [An Empak "Black History" publication. The Empak Heritage Kids, Kumi and Chanti, tell the story of Bessie Coleman]. Picture book of the life of Bessie Coleman.

75. Kelly, John. "Those Barnstorming Women." *The Sun (Washington, D.C.)* (April 9, 1984): D1, 3. Information about Bessie Coleman on p. D3, in a review of *United States Women in Aviation, 1919-1929* by Kathleen Brooks-Pazmany.

76. King, Anita. "Brave Bessie: First Black Pilot." *Essence* 7 (May 1976; June 1976): 36, 48. One of the earliest and fullest accounts of Coleman's life. In two parts.

77. Kriz, Marjorie. "Black Bessie: A Pioneer in Aviation." *Chicago Defender* (February 5, 1980): 11. Kriz provides historical background, especially for the activities in Chicago.

78. Kriz, Marjorie. "First Licensed Black Pilot is a Woman." [U.S.Department of Transportatiion News: Federal Aviation Administratiion, Great Lakes Region. Press release ?, 4 pages]. Biographical information.

79. "LTE on why Bessie Coleman Should have a Stamp Honoring Her." *Chicago Defender* (March 25, 1985): 10.

80. Molotsky, Irwin. "Pioneers: Women who Led the Way in Aviation." *New York Times* (November 25, 1985): C 12. Coleman is included in *United States Women in Aviation: 1930-1939* by Claudia M. Oakes, a series published by the Smithsonian Institution.

81. Moolman, Valerie. *Women Aloft*. Alexandria, VA: Time-Life Books, 1981. Bessie Coleman, pp.44-45.

82. "Negress in Flying Show." *New York Times* (August 27, 1922): 2. Bessie Coleman will give an exhibition this afternoon at Curtiss Field, New York. According to German newspapers she flew, without a lesson, the largest plane ever piloted by a woman. She also flew a seaplane which required unusual aeronautical skill.

83. "Negress Pilots Airplane." *New York Times* (September 4, 1922): 9. Bessie Coleman made three short flights at Curtiss Field, Garden City, L.I. This was her first experience with an American machine. The exhibition was in honor of the Fifteenth Infantry regiment. The regiment is described as negro [*sic*]. Hubert Julian, an officer of the Negro Improvement Association, made a parachute jump. There were 1,000 spectators, mostly negroes [*sic*].

84. "Negro Aviatrix Arrives." *New York Times* (August 14, 1922): 4. Bessie Coleman, termed by leading French and German aviators one of the best flyers they had seen, returned from Europe yesterday.

85. "Negro Aviatrix to Tour the Country." *Air Service News Letter* (November 1, 1921): 11. Report on the return of Bessie Coleman from France, as a full-fledged aviatrix, said to be the first of her race. She plans to engage in exhibition flying.

86. Patterson, Elois. *Memoirs of the Late Bessie Coleman Aviatrix: Pioneer of the Negro People in Aviation*. : The author, 1969. [As far as can be determined, this 13-page pamphlet is only at the Library of Congress and on microfiche at the Schomburg Center for Research in Black Culture, New York Public Library]. Patterson, Coleman's sister, covers her life and includes many personal stories and descriptions of the family, and of Coleman's childhood.

87. "Plans Flight." *Chicago Defender* (September 22, 1923). Bessie Coleman will make an exhibition flight at Chicago Air Park, after which she will take passengers up at $5 each. She has just returned from an exhibition in Columbus, and will leave immediately for an exhibition tour of the south.

88. Poindexter, J. Blaine. "Bessie Coleman Makes Initial Aerial Flight." *Chicago Defender* (October 21, 1922). Bessie Coleman performed stunts for a crowd of 2,000 spectators at Checkerboard airdrome. Some of the stunts were the Spanish Bertha Costa Climb, the American Curtis McMullen Turn, the Eddie Rickenbacker Straightenup, and the Richtofer German Glide. She has given engagements in five different cities.

89. "Recalls Exploits of Brave Bessie Coleman on 10th Anniversary of Tragedy." *Chicago Defender* (May 9, 1936): 12. Biographical article.

90. Rich, Doris L. *Queen Bess: African American Aviator*. Washington, D.C.: Smithsonian Institution Press, 1993. [Rich is the author of a biography of Amelia Earhart]. This biography of Bessie Coleman is scheduled for publication for fall 1993.

91. Robb, Frederic H. *The Negro in Chicago 1779-1927*. Chicago: Washington Intercollegiate Club, 1927. [Also called the 1927 Intercollegian Wonder Book]. Photographs of Bessie Coleman, the Martyr of the Air, and Dr. Davis of Kansas City, an active physician and pioneer aviator on p. 64; poem by Glynn Phillips about Coleman as well as a photograph, and a photograph of William J. Powell, owner of garage and oil stations. Powell had not yet become a pilot.

92. "Salute to a Nervy Lady." *Chicago Tribune* (May 8, 1980). The old custom of dropping flowers on Bessie Coleman's grave was revived last week. Rufus Hunt, a technician and pilot, brought his plane low over the cemetery and dropped a wreath on the site of the grave. In attendance were relatives of Coleman: Arthur Freeman, nephew; Vera Ramey, great niece; and Marian Coleman, niece. The custom died out when the Challenger Air Pilots retired from active flying.

93. "'Shuffle Along' Company Gives Fair Flyer Cup." *Chicago Defender* (October 8, 1921). Photograph of Mrs. Susan Coleman, holding the cup given to her daughter Bessie for her achievement in aviation, just after her arrival in New York from France.

94. St. Laurent, Philip. "Bessie Coleman, Aviator." *Tuesday* (January 1973): 11-12. A great deal of biographical information is given, and Coleman is put into context with other early women aviators.

95. "Students Commemorate First Black Pilot." *Chronicle of Higher Education* (May 20, 1992): A5. Students at Miami University in Oxford, Ohio have begun a drive to have Bessie Coleman commemorated on a stamp. They participated in this year's flyover at her grave in Chicago.

96. Taitt, John. *The Souvenir of Negro Progress, Chicago, 1779-1925.* Chicago: The DeSaible Association, Inc., [1925]. There are two photos of Powell's Garage and Oil Filling Station and one of William J. Powell before he became interested in aviation and went to Los Angeles, p. 51. Located at 46th Street and Wabash, the business cost $100,000 to build. On p. 61 there are two photos of Bessie Coleman in Berlin, and she is quoted as saying she wants to turn Uncle Tom's cabin into a hangar.

97. "They Take to the Sky." *Ebony* (May 1977): 89-96. The Bessie Coleman Aviators are a group of sixteen women in the midwest. They are learning to fly and hope to attract other black and minority women to aviation. Biographical information on Bessie Coleman. Carmelita Rhymer is the only licensed pilot. The others, students, are: Audrey Lee, Marilyn Smith, Diana Sims, Glenda McKissick, Dorothea Drew, Hatshepsut Thomas, Janyce Givens, Diane Ross Boswell, Philippa Neal, and Patricia Handy.

98. Waterford, Janet Harmon. "Race Interest in Aviation in Actuality Begins with Advent of Bessie Coleman." *Chicago Defender* (March 28, 1936). Biographical information on Bessie Coleman. "Deeds of intrepid young aviatrix light torch of black flyers here [Chicago]."

99. "Yesterday in Negro History." *Jet* (May 2, 1968): 11. Bessie Coleman was killed in an air show in Jacksonville, FL, on April 30, 1926.

Other Individuals and Events

100. Hart, Philip S. *Flying Free: America's First Black Aviators.* Minneapolis: Lerner, 1992. The story of blacks in aviation for children. Separate chapters on Bessie Coleman, William J. Powell, James Herman Banning, Hubert Fauntleroy Julian, the Chicago flyers, and the Tuskegee Airmen.

101. Pisano, Dominick A. *Legend, Memory and the Great War in the Air.* Seattle: University of Washington Press, 1992. There is a photograph on p. 98 which shows African mechanics from Germany's East African colonies maintaining German aircraft.

Between World Wars

Thomas C. Allen and J. Herman Banning

102. "Air Conqueror." (March 31, 1928). [Gumby Collection, Columbia University, Scrapbook #1]. Photograph of James H. Banning, licensed pilot of Ames, Iowa, who has done commercial flying in the mid west for the past four years. He constructed a plane, and then bought two others.

103. "Aircraft Co. Gets Permit to Sell $500,000 Stock." *Chicago Defender* (September 20, 1941). 6. El Capitan Aircraft Corporation has been granted a charter and permission to sell stock. The man behind this is Thomas C. Allen. The corporation is at 1251 East Olympic Boulevard in Los Angeles.

104. "Aviator Hurt When Plane Falls in Iowa." *Chicago Defender* (October 20, 1928). James H. Banning, owner of a commercial air fleet, suffered a broken leg and three broken ribs when his plane crashed during stunting in Ames.

105. Banning, J. Herman, and Thomas C. Allen. "Coast-to-Coast Via the Aerial Highways." *Pittsburgh Courier* (October 22, 1932). [This is the first of four articles by the "first airmen of race to span nation, reveal vivid story of flight." The other articles appeared October 29, November 5 and 12, all on p. 1 of the second section]. Banning and Allen recount their adventures in a swift-paced exciting way in this series. "Put on your flying togs, kind friend, because you are going to be our imaginary passenger on a very real flight. In fact, you are actually going to pilot the ship, yourself. Parachutes? No. Too much extra weight."

106. Bearden, Bessye J. "Two Fly from Coast to Coast in an Old Plane." *Chicago Defender* (October 15, 1932): 2. [Author is the mother of Romare

Bearden]. Thomas C. Allen and J. Herman Banning flew from Dycer Airport in California to Valley Stream Airport in New York. The trip took from Sept. 21 to Oct. 9, 1932, with many stops for repairs and fund raising.

107. Boettcher, Thomas D. "The Hard-Won Successes of Pioneer Black Pilots." *Christian Science Monitor* (September 30, 1982): 15. [The entire article was reprinted in the *Los Angeles Times*, October 7, 1982, Part V, p. 10]. A lengthy discussion of the exhibition "Black Wings: The American Black in Aviation" at the National Air and Space Museum. The curator, Von Hardesty, commented that the story is not merely about technological events, but "shaped and conditioned by nothing less than racism." Thomas C. Allen is interviewed, as are William Fuller and William R. Thompson, whose many photographs are part of the exhibit.

108. Bradford, Gardner. "Our Gay Black Way: Central Avenue." *Los Angeles Times* (June 18, 1933): 5-6, 10. [Magazine section]. Among the prominent black Angelinos mentioned are J. Herman Banning and Thomas C. Allen.

109. Bunch, Lonnie G. III. "In Search of a Dream: The Flight of [James] Herman Banning and Thomas Allen." *Journal of American Culture* 7 (Spring/Summer 1984): 100-103. Bunche examines the significance of Banning and Allen's transcontinental flight in 1932, and brings out the dark side of aviation history. Aviation and American technology were seen as a way to change society. This was especially so for African Americans who saw black achievement as a stride toward equality. Author concludes it was a dream. In 1932 Banning was the most experienced pilot of his race.

110. Carter, Sharon. "Aviation Pioneer Thomas Allen Dies." *General Aviation News* (November 6, 1989): 7, 19. Thomas Allen died September 12, 1989 in an Oklahoma city hospital at the age of 82. Biographical information.

111. "Christopher Hart Becomes Newest Board Member." *inTSB (National Transportation Safety Board)* 1:28 (August 20, 1990). [Hart was sworn in as a Safety Board Member on August 10. It was not reported then that Hart's great-uncle, J. Herman Banning, in 1926, was the first African American to receive a pilot's license in the U.S].

112. "Coast-to-Coast Flyers Land at Local Airport." *Pittsburgh Courier* (October 8, 1932). [Clipping File, Schomburg Center for Research in Black Culture, New York Public Library]. Article is incomplete; lauds the achievement of J. Herman Banning and Thomas C. Allen, "glorious hoboes of the uncharted skies...flirting hourly with the Grim Reaper in a plane whose motor is eight years old."

113. "Died." *Crisis* 40 (April 1933): 92. J. Herman Banning died in a plane crash at Camp Kearney, CA. He was a passenger, not the pilot, because he was not permitted to fly because of his race.

114. "Exhibition Traces Role of Blacks in Aviation." *New York Times* (September 26, 1982): 35. Report on the opening of the exhibition, Black Wings: The American Black in Aviation, at the National Air and Space Museum. "The history of blacks in aviation, not documented in most history books, includes a bit of the romance of early aerial combat and a great deal of the struggle over segregation." Among those in attendance were pioneers Thomas Allen and Benjamin O. Davis Jr.

115. "Famous Coast-to-Coast Trail Blazer Killed as Plane Crashes in West." *Pittsburgh Courier* (February 11, 1933). An account of the death of J. Herman Banning, which includes biographical information.

116. Fentress, J. Cullen. "1st Negro Cross Country Flier Plans to Open School." (October 28, 1939). [Claude A. Barnett Papers, Chicago Historical Society]. The Thomas C. Allen Aviation School has been incorporated in Los Angeles, with plans to open in January. It will be open to all, regardless of race, creed, or color. Allen feels the Negro should be trained in aviation now "for any openings that may eventually appear."

117. "First Negro Transcontinental Flyer to Fly around the World." (May 8, 1949). [Associated Negro Press (ANP) release, Claude Barnett Papers, Chicago Historical Society]. Allen plans a round-the-world airplane flight, through his own initiative without benefit of commercial promoters. He plans to drop off letters from the United States to people of other nations.

118. "Harlem Honors Coast-to-Coast Negro Flyers." *New York Herald Tribune* (October 1932). [Date may be October 7, or shortly thereafter. Claude A. Barnett Papers, Chicago Historical Society]. Dinner held for Allen and Banning at the Sunset [ ]rlbrooke Cafe at 2256 Seventh Avenue. The

flyers detailed their experiences to a cordial if not demonstrative group of leading Negro businessmen, editors, and men about Harlem.

119. Hart, Philip S. "Telling the Story of the Early Black Aviators." *Trotter Institute Review* 3:1 (Winter 1989): 4-7. While researching family history, Hart uncovered information about the early days of blacks in aviation. His maternal great-uncle was J. Herman Banning. He credits the National Air and Space Museum with presenting the first visual documentation on the subject with their exhibition, "Black Wings." He then decided to make a 60-minute documentary on early black aviators. The article then recounts the difficulties of getting the project funded and the general lack of interest in it. Information about Bessie Coleman, William J. Powell, Marie Coker, Harold Hurd, Cornelius Coffey, and Hubert Julian.

120. Lynn, Jack. *The Hallelujah Flight*. New York: St. Martin's Press, 1989. A fictionalized version of the 1932 cross-country flight by Thomas C. Allen and James Herman Banning.

121. "New York Gives 'Em a Royal Welcome." (1932). [Dateline is October 13; Clipping File, National Air & Space Museum]. Brief article describing the arrival of Banning and Allen after their flight from California.

122. "Noted Aviators in Exhibition at Bettis Airport." (October 1932). [Claude A. Barnett Papers, Chicago Historical Society]. Banning and Allen, intrepid birdmen, will show the safety of air travel through stunts at airport near McKeesport, near Pittsburgh.

123. "This Week in Black History." *Jet* 67:22 (February 11, 1985): 32. J. Herman Banning died February 5, 1933. He was the first black aviator to be licensed by the U.S. Department of Commerce. He was a charter member and chief pilot of the Bessie Coleman Aero Clubs in Los Angeles.

124. Zito, Tom. "Blacks in Aviation." *Washington Post* (September 23, 1982): D9. A preview of the exhibition "Black Wings." Three of the pioneers were there: Benjamin O. Davis Jr., Clarence "Lucky" Lester, and Thomas C. Allen. Allen pointed out the absence of of information about Paul Lawrence Dunbar, who worked with Wright brothers in their bicycle shop. He is thought to have assisted with their experiments in aviation.

C. Alfred Anderson and Albert E. Forsythe

125. Allen, Cleveland G. "Hop-Off Near for Good Will S. Amer. Flight."
(August 9, 1934). [Gumby Collection, Columbia University, Scrapbook
#1]. Dr. Albert E. Forsythe told the congregation of the St. James Presby-
terian Church, about the flight he and C. Alfred Anderson will make to
mark the 100th anniversary of emancipation in the West Indies. Article
discusses the series of good will flights.

126. "Bizplane People." *Aviation International News (Midland Park, NJ)* (May
1, 1985): 157. Four pilots from New Jersey have been nominated for in-
duction into the Aviation Hall of Fame at Teterboro. One of them is Dr.
Albert E. Forsythe.

127. "Black Pilot is Honored as Pioneer." *USA Today* (October 16, 1986).
Charles Anderson was awarded the Frank G. Brewer Trophy by the National Aeronautic Association. It is the nation's highest award for aviation education. The presenter was Chuck Yeager.

128. Brock, Pope. "Chief Anderson." *People* (November 28, 1988): 149 +.
Five pages of biographical information on Charles Alfred "Chief" Anderson, now 81. He speaks of what he endured to fulfill his dream of flight:
actual sabotage to his planes and discrimination. He describes life at Tuskegee, his good will flights with Albert Forsythe. Spann Watson is
quoted. Statistics are given: of 50,000 commercial pilots, fewer than 200
are black; United Airlines has 26 black pilots out of 6,300 and TWA has
15 out of 2,700.

129. "'Chief' Anderson Receives Brewer Trophy." *Aviation International News
(Midland Park, NJ)* (November 1, 1986): 116. C. Alfred Anderson is the
first black person to receive the prestigious award since its establishment
in 1943. Information about Anderson and about aviation in general. Anderson was the first black airline transport pilot.

130. "Dr. Albert Forsythe, 88, Dies; Among First Black Aviators." *New York
Times* (May 9, 1986): D22. Dr. Albert E. Forsythe died on May 6 in
Newark where he lived. The purpose of the flights Forsythe made with C.
Alfred Anderson between 1932 and 1935 were to break down the color
barrier in aviation. He then practiced medicine until his retirement in
1977.

131. "Flying Across Nation." *Evening Star (Washington, D.C.)* (July 17, 1933). [Other brief articles charting their progress appeared in the same paper July 18, July 20, and perhaps on other days too]. C. Alfred Anderson and Albert E. Forsythe took off from Atlantic City today, hoping to be the first of their race to span the continent by air. The plane is called the "Pride of Atlantic City."

132. "Four Added to Aviation Hall of Fame." *NJ Historical Commission Newsletter* (April 1985): 2. One of the four is Dr. Albert Forsythe, one of the first blacks to fly across the continental U.S., Canada, and the Caribbean.

133. "The Goodwill Flyers Call on the Governor." *Daily Gleaner (Jamaica)* (November 14, 1934). Dr. Albert E. Forsythe and C. Alfred Anderson were received by the Governor, as they stopped here on their extensive goodwill flights to the West Indies and Central and South America. Their monoplane is called the "Booker T. Washington." Article lists sponsors of the trip, describes the receptions accorded the flyers, and mentions their experiences.

134. Hunt, Rufus. "Among the First Black Aviation pioneers." *Chicago Defender* (August 18, 1981): 6. A pilot and aviation historian, Hunt provides a biographical sketch of Charles Alfred "Chief" Anderson, who was born February 7, 1909. He flew for over a year (he had to buy his own plane) before receiving any instruction. On August 6, the Winky Fix near Moton Airport, Tuskegee, Alabama, will be renamed the Ander Fix to honor Anderson. A navigational fix is a geographical location determined by electronic means, and is limited to five letters.

135. "Manifest." *Professional Pilot* 20:12 (December 1986): 107. Charles Alfred "Chief" Anderson received the Frank G. Brewer Trophy at the National Air and Space Museum. Retired Gen. Chuck Yaeger was the presenter.

136. McKelway, John. "They Had a Dream and Gave It Wings." *Washington Star* (January 11, 1980). Report of a symposium held at the National Air and Space Museum the day before. Reminiscences and opinions of Lee A. Archer Jr., C. Alfred Anderson, and Benjamin O. Davis Jr.

137. McKenzie, Alecia, and Karen Turner. "The Father of Black Aviation." *Everybody's* 9:1 (January/February 1985): 22-24. Dr. Albert E. Forsythe, born in the Bahamas and raised in Jamaica, is profiled. He and C. Alfred

Anderson were the first two blacks to make a cross-country flight in a single engine plane. This occurred in July 1933, from Bader Field in Atlantic City, New Jersey to Los Angeles and back in September. There is biographical information on Anderson as well, their Goodwill flights undertaken to prove blacks could fly, and Leslie Morris of Eastern Airlines is interviewed. Forsythe taught his wife Frances to fly.

138. "Nassau Welcomes Goodwill Fliers." *Nassau Daily Tribune (Bahamas)* (November 10, 1934): 1, 2. [Claude A. Barnett Papers, Chicago Historical Society]. An immensely detailed account of the arrival of the Goodwill Flyers, C. Alfred Anderson and Dr. Albert E. Forsythe. Some of the details include the dramatic night landing, and the names and titles of almost everyone present at the landing and subsequent reception and dinner. Dr. Forsythe describes some of the events of the flight. The text of the Goodwill message, presented to the Governor, is included.

139. "Negro Fliers at Trinidad." *New York Times* (December 14, 1934). [There were brief, almost daily reports in the paper]. The goodwill fliers C. Alfred Anderson and Albert G. [*sic*] Forsythe landed at Port of Spain and were received at a reception by the Governor. Anderson and Forsythe presented a scroll to him, as they have been doing at their other stops.

140. "Negro Fliers in Havana." *New York Times* (November 10, 1934). Albert C. [*sic*] Forsythe and C. Alfred Anderson landed at Havana after a flight from Nassau. The trip is sponsored by Tuskegee Institute and the Inter-Racial Good-Will Aviation Committee of Atlanta.

141. "Negro Fliers Land in Dominican Hills." *New York Times* (November 18, 1934). Albert C. [*sic*] Forsythe and C. Alfred Anderson had to make a forced landing. This flight is part of their Good Will Tour of 13,665 miles.

142. "Negro Fliers Make Miami-Nassau Hop." *New York Times* (November 9, 1934). Dr. Albert E. Forsythe and C. Alfred Anderson completed the first hop of their goodwill flight to Latin America. They plan to leave for Havana tomorrow. More than 5,000 people were present to see the night landing, the runway lit with automobile headlights.

143. "Negroes End Flight." *New York Times* (July 29, 1933). C. Alfred Anderson and Albert E. Forsythe completed the first airplane flight to the Pacific Coast and back ever made by Negro flyers. They left on July 17 for

Los Angeles and returned to Atlantic City. They were welcomed by 1,000 people on their return.

144. Poston, Ted. "Ted Poston Learns Why School Was Last to be Okayed." *Pittsburgh Courier* (December 7, 1939). Howard University was the last school to apply for the training program of the Civil Aeronautics Association. The reasons had to do with Board of Trustees meetings and Howard's relation to the federal government, and is spelled out in detail. Influential in the negotiations was C. Alfred Anderson, president of the Washington Airmen's Club.

145. "Redd Foxx: 'Auntie Eleanor' Film Tells How President's Wife Proved Blacks Could Fly U.S. Planes." *Jet* 66:4 (April 2, 1984): 58-61. [Cover story]. In a forthcoming film Redd Foxx will play Judge William H. Hastie, who fought for equality in the armed forces. One incident in the film will show Eleanor Roosevelt going up in a plane despite the protests of her secret service agents. C. Alfred Anderson was the pilot who flew the plane over Moton Field at Tuskegee.

146. Robertson, Blair. "Black Pilots Honor Aviation Pioneer." *Birmingham Post-Herald* (May 24, 1992): 1B-2B. Airport Road in Tuskegee, Alabama, was renamed Chief Anderson Street for C. Alfred "Chief" Anderson, the head instructor of the Tuskegee Airmen. Anderson, 85, "still flies almost every day and is considered something of a saint by the pilots gathered at Moton Field Airport." The gathering was the 22nd Annual Memorial Day Fly-in of the Negro Airmen International (NAI). Pilots with stories about Chief Anderson include: Leslie A. Morris, president of NAI, Johnny Ford, Tuskegee's Mayor and a pilot, Palmer Sullins Jr., who was taught by Anderson when he was nine years old, and Roosevelt Lewis, a retired colonel, who now manages the airport.

147. "The Story of 'Alf' Anderson Who Paid $6,000 to Learn to Fly." *Pittsburgh Courier* ([December 8, 1939]). [The date may not be correct. The article is from the Claude A. Barnett Papers, Chicago Historical Society]. Biographical Information on C. Alfred Anderson.

148. "Transport License Given Negro Pilot." *Washington Post* (February 28, 1932). [C. Alfred Anderson is the only American Negro qualified as a transport air pilot by the Department of Commerce. The Quaker City lodge of the colored Elks takes credit for his award because they

purchased a plane and secured instruction so Anderson could complete 200 solo flying hours].

149. Voss, Dorothy. "He Pioneered Black Aviation." *Tel-news [New Jersey Bell]* (January 1986). [This was an insert in a telephone bill]. Biographical information on Dr. Albert Forsythe who began flying in 1930. He and "Chief" Anderson flew from Atlantic City to Los Angeles and back in 1933. They had a compass and an altimeter, but no radio, lights, or parachutes. Last year Forsythe was inducted into the Aviation Hall of Fame at Teterboro Airport in New Jersey. A painting in color of the two aviators by Roy LaGrone is included.

150. Washington, Mary J. "A Race Soars Upward." *Opportunity* 12:10 (October 1934): 300-301. An account of the first of a series of "goodwill flights" by colored aviators. Launched by the National Negro Aeronautical Society (name changed to Interracial Goodwill Aviation Committee), the purpose of the flights is to use aviation's tremendous and dramatic possibilities to help the race win world-wide respect. "The Negro aviator is to be the adventurous salesman who goes forth to carry his own message... and his own interpretation to his neighbors." The first flight was made by C. Alfred Anderson and Dr. Albert E. Forsythe on July 17, 1933. Technical information.

151. White, John C. "Father of Black Aviation Still Flying, Teaching at 75." *Chicago Tribune* (May 23, 1982): 13. [Section 3]. Lengthy profile of C. Alfred (Chief) Anderson, who recounts his experiences, many of them marked by discrimination. In over 50 years of flying Anderson trained more than 1,000 black pilots.

152. "Young Transport Pilot Joins Ranks of Scottsboro Defense." *New York Amsterdam News* (May 3, 1933). C. Alfred Anderson offered his services as a pilot to lawyers or reporters.

Hubert F. Julian

153. "Abyssinian Official Repudiates Julian." *New York Amsterdam News* (August 27, 1930). Says Julian is not authorized to represent the Abyssinian government.

154. "Aviation." *Opportunity* 9:9 (September 1931): 286. Hubert Julian, whose aviation exploits have furnished the daily press with news copy for a number of years, has recently been granted a pilot's license by the Department of Commerce. He hopes to make a non-stop flight to Africa.

155. "'Black Eagle' a Citizen." *New York Journal American* (September 29, 1942). Julian is also a sergeant in the Army Air Corps.

156. "'Black Eagle' Adopts Italian Appellation." *New York Times* (June 19, 1936). Hubert Fauntleroy Julian changed his name to Huberto Fauntleroyana Juliano, as he is now an Italian citizen by conquest. He has come to Italy to realize his dream of a flight between Rome and New York.

157. "'Black Eagle' Blasts U.S. Refusal to Sell Arms to Guatemala." (May 26, 1954). [ANP release, Claude Barnett Papers, Chicago Historical Society]. U. S. Customs officials seized $91,000 worth of arms Julian had purchased for Guatemala. Some biographical information.

158. "'Black Eagle' Dashes in on Mule to Help Emperor Retake Adowa." *Herald Tribune* (November 14, 1935).

159. "Black Eagle Finds Jamaica Warm, Glides to Haitian Republic." *The Voice* (October 5, 1963): 6. Julian says he is in Haiti because he is ill, but the article implies strongly he is there to buy arms for the Haitian government.

160. "Black Eagle Flying Again, Gets Passport." *New York Amsterdam News* (July 17, 1954): 1. Julian's passport was picked up on June 17 by the State Department after he was accused of selling military suppplies to Guatemala. It was restored, and Julian is off to England to complete a $36,000 business deal. Julian says he suffered heavy financial loss, including his Rolls Royce, because of the seizure of his passport.

161. "Black Eagle Gets the Air in Ethiopia." [Gumby Collection, Columbia University, Scrapbook #1].

162. "Black Eagle in Huff Quits Ethiop Army." (November 15). [Gumby Collection, Columbia University, Scrapbook #1]. Julian asked to be relieved of all military and aviation duties because his authority was not respected.

163. "Black Eagle Loses Wings and Stripes." *Sunday News [New York]* (August 11, 1935).

164. "The Black Eagle of Harlem." *Chicago Tribune* (July 23, 1972): 3. [Section 1A - Perspective]. This is a side bar to a larger article on arms merchants. Julian is quoted as saying, "It's disgraceful to think that munitions dealers can be millionaires. When you think of all those un-heralded scientists working to cure disease, earning a pittance, its dis-graceful. It's a crime that we spend so much money on arms." Julian also says that Sidney Poitier will soon star in a film about him.

165. "'Black Eagle' Plans Sea Flight to Cairo." *Newark Star-Eagle* (March 27, 1931). Col. Julian sorry friends are slow with nickels.

166. "Black Eagle Plans World Flight." (1935). [Gumby Collection, Columbia University, Scrapbook #1].

167. "Black Eagle Renounces Citizenship." *New York Amsterdam News* (October 29, 1975): 1. Hubert F. Julian turned in his passport on August 19, at the American Embassy in London. No reason is stated. Julian is described as Chairman of the Black Eagle Corporation at 1630 Sedgwick Avenue in the Bronx. This is also his home address. Col. Julian plans to visit member states of the United Nations.

168. "Black Eagle Returns Railing at Ethiopia." *Daily News* (December 14, 1935).

169. "The Black Eagle Returns." *Our World* 4:5 (May 1949): 26-28. Hubert Julian returned from a 25,000 mile trip to the Far East. Julian returned on the Queen Mary and held a press conference to discuss the problems of the Dutch and the Indonesians. Julian traveled as the correspondent for *Our World*, and there is a great deal about his wardrobe, i.e., his custom-made hats.

170. "'Black Eagle' Returns From Jail In Congo." (August 24, 1962). [No source, but may be *New York Times*. Claude A. Barnett Papers, Chicago Historical Society]. The United Nations obtained the freedom of Hubert F. Julian, after he was arrested as a mercenary in Katanga. Rather than receiving pay from the government, Julian said they owe him $35,000 for medical supplies and shoes shipped in March. Other information.

171. "'Black Eagle' Says He Was Too 'Efficient'." *Newark Evening News* (November 12, 1930). Julian, in Paris, before sailing to New York, recounts experiences in Ethiopia.

172. "Black Eagle Says 'I'll Sue the City for $1,000 a Second!'." *New York Amsterdam News* (September 8, 1962): 1-2. Julian was falsely arrested in a parking violation, and was held in custody three hours, eighteen minutes and 40 seconds. The affidavit of the person responsible is reproduced on p. 2.

173. "Black Eagle Screams 'Not Guilty'." *New York Amsterdam News* (July 11, 1959): 1. Julian vehemently denied the charge by the Cuban ambassador in London that he had been selling arms to the Dominican Republic. Julian said that if he had done so, the State Department would have revoked his license. Instead they renewed it. The same story appears in the *Pittsburgh Courier* (July 18, 1959), p.3.

174. "'Black Eagle' Signs Up." *New York American* (July 13, 1935). Julian to fly for Ethiopia. Photograph of Julian with State Senator A. Spencer Feld.

175. "'Black Eagle' Spreads Wings in Village Aerie." *Herald Tribune* (August 10, 1930). [Gumby Collection, Columbia University, Scrapbook #1 contains invitation and guest list; Gumby was the Master of Ceremonies]. A party to welcome Julian home from Ethiopia held at 106 Waverly Place. Julian describes the Emperor and life in Abyssinia. His aim is to make Abyssinia air minded.

176. "Black Eagle to Live Abroad." *Pittsburgh Courier* (September 24, 1955): 9. Hubert Julian plans to live in Trinidad.

177. Booker, James. "Where is Col. Julian Harlem's Black Eagle ?" *New York Amsterdam News* (June 23, 1962): 1-2. Julian has been in U.N. custody since April 19. Mrs. Julian says nobody will tell her the charges; there is "a curtain of silence and secrecy." They parted in Rome on April 17, when he left for the Congo.

178. Chamberlin, Clarence D. *Record Flights*. Philadelphia: Dorrance, 1928. Chapter XV, "Two Black Crows," pp.232-246, is a racist "humorous" account of two unnamed flyers Chamberlin piloted so they could make parachute jumps. One of the flyers is Hubert F. Julian. This chapter is

omitted from the 1942 edition (New York: Beechwood) to which is added Book II, Give 'Em Hell!

179. Chase, Bill. "All Ears." (May 15, 1943). [Chase is a black reporter. Gumby Collection, Columbia Univ., Scrapbook #1]. Sgt. Hubert Julian called from Lincoln, Nebraska (Army Air Force Technical School) to say he had been appointed captain because of his unusually high rating - 93 percent.

180. "Col. and Mrs. Julian." *New York Amsterdam News* (December 10, 1930). Photograph on the occasion of their visit to the Nazarene Congregational Church.

181. "Col. Hubert Julian, Now Air Chief for Abyssinian Emperor, to Purchase Ships." *New York Amsterdam News* (August 6, 1930). Julian parachutes at the feet of Haile Selassie, is rewarded with money, a medal, and is made colonel, as well as an Ethiopian citizen.

182. "Col. Hubert Julian Wins Libel Suit Against Hearst Publication; Gets Cash and Full Page Retraction." *New York Age* (December 30, 1933). Julian's suit was based on the *American*'s published statement on December 1, 1930, that he was kicked out of Abyssinia. Biographical information, Hearst's actions and descriptions of planes are included.

183. "Col. Julian Changes 'Uncles'." [Gumby Collection, Columbia University, Scrapbook #1]. Now out of the army and working at Willow Run, Henry Ford's plant. He is assistant to Paul Collier, director of employer/employee relations.

184. "Col. Julian is Off." *New York Sun* (June 6, 1936). Now an Italian citizen by conquest, Julian sailed for Italy on the Vulcania.

185. "Col. Julian Leaving America." *New York Amsterdam News* (November 2, 1968): 2. Julian left for London to accept a $2,400,000 offer to move his weapons business. This is the Black Eagle's 28th crossing on the Queen Mary. The Black Eagle International Association, of which Julian is president, is the only black-owned company registered with the State Department to sell arms and military equipment. Julian says he fought with the Royal Canadian Air Force (RCAF) during World War I.

186. "Col. Julian Passes British Test; is Admitted to RAF." *New York Star-Amsterdam News* (January 11, 1941).

187. "Col. Julian Sails for Finland." [Gumby Collection, Columbia University, Scrapbook #1]. Photograph of Julian, his wife, others and the radio that Louis Armstrong gave him.

188. "Col. Julian Wins $93,000 Shipment." *New York Amsterdam News* (June 22, 1957): 1, 25. The State Department returned the arms shipment it seized three years ago on October 16, 1953. Julian acted as his own lawyer, and said it was the first time the State Department released a seized shipment to an individual without penalty. Julian will sue the shipping company for stopping in New York when the shipment was to have gone from Naples to Guatemala without stopping.

189. "Col. Julian's $30,000 Auto Steals N.Y. Show." *Jet* (February 18, 1954): 18-19. Col. Hubert F. Julian, importer-exporter and soldier of fortune, displayed his custom-built Rolls-Royce. The car has gold appointments, is trimmed in silver and has been enameled royal blue. The customs charge was $8,900. Further description and photographs.

190. "Colonel Hubert Fauntleroy Julian 'The Black Eagle'." *Afro-American Journal (Indianapolis)* 3:5 (September/October 1975): 8. In one page and three photographs a great deal of biographical information is covered.

191. "Colonel Julian." *New York Amsterdam News* (November 26, 1930). [Disapproving editorial].

192. "Colonel Julian Honors Poets." *New York News and Harlem Journal* (November 29, 1930). A Thanksgiving gala meeting of the Poets Round Table, reported in a light-hearted, gently satirical way. The guest list is included, and the poets "gazed in awe" at the "two lights," Colonel Julian and George Schuyler.

193. "Colonel Julian Makes 23-Minute Solo Flight While 1,200 Watch Air Circus." *New York Amsterdam News*. [Gumby Collection, Columbia University, Scrapbook #1]. The event took place at Glenn Curtiss airport.

194. "Colonel Julian Ordered to Pay $30,311 Judgement." *Jet* (February 2, 1956): 6. The New York Supreme Court ordered Julian to make restitution to a West Hartford, Connecticut businessman. Treasury bonds stolen

from the man's safe in 1949 were sold by Julian to a Havana, Cuba, syndicate.

195. Curtis, Constance. "Colonel Julian Frightens Man-Eating Tiger in Java." *New York Amsterdam News* (January 29, 1949): 1, 15. Notably short on details, this article expects Julian to come back with good stories about his adventures in Sumatra. He is referred to as an "old world gallant and Harlem harlequin ... [who] keeps the ladies goggle-eyed and the gentlemen glum."

196. "Do You Remember The Black Eagle." *Negro Digest* (March 1951): 36-37. Biographical information. "Today, fiftyish and still nimble as a college athlete, Col. Julian ..." is chairman of the purchasing board for the Guatemalan Air Force. He hopes to use his influence to alter that country's laws that bar entry to Negroes.

197. "Eagle's Wings Clipped by U.S." *Pittsburgh Courier* (June 26, 1954): 1, 4. Hubert F. Julian had his passport revoked because of Guatemalan arms shipments. Julian says he is Guatemala's military purchasing agent, and he will seek denaturalization.

198. Ellis, R. H. "Hailed as 'Bronze Lindy'." *Pittsburgh Courier* (March 24, 1928): 1. [Second section]. Lt. Hubert Julian plans a flight to Paris and back in June. He hopes his success will help establish schools where Negroes may be taught to fly - free.

199. Ellis, R. H. "Negro American Plans Flight to Paris and Return Trip." *New York Evening Graphic* (March 17, 1928). [Magazine section]. Long biographical article. Julian's trip is scheduled for June, and he hopes to be the "Lindy" of his people. "The sole purpose of my flight is to stimulate a greater interest in aviation among my own people." Article states Julian is the only Negro pilot licensed by the National Aeronautic Association, of which Orville Wright is the president.

200. "'The Emperor and I are Pals' Says Harlem's Own Eagle." *Newark Ledger* (November 19, 1930). Returns from Ethiopia because of plots against him.

201. "Former Selassie Aide Makes Cash Bid to Free Emperor." *Jet* 47:8 (November 14, 1974): 30. Hubert F. Julian offered the Ethiopian government $1.45 million to release Selassie from military custody. The

77-year-old Julian who now runs a sugar brokerage firm in New York said, "I owe my prominence and stature to the benevolence of His Imperial Majesty and was very distressed to learn of his situation."

202. Hall, Herman. *200 Years of West Indian Contributions.* Brooklyn, NY: Herman Hall Associates, 1976. Biographical information on Hubert F. Julian, including a description of the first aerial "streak," in Atlantic City, New Jersey, p.25.

203. "Harlem 'Black Eagle' Barred from Country; Visa of Julian, Now an Ethiopian, Faulty." *New York Times* (January 24, 1936). Good deal of biographical information: Julian, convinced he will be assassinated, took one of his sons to France for schooling; the family lives at 118 W.119th Street.

204. "Harlem Cheers Negro Flyer in Leap to Roof." *The Daily Star [Queens Borough]* (July 5, 1924). [This article is reprinted in Allon Schoener, *Harlem on My Mind:Cultural Capital of Black America, 1900-1968,* New York: Random House, 1968, pp.60-61, as "Champion Daredevil Parachutes to Tenement."] Lieutenant Hubert Julian, M.D. [Mechanical Designer], did a death and police defying parachute jump over City College to advertise a five and ten cent store. He was served a summons for violation of the Sunday law. But first the police had to go through a crowd whose pressure had bent iron gates and smashed show windows, to reach Julian, riding on the shoulders of admirers. Two other airplanes had dropped smoke bombs to herald Julian's jump.

205. "'Harlem Eagle' Passes U. S. Test for Pilot's Rank." *Herald Tribune* (July 31, 1931). Two-column article covers facets of Julian's life and personality.

206. Harrington, Ollie. "How Bootsie Was Born." *Freedomways* 3:4 (Fall 1963): 518-524. Harrington evokes Harlem in 1936, the inspiration for his cartoon character Bootsie. He mentions "The Black Eagle" getting his hair cut at the Elite Barber Shop where "America's top second-class citizens" met to discuss the issues of the day. He also claims to have the inside story of Hubert Julian's challenge to Goering to fight an air duel. It was proposed by Ted Poston, a reporter for the *Pittsburgh Courier* who needed a story. A bottle of Scotch whiskey was involved. "A little light signifying and Goering was a challenged cat."

207. "'I'm No Mercenary!' Col. Julian." *New York Amsterdam News* (September 1, 1962): 1, 26. Exclusive interview with Julian after his four months of detention by the United Nations in Leopoldville, Congo. This included a hospital stay. Julian vehemently denied he was attempting to bring arms in. He gives his views on peace in Africa.

208. Jackson, Neale. "Black Eagle." *Bronzeman: A Popular Magazine for All [Chicago]* 2:11 (October 1931): 23-24, 32; 2:12 (November 1931): 14-15, 29, 34. [This is a two-part article]. Biographical information about Hubert F. Julian.

209. Johnson, Irving. "How the Black Eagle Plotted Duce's Death." *New York World Telegram* (May 2, 1944): 1, 7. On his return from traffic court, Julian recounts his unsuccessful plan to kill Mussolini in 1934.

210. "Julian Back in New Role." *New York Amsterdam News* (December 4, 1937). Julian arrived on the Queen Mary with an Egyptian princess and the corpse of her father. They will accompany the body to Johns Hopkins Hospital for an autopsy to explain his double stomach.

211. "Julian, Back, Reveals Narrow Death Escape." *New York Amsterdam News* (December 8, 1934). The flier was trapped over the English Channel in a fierce storm. Julian returned with clippings from French and English newspapers, which deplored the tendency of American papers to spoof Julian, and suggested his serious dignified manner and his abilty deserved better treatment.

212. "Julian Comes to Town with Usual Flourish." *The People's Voice* (June 12, 1943). Julian returned from Army Air Force Technical School at Lincoln, Nebraska, with a 91 percent rating and letters of recommendation.

213. "Julian Ends Tiff with Emperor." *New York Times* (November 9, 1935).

214. "Julian Escaped 'Enemy's Poison' and Air Death." *New York News and Harlem Journal* (November 22, 1930). Julian denies smashing the Imperial plane. He displays rare gifts acquired on his travels.

215. "Julian Has a Scrap in Ethiopian Hotel." *New York World Telegram* (August 8, 1935). Hubert Julian accused John C. Robinson, an aviator, of being connected with an unfavorable article. Robinson denied it and they fought.

216. Julian, Hubert. *Black Eagle*. London: Jarrolds, 1964. [As told to John Bulloch]. Julian's own account of his life, and his versions of the many newspaper stories about him. He emerges as not only an adventurer, but also as a daring entrepreneur, sensitive, intelligent and a fighter for his race in his own way. There was another edition of this book, also published in London, in 1965 by the Adventurers Club.

217. Julian, Hubert F. "Hubert Julian at War Front." *New York Amsterdam News* (September 9, 1939). [Julian is "now at the front with the French army covering the new World War for the *New York Amsterdam News*. He is the only correspondent for a Negro newspaper in the war zone"]. Julian reports admiringly the French inclusion of black men from the French West Indies in the army. He writes of life in Paris under siege.

218. "Julian Maintains His Story is True." *New York Amsterdam News* (December 18, 1937). Accuses the newspaper of perpetrating falsehoods against him.

219. "Julian Meets Chief." *New York Amsterdam News* (September 22, 1934): 3. A photo of Julian in London giving Sir Offori Atta, paramount chief of the Gold Coast, a few pointers on aviation. The chief was knighted by King George.

220. "Julian Set to Fly in Melbourne Race." *New York Amsterdam News* (September 22, 1934): 3. Julian flew from London to Paris where an official from Abyssinia met him. He hopes to represent Abyssinia in the forthcoming air race from London to Melbourne.

221. "Julien [*sic*] Again in Court." *Topeka Plaindealer (Kansas)* (August 31, 1923): 1. [Datelined New York, K.N.F. Service, Aug. 23]. Lieut. Herbert [*sic*] Julien [*sic*], the daredevil astronaut, was again called into court last Monday, charged with assaulting his former partner, Simon Bernard, 3441 Seventh Ave., over the payment of some money. Julian offered to pay his partner's doctor bills, but the magistrate refused this request. The case was postponed until a later date and Julian was paroled.

222. Kellner, Bruce. *The Harlem Renaissance: A Historical Dictionary for the Era*. Westport, CT: Greenwood Press, 1984. Hubert F. Julian is described on p. 207.

223. Lamparski, Richard. *Whatever Became of...?* New York: Crown Publishers, 1967. Hubert F. Julian: The "Black Eagle," pp. 94-95.

224. Lewis, David Levering. *When Harlem Was in Vogue.* New York: Random House, 1982. Hubert Julian's exploits are colorfully described on pp.111-112, and sources are included.

225. Lincoln, Richard. "Black Eagle Raps Mag for Slurs." *New York Amsterdam News* (November 15, 1952): 1, 22. Hubert Julian sues *Time* for $600,000 for its November 3rd story calling him a coward, stuntster, sham, etc. Julian blasted the story as "editorial melodrama." The names of his lawyer and three editors of the magazine are given.

226. Loose Jaws. "The Tattler." *New York Amsterdam News* (October 1, 1983): 16. Gossip columnist states that Hubert Julian's death was unreported for six months because his young wife disliked his reputation as the Black Eagle. He died in the Veterans Hospital in the Bronx and was buried by the Walter B. Cooke Funeral Home.

227. Markey, Morris. "The Black Eagle." *The New Yorker* (July 11, 1931): 22-25. [The second part of the profile is in the issue of July 18, 1931, pp. 20-23]. The first part of this profile narrates Julian's association with Clarence Chamberlin, and describes his failed flight to Liberia on July 4, 1924. The second part concerns Julian's invitation to come to Ethiopia and his reception there. Julian is quoted "And I wish to say that I consider will power and personality the alpha and the axis of my success."

228. "Mrs. Hubert Julian Dies." *New York Amsterdam News* (January 11, 1975): A1, 3. Mrs. Essie M. Julian died [January 4] at the age of 79. She is buried in Woodlawn Cemetery. Biographical information about her and list of survivors, other than Julian.

229. Neely, William. *Pilots! The Romance of the Air: Pilots Speak About the Triumphs and Tragedies, Fears and Joys of Flying.* New York: Simon & Schuster, 1991. Mention of Hubert F. Julian, the first black mercenary pilot, on p. 65, and his experiences in Ethiopia.

230. "Negro Aviator Injured in Fall in Flushing Bay." (July 5, 1924). [Gumby Collection, Columbia University, Scrapbook #1]. Engine trouble cut short Hubert Julian's flight to the West Indies from College Point. Fred Hess, a machinist on a motor boat, rescued Julian, who was unconscious.

231. "Negro Aviator Plans Flight to Continent." *Sunday Call (Newark)* (June 17, 1928). Hubert Julian will attempt a flight to Paris or Rome at the end of July.

232. "Negro Aviator Seeks $25,000 and Good Map." *Herald Tribune* (June 21, 1928). Like many articles about Julian, this one is somewhat satirical, grudgingly admiring, and offering some information. Includes some comments by Clarence Chamberlin, Julian's pilot when he parachutes.

233. "Negro in Parachute Hits Police Station." *New York Times* (November 6, 1923). Hubert Julian had planned to land in St. Nicholas Park to advertise a political rally at Liberty Hall, 140th St. and Lenox Ave. Unfavorable currents set him atop the police station at 123rd St. Clarence Chamberlin was the pilot.

234. "Negroes' Air Hero Asks Fund for Hop." *World* (May 13, 1928). Rome and return latest project of Lieut. Hubert Julian. Clarence E. Lorraine, of Danville, Virginia, is building a plane to operate on compressed air, instead of fuel. He hopes to accompany Julian as radio operator.

235. "Notables Felicitate the Black Eagle." [*New York Amsterdam News* ?] (November 15, 1933). A banquet was held for Col. Hubert Julian at the 135th St. YMCA on November 11. Julian plans to fly to Aden, Arabia.

236. Nugent, John Peer. *The Black Eagle*. New York: Stein and Day, 1971. [There is neither an index nor a bibliography]. The fullest account of Julian's life, written seven years after Julian's autobiography. Nugent admires Julian for his intelligence and nerve.

237. Nugent, John Peer. "The Madcap Odyssey of a Soldier of Fortune." *Ebony* (April 1972): 104-106, 108, 110, 112. Known as the Black Eagle of Harlem, Julian has been a gun runner, mercenary, stunt flyer, diplomat and foreign correspondent, as well as one of the earliest black pilots. Biographical article declares him still flamboyant and swashbuckling.

238. "One-Man Air Force Returns to Harlem." *New York Times* (November 19, 1930). [Photo of Julian "clad faultlessly in morning dress"]. Col. Julian denies Abyssinia ejected him for breaking up plane.

239. Ottley, Roi. *Black Odyssey: The Story of the Negro in America.* New York: Scribner's, 1948. Hubert F. Julian is briefly mentioned as the "Black Ace," p. 245.

240. Ottley, Roi. *'New World A-Coming': Inside Black America.* Boston: Houghton-Mifflin, 1943. Ottley briefly outlines Julian's more famous exploits, calls him tall, tan, terrific, and daredevil of the air, pp.107-109.

241. Pearson, Drew. "Harry Vaughan, Influence Man." [Dateline is July 29. From internal evidence the year may be 1948. Claude A. Barnett Papers, Chicago Historical Society]. Pearson takes aim at General Vaughan, President Truman's military aide, for meddling in contracts that do not concern him. Vaughan apparently "went to bat for Colonel Hubert Fauntleroy Julian," who had connections with a shady company. The endorsement was so strong that Julian, when he went to Germany, was given a special military aide, had an hour's conference with General Clay, and toured the American zone as a guest of the United States Army. Further details of a plan to sell stale cigarettes to the Japanese. Photograph of Julian.

242. "[Photograph]." *Daily Telegraph (London)* (December 12, 1935). The Negro pilot, Col. Herbert [*sic*] Julian of Harlem, New York, who plans to supply Abyssinia with two fighting planes.

243. Poindexter, Malcolm. "Famed 'Black Eagle' Seeks Funds for West Indies." (April 4, 1956). [ANP release, Claude A. Barnett Papers, Chicago Historical Society]. Julian negotiated with Vice President Nixon for additional aid to the West Indies Hurricane Fund. Since October of last year he has had sent $250,000 worth of medical supplies and equipment to Grenada and Barbados. Description of his reception there.

244. "Police Clip Black Eagle." *New York Journal American* (April 26, 1944): 24. Hubert Julian receives a parking ticket for holding up traffic. Reporter notes snappy dialogue between Julian and the policeman.

245. "'Princess' Ali Loses Royalty." *New York Amsterdam News* (December 11, 1937). The case of Hubert Julian, the corpse and the princess is revealed to be a hoax. Ali, the corpse thought to be the father of the princess, was a vaudevillian.

246. "RAS Sends Flyer Back to Harlem." *New York Sun* (October 31, 1930). Emperor Ras Tafari sent Julian home because he cracked up the plane reserved for the coming coronation festivities.

247. "Ready to Leave Abyssinia, Says Harlem Aviator." *New York Times* (March 3, 1934).

248. "Ruling on Julian." *New York Sun* (January 23, 1936). Secretary of Labor will rule on whether Julian may be admitted to the U.S. Julian returned from England after arranging for the education of his nineteen-year old son.

249. Schuyler, George S. "Views and Reviews." *National News* (March 31, 1932): 7. [This newspaper was published only from February to June. Since Schuyler's column was syndicated this is likely to be found in other newspapers, such as the *Pittsburgh Courier*]. Leon D. F. Paris, who owns his own airplane, is planning a flight from New York to Haiti. Schuyler comments he is modest and unassuming, unlike that notorious chiseler, "Colonel" Hubert Julian, who seems to have flown everywhere but in the air. Schuyler notes there are close to two dozen licensed Negro aviators in the United States.

250. Scott, William R. *The Sons of Sheba's Race: African Americans and the Italo-Ethiopian War, 1935-1941.* Bloomington, Indiana: Indiana University Press, 1993. Chapter 6, "The Brown Condor," pp. 69-80, refers to John C. Robinson. Pages 233-236 contain 71 footnotes. Chapter 7, "The Eagle and the Lion," pp. 81-95, concerns Hubert F. Julian. Pages 236-240 contain 97 footnotes.

251. Scribner, Kimball J. *Adventures in Aviation: An autobiography of Captain Kimball J. Scribner.* Long Beach, CA: Mansfield Publishing, 1990. Captain Scribner describes his meeting Hubert F. Julian who was a passenger on the plane Scribner was flying from Rio to Miami. Various adventures of Julian's are discussed, and Scribner concludes, "Among the annals of the early international aviators, Colonel Julian remains one of the most interesting and memorable figures I ever met." The account is on pp. 118-120.

252. Sincere Colored Man. "Letter to the Editor." (December 14, 1935). [Gumby Collection, Columbia University, Scrapbook #1]. "I am getting

tired of reading and hearing about Col. Hubert Julian, so-called Black Eagle of Harlem."

253. Smith, H. Allen. *Low Man on a Totem Pole*. Garden City, NY: Doubleday, Doran & Co., 1941. "The Black Eagle Screams," pp. 72-81. Smith recounts some of Hubert Julian's escapades, but there is no screaming in any of them. There is an incidence of Julian's charm at a party on Waverly Place, the "premiere" of a film by Oscar Micheaux, and the challenge to Hermann Goering to fight an air duel with him. Julian was furious when Goering wrote that Negroes were baboons. The text of Julian's telegram to Goering is included. Smith continues to write about him, despite the opinions of his friends, because "He is a ball of fire in every contingency."

254. "Spreading His Wings." *New York Amsterdam News* (July 9, 1949). Photograph of Hubert Julian about to board a Pan Am clipper. Now president of Black Eagle Airlines, Julian plans to inspect his company's factories in France and Italy.

255. "State Department Gets 'Advices' of Black Eagle." *Herald Tribune* (December 24, 1935). 'Late Colonel' Julian's 'unanimous' view is to keep out [of Ethiopia's affairs]. This article, like many others, describes Julian's clothing in great detail.

256. "State Department Lifts Col. Julian's Passport." *Jet* (July 1, 1954): 5. Julian was asked to surrender his passport on his return from Sweden where he had attempted to purchase arms for the Communist-led government of Guatemala. Julian said he would apply for cancellation of his citizenship.

257. "Tiger Flowers Promises to Aid Well Known Aviator." *Empire State Gazette* (July 11, 1926). Photograph of Flowers, the boxer, Hubert Julian, and a crowd viewing a plane on 139th St. near Seventh Ave. "about a year ago."

258. Wells, Linton. "Appetite Shoves Black Eagle in Debt and Imperial Disfavor." *Herald Tribune* (November 14, 1935). Satirical story about Julian's financial difficulties in Ethiopia.

259. Wells, Linton. "Haile Selassie Gets Swan Song of Black Eagle." *Herald Tribune* (November 17, 1935). Col. Julian delays his sad leave taking a day, and pledges fealty to the Negus.

John C. Robinson

260. Allen, Cleveland G. "Col. Robinson Exhibits His Leadership." *Chicago Defender* (May 30, 1936): 7. News article describes how Robinson quieted a noisy crowd of 5,000 people who took umbrage at remarks of Miss Paula Le Claire, a white newspaper reporter in Ethiopia.

261. "American Negro Pilot Bests Two Italian Planes." *New York Times* (October 5, 1935). John C. Robinson in the Italo-Ethiopian war.

262. "Americans in Ethiopia." *Ebony* (May 1951): 79-83. John C. Robinson is featured as the best known American living in Ethiopia. Until he was forced out in 1948, Robinson was the commander of Ethiopia's 25-plane air force. The article states his mother was born in Ethiopia.

263. "Aviatrices Welcome Col. John Robinson." *Chicago Defender* (May 30, 1936): 9. Janet Waterford and Willa Brown presented two beautiful bouquets of peonies to John C. Robinson, as he stepped from a TWA plane Sunday. The flowers were a gift of the Challenger Air Pilots Association, which was founded by Robinson.

264. "'Brown Condor' Steals 'Black Eagle's' Stuff." *Herald Tribune* (October 10, 1935). John C. Robinson of Chicago has replaced Hubert Julian in the Ethiopian Air Force. Robinson was the first American to volunteer in Haile Selassie's army. Julian has been sent 400 miles from Addis Ababa to drill recruits.

265. "Chicago Flyer in African War Returns a Hero." *Chicago Daily Tribune* (May 25, 1936). Col. John C. Robinson acclaimed by cheering throng.

266. "Col. Robinson, Haile's Flyer, Welcomed Here." *News (Chicago)* (May 25, 1936). Robinson returned to Chicago after 13 months in Ethiopia. He predicted guerilla warfare will continue against the Italians. His garage, at East 47th Street, was managed by his wife while he was away.

267. "Col. Robinson Starts own Aviation College." *New York Amsterdam News* (October 3, 1936): 24. The John C. Robinson National Air College and School of Automotive Engineering opened September 28, at Poro College on South Parkway.

268. "Colored U.S. Mechanic Hailed as Hero of Selassie's Pilots." *Star (Washington, D.C.)* (May 25, 1936). Brief article describes tumultous welcome accorded John C. Robinson. A plane piloted by Dr. Earl Renfroe, "flying colored dentist," escorted the big airliner to the airport. This Associated Press news release shows the denigration reserved for accomplishments by blacks, both by its headline and by its brevity.

269. Diamond, Jack. "Haile Selassie's Ace Airman Back in New York, Glad War Days Ended." *Enterprise (Riverside, California)* (May 21, 1936). An interview with John C. Robinson who says his luxuries in Ethiopia never became part of him. He reports on the fighting and on his health - he was gassed.

270. "Ethiopia Honors Dead U. S. Flyer." *New York Amsterdam News* (April 3, 1954): 1-2. Col. John C. Robinson was buried with high military honors in Addis Ababa. He died after a plane crash. Biographical information.

271. "Ethiops' Rabble Army Won All Frays - Flyer." *Afro-American (Baltimore)* (June 13, 1936). John C. Robinson spoke at the Metropolitan Baptist Church in Washington, D.C., relating Ethiopia's difficulties in procuring modern planes and weapons, the character of the natives and the land. He was met by Dr. Leo Hansberry, Dr. Charles H. Wesley, and James Browning.

272. "Extend Fete for 'Brown Condor'." *Daily Times (Chicago)* (May 25, 1936). John C. Robinson owns a garage at 47 E. 47, which his wife managed in his absence of 13 months. He is undecided whether to remain in Chicago or to go to Tuskegee to teach.

273. "Famed 'Brown Condor' Injured in Ethiopian Crash." (March 15, 1954). [ANP release, Claude A. Barnett Papers, Box 171, Fd. 6, Chicago Historical Society]. John C. Robinson was hurt when a training plane he was flying crashed and burned. The Italian engineer with him died. The article also tells of an incident in 1947 in which Robinson was sentenced to prison for punching Count Gustaf Von Rosen, the Swedish Commander

of the Ethiopian Air Force. There are numerous ANP releases about this incident in this box, variously dated for September 1947.

274. Fields, A. N. "Editor Abbott in Tribute to Col. Robinson." *Chicago Defender* (May 30, 1936): 2. Robert S. Abbott, editor and publisher of the newspaper, introduced Robinson from the balcony of the Grand Hotel in Chicago. Abbott always supported aviation activities among blacks with money and publicity. His tribute was more than a welcome address. "It was a resume of our racial hope, opportunities and ambitions."

275. Fleming, G. James. "Col. Robinson Acclaimed as Ethiopia Hero." *New York Amsterdam News* (May 23, 1926): 1, 13.

276. Hall, Chatwood. "Col. Robinson Launches East African Airlines." *Chicago Defender* (February 21, 1948): 13. Sultan Airways, Ltd. is under the direct management of John C. Robinson. Its offices are in Addis Ababa. It uses Douglas DC 3's and the pilots are former RAF flyers.

277. Kellum, David W. "City Heralds Robinson on Return Home." *Chicago Defender* (May 30, 1936): 1. More stories about John C. Robinson on pp. 3, 6, 8, 9.

278. Kellum, David W. "Defender Scribe Greets Robinson." *Chicago Defender* (May 23, 1936): 1, 2. Exclusive pictures in this issue were taken aboard the ship Europa as Col. John C. Robinson arrived from Ethiopia. Robinson blames the defeat of Ethiopia on "not so much the military skill of the Italians, but the rebellion of the various native tribes." He said Ras Hailu was the instigator. Biographical information, his plans, his war wounds.

279. Kellum, David W. "Twenty Thousand Greet 'Brown Condor' on Return." *Chicago Defender* (May 30, 1936): 1, 2. [Pictures on p.7]. Long article of details of Robinson's life, activities, plans, etc.

280. McIntyre, William A. *Library Journal* (June 15, 1988): 55. A book review of *The Brown Condor: The True Adventures of John C. Robinson* by Thomas E. Simmons. "More than a biography about a black pilot who became an U.S. hero, this book is a social history of racial conditions in the first half of the 20th century."

281. "Negro Flyer in Center of Adowa Fight." *New York Amsterdam News* (October 19, 1935). John C. Robinson describes an aerial battle with Italian planes.

282. "Negro Flyer Returns." *Union-Star (Schenectady, NY)* (May 19, 1936). Col. John C. Robinson will leave New York today for Chicago. Describes triumphal return: "750 cheering negroes [*sic*] greeted him, and he was carried on the shoulders of admirers." Discussion of the war in Ethiopia.

283. "Negro Flyer to Keep Beard; Made Him Ethiopia's Hero." *World-Telegram* (May 19, 1936). Life in Tuskegee will never be what it was in Addis, where John C. Robinson had an eight-room house with six servants and a private car for piloting Haile Selassie. Some description of life in Ethiopia.

284. Norman, Charles. "'Brown Condor,' Pilot of Selassie, Feted as Harlem's Newest Hero." *Progress (Jacksonville, Texas)* (May 25, 1936). [This article also appeared in the *Jersey City Journal*, same date]. A report from AP with the sarcastic tone usually used in stories about Hubert F. Julian. When he was asked about Julian, Robinson said, "I guess I just have nothing in common with him." Robinson mentions his work delivering medical supplies and doctors to the front.

285. Schuyler, George S. "Negroes in the Air." *American Mercury* 39 (December 1936): xxviii, xxx. [Letter to the editor, The Open Forum]. Schuyler replies to an article by Kenneth Brown Collings in which he wrote "Negroes cannot fly." Schuyler mentions Negro aviators in Colombia, Brazil, Venezuela, and France. He also refers to Bullard, Coleman, and Robinson. "This simply is not true and I trust his misstatement is not indicative of the general accuracy of his article." Schuyler further posits a conspiracy in America to keep the Negro out of aviation as well as other areas of endeavor. Brown replies that he met John C. Robinson in Ethiopia and that just proves there are exceptions to every rule.

286. Scott, William R. "Colonel John C. Robinson: The Condor of Ethiopia." *Pan-African Journal* 5:1 (Spring 1972): 59-69. A long biographical article, with 64 footnotes for further research. Robinson owned an auto repair shop in Chicago. He became the first black student at the Curtiss-Wright Aero School, and then became an instructor for other black students he had recruited. Thus, he was an early advocate for

blacks in aviation. He was the private pilot of the Duke of Harar, Haile Selassie's grandson. There is also mention of Janet Waterford.

287. "Selassie Air Ace Just 'Had to Run'." *Evening Post (New York)* (May 19, 1936). Interview with John C. Robinson about his actions in the Italo-Ethiopian War.

288. "Selassie Pilot Arrives Today." *New York Journal* (May 16, 1936). Brief article about John C. Robinson.

289. "Selassie's Air Aide Back from Africa." *New York Times* (May 19, 1936). Col. John C. Robinson returns to teach aviation at Tuskegee, his alma mater. Discusses the Italo-Ethiopian war, lays collapse of defense to revolution led by Ras Hailu.

290. Simmons, Thomas E. *The Brown Condor: The True Adventures of John C. Robinson*. Silver Spring, MD: Bartleby Press, 1988. A biography of Robinson with an overview of the Italo-Ethiopian War and descriptions of Ethiopia.

291. Slaughter, Vera B. "20,000 Greet 'Brown Condor' at Airport." *Chicago Defender* (May 30, 1936): 9. Return of John C. Robinson from Ethiopia. Information about him and the Italo-Ethiopian War. Photo captions: "Welcome Home Colonel," "I'm Glad to be Back."

292. Walden, Goldie M. "Socialites Greet Hero at Airport." *Chicago Defender* (May 30, 1936): 7. Return of John C. Robinson from the Italo-Ethiopian War. Photo captions: "Flyer Dinner Guest of the Abbotts," "Flyer to Linotypist."

293. Waterford, Janet. "John Robinson Wings His Way Down to Tuskegee." *Chicago Defender* (May 9, 1936): 12. Recounts a trip to Tuskegee.

294. Waterford, Janet. "The Real Story of Col. John Robinson, or How a Gulfport, Miss. Boy Grew to be the No. 1 Flyer of His Race." *Chicago Defender* ([May 16, 1936]): 14. [Caption under a photo of Waterford states she began a series of articles on the Negro in aviation last week. Next week: "Robinson Organized a Flying Club."]. Biographical data on Robinson, who was once a circus motorcycle rider, in an act called "Death Valley."

295. Waterford, Janet. "Robinson Arouses Race Interest in Aviation." *Chicago Defender* (n.d.). [One of a series of articles Waterford wrote in April and May 1936]. Tells how John C. Robinson became an instuctor at the Curtiss-Wright School, recruiting twenty black students as well. Describes class work and the building of an airport at Robbins, an all-black town.

296. Waterford, Janet. "Robinson Excelled as an Instructor in Aviation Because of his Keen Insistence on Real Discipline." *Chicago Defender* (April 25, 1936): 12. Waterford, herself a pilot, recounts a personal instance when she did not follow his instructions while they were co-piloting a plane.

297. Waterford, Janet. "Robinson Organizes Brown Eagle Aero Club in Effort to Interest Race in Flying." *Chicago Defender* (May 23, 1936). [The date is based on information in an earlier article, and may not be correct]. The article tells of Robinson's efforts to organize a club for young people, and of his efforts to raise money from local businessmen and by holding dances.

298. "'We'll Sing Ethiopia,' Song Dedicated to Col. John C. Robinson, Honors Returning War Hero." (1936). [Dateline New York City - June. ANP release, Claude A. Barnett Papers, Chicago Historical Society]. This song, composed by Rev. William Lloyd Imes, with music by Luckeyeth Roberts, was in the Flying Colonel's honor for his valiant efforts in Ethiopia's struggle to maintain independence. The text is given. Copies were distributed among the audience at Rockland Palace, 155th Street and 8th Avenue at the huge mass meeting held for Robinson.

299. White, A. E. "Harlem in Wild Acclaim Over Return of 'Brown Condor'." (1936). [Claude A. Barnett Papers, Chicago Historical Society]. A very full article reporting on the reception for John C. Robinson. Remarks by eight speakers quoted heavily, and there are long descriptions by Robinson of the Italo-Ethiopian War.

300. "Youthful Aviator Makes Initial Flight." (February 3, 1930). [Claude A. Barnett Papers, Chicago Historical Society]. Johnnie Robinson made his initial flight even though the temperature was below zero. It was successful, but his arms and legs were frozen. Sometime earlier he had constructed an airplane from automobile parts.

Willa B. Brown

301. "About People." *Essence* (April 1988): 46. Biographical information about Willa Brown.

302. Alston. "Lieut. Willa Brown." *Philadelphia Tribune* (February 26, 1944). Cartoon, with biographical information.

303. "Aviatrix is Cited in 'Time'." *Pittsburgh Courier* (October 7, 1939). Chicago's Southside aeronautical colony pleased at the honor paid one of its best liked members, Willa B. Brown. Biographical information.

304. "Aviatrix Visits at W. Va. State." *Chicago Defender* (Novenber 22, 1941): 5. Willa B. Brown, president of the National Airmen's Association, visited West Virginia State College en route to Chicago. She was returning from the Civilian Pilot Training Conference for Negro Colleges, which was held at Hampton Institute November 8-9.

305. "Aviatrix-Instuctor." *Chicago Bee* (February 1940). Willa B. Brown is appointed Director of Flight Training for the Negro community in Chicago. Thirty young men and women from all parts of the U.S. will be taught to fly through scholarships from the Civil Aeronautics Authority. Her appointment is based on her outstanding ability in aeronautical circles and her understanding of the Negro's problems in aviation. She is the first Negro woman to receive full-time employment in the aviation industry. Other biographical information.

306. "Black Aviation Pioneer Dead at 86." *Daily Challenge (New York)* (July 21, 1992): 2. Obituary of Willa Brown Chappell, the first black woman to earn a commercial pilot's license. She died in Chicago at Bernard Mitchell Hospital and she will be buried in Lincoln Cemetery. Biographical information.

307. "Coffey Air School May Be Closed." [No source or date. Claude Barnett Papers, Chicago Historical Society]. Article blames government red tape. Notes Willa B. Brown's trip to Washington to try to save only flight school where Negroes can get flight training free of discrimination.

308. Downs, Karl E. *Meet the Negro*. Pasadena, CA: Login Press, 1943. "Willa B. Brown: Vivacious Aviatrix," pp.54-55.

309. Heise, Kenan. "Willa Chappell, Pioneer Black Pilot." *Chicago Tribune* (July 21, 1992): Section 2, 9. [Obituary, died July 18, 1992].

310. Holden, Henry M., and Lori Griffith. *Ladybirds II: The Continuing Story of American Women in Aviation*. Mt. Freedom, New Jersey: Black Hawk Publishing Company, 1993. Biographical information on Janet Harmon Waterford Bragg, pp. 47-49; Willa C. [*sic*] Brown Chapell, pp.303-305. Errors in dates, spelling of names.

311. Horton, Luci. "1st Black Woman Commercial Pilot Joins FAA Panel." [Claude A. Barnett Papers, Chicago Historical Society]. Willa Brown achieves another first: she is the first black woman on the Federal Aviation Agency's Women's Advisory Committee on Aviation. Biographical information.

312. "Instructs Aviation Class." *Chicago Defender* (March 22, 1940). Photo of Willa Brown and her students. Some text.

313. May, Charles Paul. *Women in Aeronautics*. New York: Nelson, 1962. Information about Willa Brown on p. 170.

314. Morgan, Gene. "30 Take to Air as Negro Pilot Course Starts." [Newspaper article with no date or source, three columns. Mentions the school gave a demonstration in 1941 to convince the Air Force that Negroes could be trained as pilots. Also, the Coffey School is ten years old. Claude A. Barnett Papers, Chicago Historical Society]. Description of the course of study and the equipment. Graduates may be inducted into the Army Air Forces enlisted reserve but their call to duty is not contemplated in the near future. Interview with Willa Brown. Names of Chicago youths enrolled are given.

315. *Opportunity* 19:3 (March 1941). [Cover photo of Willa B. Brown. There is no story].

316. Peckham, Betty. *Women in Aviation*. New York: Nelson, 1945. Willa B. Brown is profiled on pp. 35-36.

317. "Pioneer in Aviation Willa Chappell, 86, Dies; Trained Black WW II Pilots." *Jet* 82:15 (August 3, 1992): 18. [Obituary of Willa B. Brown].

318. "School for Willa." *Time* (September 25, 1939): 16. The non-military Ci-
     vilian Aeronautics Authority certified 220 U.S. colleges and universities
     for its pilot-training program. While giving a great deal of information
     about the program and thought behind it, the article features Willa Bea-
     trice Brown, including a photograph. Of the 62,000 pilots licensed by the
     C.A.A., only 130 are Negroes.

319. "To Organize Junior Birdmen; Young Aviatrix to Teach Air-Minded Bil-
     likens the Principles of Aviation." *Chicago Defender* (May 16, 1936): 1.
     Willa Brown will establish a young people's group to study aviation pri-
     ciples, make model planes, take weekly trips to the Municipal Airport,
     and hear talks by outstanding pilots.

320. Travis, Dempsey J. *An Autobiography of Black Chicago*. Chicago: Urban
     Research Institute, 1981. On pp. 88-89 Travis recounts his study at an
     aviation mechanics program. Willa Brown was the teacher.

321. "Wants to Fly Bombers." *Pittsburgh Courier* (January 18, 1936): 1. Two
     photographs of Willa B. Brown in aviation dress, one shows her reading
     a book. Horrified by Italian attacks on Ethiopia, Brown wants to answer
     the call to Ethiopia. At present she is employed as a cashier by Wal-
     green's in Chicago.

322. Waters, Enoc P. Jr. "Peacetime Flyers." 13, 15. [No source or date, but
     from internal evidence it is 1941. Claude A.Barnett Papers, Chicago
     Historical Society]. A detailed description of the Coffey School of Aero-
     nautics: its origins, programs, students and principals, Willa B. Brown
     and Cornelius R. Coffey. This well-outfitted school is the result of the
     cooperation of the National Airmen's Association (Coffey is president
     and Brown is secretary), Chicago Board of Education, Civil Aeronautics
     Authority, and the Works Project Administration. Notes opposition to the
     government's plans to set up a jim crow air squadron at Tuskegee.

323. "Willa B. Brown Named Member Of Civil Air Patrol in Illinois."
     (March). [ANP release, no year, Claude A. Barnett Papers, Chicago His-
     torical Society]. Brown was the first Negro member of the Civil Air Pa-
     trol in Illinois.

324. "Willa Brown Chappell, 86, Trained Black WW II Pilots." *Chicago Sun
     Times* (July 20, 1992): 41. [Obituary, died July 18, 1992].

325. "Willa Brown Chappell." *Daily News* (July 22, 1992): 34. Obituary states she died of a stroke.

326. "Willa Brown, Famed Aviatrix, Returns to Chicago Teaching." *Baltimore Afro-American* (May 5, 1962): 18. Now the wife of Rev. J. H. Chappell, Brown is teaching shorthand and typing at Crane High School.

327. "Willa Brown Praised by CAA Chief Visiting Air School." *Nashville Defender* (June 22, 1940). Describes the work of the Coffey school in Chicago. Lewis A. Jackson is chief instructor for college students.

328. "Wings Speaker." *[Chicago Defender?]* (August 22, 1941). [Biographical sketch of Willa Brown, and photo before a microphone with call letters WGAR]. Brown's entire speech, delivered on August 17, 1941 in Cleveland, Ohio, is included. It is a moving history of Negroes in aviation, only 20 years.

329. "Women in Uniform." *Journal and Guide (Norfolk, VA)* (June 19, 1943). Brief information about Willa B. Brown, who is in Washington, D.C. for a short stay. Mentions that Brown took part in a recent "sham" bombing of Chicago.

Cornelius R. Coffey

330. "Aerial Honors." *Flying* (January 1981): 17. The FAA renamed Calum Intersection, over the south side of Chicago, to honor Cornelius Coffey. It is spelled as Cofey Intersection to conform to computer mandates.

331. Allen, Henry. "To Fly, to Brave the Wind." *Washington Post* (September 26, 1979): B1, 6. Biographical information on Cornelius Coffey, now 76, along with many comments by Coffey, in Washington to be honored at the National Air and Space Museum.

332. "Aviation Pioneers Honored." *Chicago Metro News* (November 17, 1984): 10. The Second Annual Illinois Aviation Recognition Banquet was held recently [September 7, 1984] at Springfield. The 1984 honorees elected to the Illinois Aviation Honor Roll were Oliver L. Parks Sr., Thomas Young, and Cornelius R. Coffey. They were honored for their contribution to Illinois aviation history. Rufus A. Hunt, aviation historian, is pictured in a plane.

333. "Flyer Gets Coveted Award." *Chicago Defender* (September 20, 1941): 1. Cornelius R. Coffey was presented with the Dwight Green Trophy. It is an award given by the National Airmen's Association for the greatest contribution to the field of aviation. Coffey won it for 1940. The donor is Dwight Green, a governor of Illinois and a pilot. The presenter was Rachel Carter, the first girl to graduate from civilian pilot training in Chicago.

334. "Flying Past Prejudice." *National Air and Space Museum Events* (September 1990): 1. [The General Electric Aviation Lecture]. Cornelius R. Coffey will speak on September 20. "Here is a rare opportunity to meet an aviation pioneer. Join Coffey as he relates the struggles and triumphs of an exciting era."

334a. Golab, Art. "Black Aviator Still Flies High." *Chicago Sun-Times* (July 14, 1993): 24. The Cornelius R. Coffey Aviation Education Foundation has just been established at American Airlines Maintenance Academy in Chicago. It honors Coffey, now 89, who stills flies his plane. Coffey in 1932 became the first black to be certified as an aircraft mechanic. Biographical information.

334b. Grossman, Ron. "A Flight Against the Wind." *Chicago Tribune* (July 25, 1993): 1,6. A lengthy biographical article on Cornelius R. Coffey, born in 1903. Admirers recently set up the Cornelius R. Coffey Aviation Education Foundation to offer scholarships to a younger generation. Coffey stated, "My spirit was kindled to go into a line of work where I wouldn't be bound by the limitations my father had to put up with."

335. Hunt, Rufus A. *The Cofey Intersection.* Chicago: J.R.D.B. Enterprises, 1982. A detailed account of the efforts of Rufus Hunt to honor the aviation pioneer, Cornelius R. Coffey. Biographical information, copies of letters, and many photographs record Coffey's contribution to black aviation history in Chicago.

336. Hunt, Rufus A. "Cornelius R. Coffey: Pioneer Aviator, Mechanic, and Instructor." *Buffalo: For the Black American Military Professional* 1:2 (December 1980): 4-8. [Hunt is Secretary Historian of the Tuskegee Airmen Inc]. Biographical information includes Coffey's difficulties in trying to enroll in segregated Curtis-Wright School of Aeronautics in 1929. A threatened law suit gained his admission, as well as that of John C.

Robinson. Hunt recounts his part in getting the FAA to rename a "fix" for Coffey in July 1980, and to have Coffey be the first pilot to fly over the intersection newly named in his honor.

337. "Negroes Organize: National Airmen's Association of America Holds First Meeting in Chicago." *American Aviation* 3:9 (October 1, 1939): 14. Officers of the new organization are listed. Cornelius R. Coffee [*sic*] is the president. Dr. A. Porter Davis received the Dwight H. Green Trophy fro "the greatest contribution to aviation among Negroes."

338. Page, Clarence. "FAA Honors Chicago Black Aviator's Feats." *Chicago Tribune* (July 23, 1980): 6. Cornelius R. Coffey was honored for over 50 years of flying and his contribution to the training of black aviators, by the Mayor and officials from the Federal Aviation Administration. Biographical information, and description of the bronze plaque, which shows the location of the "Cofey Fix." Regulations limit the numbers of letters to five. Coffey commented, "It's nice to enjoy your flowers while you're still living."

William J. Powell

339. "Aviation." *Opportunity* 10:9 (September 1932): 291. William Powell and Dick Wells of Los Angeles entered the Pacific Division of the Cord Cup Transcontinental Derby. The flight is to end in Cleveland.

340. "Aviation." *Opportunity* 15:5 (May 1937): 156. Lieutenant William J. Powell has established a school in Los Angeles to train aviation mechanics and pilots through the Emergency Education Program of the government. A club has been formed, Student Craftsmen of Black Wings. Two planes are now under construction and 32 students have qualified for pilots' licenses. Craftsmen of Black Wings have two branches: Dyer Airport, 9401 S.Western Ave. in Los Angeles and Haitian American Appliance Company, 200 W. 135th St., New York. They publish *Craftsmen Aero News*.

341. Barton, Rebecca Chalmers. *Witnesses for Freedom: Negro Americans in Autobiography.* New York: Harper, 1948. A summary of *Black Wings* by William J. Powell is on pp.49-51. The author does not consider it an adequate autobiography because there is nothing about Powell's childhood.

But for people interested in aviation history, it offers an eye-witness account of blacks in aviation at the beginning.

342. Corn, Joseph J. *The Winged Gospel: America's Romance with Aviation, 1900-1950*. New York: Oxford University Press, 1983. Corn investigates the hopes Americans placed in aviation, expecting it to change the world for the better, i.e., even eliminate war. Black pilots in the twenties also believed that when whites saw people of color flying, prejudice would be eliminated. Mentioned are William J. Powell, pp. 35-36, and Albert Forsyth [*sic*] and C. Alfred Anderson, pp. 59-60.

343. *Craftsmen Aero News* (1937). This is the publication of Craftsmen of Black Wings, founded in Los Angeles by William J. Powell, to interest young blacks in aviation. It is a scarce journal - Powell wrote it is the first Negro trade journal in the United States. The Schomburg Center for Research in Black Culture, New York Public Library holds issues nos. 1,2,4,5,7. Some other repositories are Howard University and the Library of Congress. The July 1937 issue, pg. 12, reprints the full texts of the letters written by George S. Schuyler, William J. Powell, and Kenneth Brown Collings in the *American Mercury* about whether Negroes can fly. See entries 245, 348.

344. "Craftsmen of Black Wings." *The Sphinx* 22:3 (October 1936): 5. William J. Powell, a member of the Alpha Phi Alpha fraternity, has organized Craftsmen of Black Wings in New York and Los Angeles. Its aim is to create thousands of jobs for Negroes in a new industry, and to decrease racial prejudice by proving that Negroes can fly, build, and service planes. The efforts of other fraternity brothers are stressed, such as Dr. N. Curtis's loan of $300 when banks refused to lend to Negroes. Powell requests financial aid from fraternity members in this article.

345. "Negroes Organize National Flying Club in Los Angeles." *Air Transportation* 8:6 (July 6, 1929). [Page number not available, but article appears on the masthead page]. The Bessie Coleman Aero Clubs, 1423 W. Jefferson Blvd., have been organized, with plans for over 100 local clubs. The pilots include: Albert Warrender, Beatrice Reeves, Irvin E. Wells, William J. Powell, William Johnson, W. L. Brown, Wesley Cotton, and Leo Walker.

346. Powell, William J. *Black Wings*. Los Angeles: Ivan Deach Jr., 1934. Powell wrote this book "to stimulate interest among Negroes in a new industry, aviation, which is destined to become the most gigantic of all industries... It is a true story of the struggles of a few young Negroes bent on stirring up general interest in aviation among Negroes throughout America." There is no index, but Powell describes all the major black events and players in aviation, up to that time, in an engaging manner, giving times, places and dates. He recounts personal vignettes as well, which adds to this important source book. Among the many pilots noted are Hubert F. Julian, pp.43-50, 145; Lottie Theodore, pp. 29-32, 42-43, 143; Marie Dickerson and Mable Norford, p. 143; Bessie Coleman, pp. 143-144; and Irvin E. Wells, p. 90.

347. Powell, William J. *Black Wings*. Washington, D.C.: Smithsonian Institution Press, 1993/94. This is a new edition of Powell's 1934 book. Additional photographs and a bibliography have been added. Von Hardesty of the National Air and Space Museum has written an introduction which places the book in a historical context, and provides biographical information on Powell. Forthcoming in 1993/94.

348. Powell, William J. "Negroes in the Air." *American Mercury* 41 (May 1937): 127. [Letter to the editor, The Open Forum]. Powell replies to Kenneth Brown Collings' reply to George Schuyler's criticism of his article in which he states Negroes cannot fly. Powell takes particular issue with Brown's statement that obstacles have not been placed in the way of would-be Negro aviators. He recounts his own experiences of being turned down by many schools across the country, before being accepted in Paris and Los Angeles. He also has letters from over 300 Negroes who had similar experiences. "If given an opportunity, a Negro will outdo a white man in almost anything."

349. Schuyler, George S. "Views and Reviews." *Pittsburgh Courier* (January 30, 1937). [This appeared on the unnumbered editorial page]. The entire column deals with aviation and the part the Negro should play in this field. He begins by writing "Aviation is the big thing in industry and transportation today. Negroes should get into it - there are never enough HIGHLY TRAINED workers in ANY field." He ends with great prescience, "Who knows how great the demand for skilled mechanics and pilots may be in 1940?" He mentions Bessie Coleman, William J. Powell, and his group Craftsmen of Black Wings.

350. "Two Negro Pilots Forced Down In Lower California." *Los Angeles Times* (November 2, 1929): Part 2, p.10. J. Herman Banning and William J. Powell wandered for four days with no food and little water when their plane was forced down by lack of fuel. Mexican authorities held the men in custody until American officers in Calexico interceded in their behalf.

James L. H. Peck

351. "American Fighter Aces Swap Tales at Recent Reunion." *Sentinel (TRW Inc.)* (December 1967). [Model 35 was the code name of a top secret spy satellite]. Last month's reunion of American Fighter Aces Association, held at Miramar Naval Air Station, California, included James L. H. Peck. Peck heads Data Management for the Model 35 Spacecraft Project of TRW Systems Group. Gene A. Valencia, founder of the Association, is shown holding a portrait of Peck, which was displayed at the meeting.

352. Caidin, Martin. *The Ragged, Rugged Warriors*. New York: Dutton, 1966. [P.28]. Recounts experiences of James Lincoln Holt Peck, "a free-lance aerial soldier of fortune." He fought in the Spanish Civil War, then offered his services to the U. S. War Department, which refused. "His status as seasoned combat flier and an ace mattered little against the fact that he was a Negro."

353. Collum, Danny Duncan , ed. *African Americans in the Spanish Civil War: "This Ain't Ethiopia, But It'll Do."* Boston: G.K. Hall, 1992. Information about pilots James L. H. Peck, Paul Elisha Williams, and Patrick Roosevelt in about ten pages. Roosevelt did not fly, although he was a pilot.

354. *Current Biography*. New York: Wilson Company, 1942. James L(incoln) H(olt) Peck, pp. 653-655.

355. Groner, Joe. "'Good Old Days' in the Air." *Los Angeles Herald Examiner* (October 6, 1968). Meeting of fighter pilots from four wars. Photograph shows James L. H. Peck, although he is not mentioned in the article.

356. Herr, Allen. "American Pilots in the Spanish Civil War." *American Aviation Historical Society Journal* 22:3 (Fall 1977): 162-178. James Lincoln Holt Peck and Paul Elisha Williams are discussed on pp. 171-172.

Herr writes, "The stories written by Peck and about Peck are fraught with errors and are not corroborated by any known Spanish or American source on aviation in the Spanish Civil War."

357. Kobler, John. "This Negro is a Military Ace - But We're Not Using Him." *PM (New York)* (May 7, 1941): 15-16. Biographical information about James L. H. Peck.

358. Peck, James L. H. "579 Miles an Hour, Vertical." *Harper's* (August 1939): 311-320. Account of a test pilot's experiences while trying out a new Army plane.

359. Peck, James L. H. "Airpower for Defense." *Scientific American* (December 1940): 311-314.

360. Peck, James L. H. "America's Winged Weapons." *Scientific American* (July 1940): 5-7.

361. Peck, James L. H. *Armies with Wings*. New York: Dodd, Mead & Company, 1940. This book explains what military aviation is today. It dicusses types of airplanes, how they are built and tested, who flies them and maintains them, and about the changes in military tactics and strategy airpower will effect. This book, by a black pilot and author, is about aviation in its general sense. Peck uses material from his Spanish Civil War journal, as Loyalist airmen flew many types of European planes.

362. Peck, James L. H. "Atomic Age Air Force." *Air Trails* (December 1948). [Condensed in *Science Digest* (February 1949) 27-31. All the following articles by Peck, without annotations, were not seen].

363. Peck, James L. H. "Body Armor." *New Frontiers* (Spring 1956): 14+.

364. Peck, James L. H. "Bomber to Britain." *Harper's* (March 1941): 347-358. [Abridged in *Reader's Digest* (April 1941) 19-23]. The story of a ferry pilot's hazardous first trip to deliver an American-made plane across the Atlantic Ocean.

365. Peck, James L. H. *Bomber One: The B-1 Story*. New York: Paragon, 1993-94. Forthcoming.

366. Peck, James L. H. "Can Future Military Pilots Make It?" *Sportsman Pilot* (October 1939).

367. Peck, James L. H. "Defense Against Air Attack." *Science Digest* (June 1940): 5-9.

368. Peck, James L. H. "Dogfight - A Lifetime in Forty Minutes." *New York Times* (May 26, 1940): 4, 20. [Magazine section]. Peck is identified as a young pilot who took part in aerial battles over Spain. There is no mention of Peck's color. The article reports actual experiences of an aviator in a swift battle above the earth.

369. Peck, James L. H. "Doom on the Wing." *Popular Science* (February 1946): 84-88+.

370. Peck, James L. H. "Fifty Miles Up This Summer." *Popular Science* (May 1946): 66-71.

371. Peck, James L. H. "Flying in the Spanish Air Force." *Sportsman Pilot* (February 15, 1938). Peck, who is black, wrote articles on aviation in general. This article describes training of pilots by the French and Russians, names the twenty Americans in the Spanish Air Force, and describes his battle missions.

372. Peck, James L. H. "General Ike's Air Force." *Flying* (March 1952): 11-13+.

373. Peck, James L. H. "Helldivers." *Scientific American* (October 1940): 186-188.

374. Peck, James L. H. "Heroes in Glass Houses." *Scientific American* (January 1941): 12-14.

375. Peck, James L. H. "How Aircraft Instruments Work." *Popular Science* (March 1944): 116-123.

376. Peck, James L. H. "How Armies Hit the Silk." *Popular Science* (June 1945): 128-135.

377. Peck, James L. H. "How Fast Can We Fight?" *Popular Mechanics* (December 1950): 125-129+.

378. Peck, James L. H. "How Warplanes Fight at Night." *Popular Science* (October 1941): 82-88.

379. Peck, James L. H. "I Flew Black Market Gold." *American Legion Magazine* (October 1948): 16, 36, 40-43, 46, 49-53. [As told to James L. H. Peck]. Told by a former RAF pilot, who is a member of a ring of gold smugglers. Their base of operations includes England and France.

380. Peck, James L. H. "If War Comes." *Flying* (December 1951): 30-31+. [The joint author is Chalmers H. Goodlin].

381. Peck, James L. H. "Minute Men of '52." *Flying* (April 1952): 30-31+.

382. Peck, James L. H. "One-Horse Airlines." *Harper's* (October 1946): 317-324.

383. Peck, James L. H. "Our Navy's Air Arm." *Scientific American* (March 1942): 121-123.

384. Peck, James L. H. "Out of this World: The story of the Ionosphere." *Harper's* (June 1946): 502-509. [Abstracted under the title "Earth's Invisible Shield." in *Science Digest* (November 1946)].

385. Peck, James L. H. "Propellers for Our Fighting Planes." *Popular Science* (November 1943): 122-127+.

386. Peck, James L. H. "Radar: Magic Eye that Sees the Invisible." *Popular Science* (September 1945): 65-71+.

387. Peck, James L. H. "Radar of the Deep, Sonar." *Popular Science* (November 1945): 84-87+.

388. Peck, James L. H. "Relation of the Human Element to Safe Flying." *Aero Digest* (May 1937).

389. Peck, James L. H. "The Russian Air Force." *Flying and Popular Aviation* (October 1941): 14-17, 62-63.

390. Peck, James L. H. *So You're Going to Fly.* New York: Dodd, Mead, 1941. Aimed at young people who are going to begin aviation training, the

book first describes the training, then deals with military aviation and commercial aviation.

391. Peck, James L. H. "Soybeans and Sex." *Our World* (August 1949): 22-24.

392. Peck, James L. H. "Stalin's New Storm Bomber." *Flying* (February 1952): 12-13+.

393. Peck, James L. H. "Supersonic Combat: Today's Armament and Tactics Cannot Meet the Demands of Jet Aircraft." *Ordnance* (March/ April 1950): 311+.

394. Peck, James L. H. "Ten Miles Plus Straight Up." *True: The Man's Magazine* (November 1950). [Reprinted in Martin Caidin, *Rockets Beyond the Earth*. New York: McBride Co., 1952, pp. 132-138. Experience of Jim Peck being checked out in new T-33A jet trainer over Andrews AFB. Reached 53,000 feet to "edge of space."].

395. Peck, James L. H. "They Call it Tac." *Flying* (May 1952): 22-23+.

396. Peck, James L. H. "Tomorrow's Fighters?" *Popular Science* (April 1945): 65-67+.

397. Peck, James L. H. "Tools - The Measure of Man's Progress." *New Frontiers* (Spring 1957): 12+.

398. Peck, James L. H. "The Truth About Our Aircraft Engines." *Popular Science* (June 1943): 108-115.

399. Peck, James L. H. "Underground Exploring by Air." *Popular Science* (August 1946): 128-132.

400. Peck, James L. H. "War Moves to the Stratosphere." *Popular Science* (November 1941): 102-109.

401. Peck, James L. H. "Warbird Doctors." *Scientific American* (April 1941): 212-214.

402. Peck, James L. H. "Warplanes in Peace." *Air News* (September 1944).

403. Peck, James L. H. "Weapons of the War Planes." *Science Digest* (May 1940): 63-69.

404. Peck, James L. H. "When Do *We* Fly?" *Crisis* 47 (December 1940): 376-378, 388. Pecks comments on newspaper articles that report the setting up of a Negro air force. He states that "we are either being misled or built up for an awful let-down." He deplores the waste of man power not being trained properly. Peck further comments, "Our patriotism is, as always, so fervent that we do want to do our part in the national defense. We must lick a certain bigoted clique in Washington - and points north and south - before we can get at Adolf." Includes information on Peck and his writings.

405. Peck, James L. H. "When the AEF Throws Everything at Japan." *Popular Science* (August 1945): 78-80+.

406. Peck, James L. H. "Who is Yehudi ?" *Popular Science* (December 1945): 93-95+.

407. Peck, James L. H. "Why Our Planes Can Take It." *Popular Science* (July 1945): 118-121+.

408. Peck, James L. H. "You Can Be Hypnotized." *Ou · World* (September 1949): 32-36.

409. Peck, Jimmie. "Will Negro Aviators Ever Fly U. S. War Planes?" *Pittsburgh Courier* (July 1, 1939): 6. [This is the first of three articles with the same title. The second appeared July 8, p. 5, and the third July 15, p. 14]. Lengthy articles on the training programs of the Army Air Corps and the Civilian Aviation Authority, description of a military pilot's training for youths who may be contemplating such training, and what to expect if one is assigned to Attack - the most exacting and exciting department of military flying. Peck also discusses the problems attendant on being a Negro: the difficulties of getting the training and then what happens after. "Legislation from the White House and Congress cannot successfully combat service 'traditions.' Training fields are all in the South, some so biased there is not even a colored porter."

410. Prattis, P. L. "The Horizon." *Pittsburgh Courier* (February 10, 1940): [12]. Biographical sketch of James L. H. Peck, on the publication of his first book, *Armies With Wings*.

411. Steiner, Herbert. "Bailing Out." *Daily Worker* (March 6, 1938): 6.
[Magazine section]. "Leaping for life from a wrecked plane was only an
incident in the exciting life of Paul Williams, Negro pilot." A biographi-
cal article on Williams, born 1909, flyer for the Loyalist Air Force in
Spain, and the only Negro flyer to attain the rank of Lieutenant, Junior
Grade, in the Navy. Williams attended Carnegie Tech and the Ohio
School of Aeronautical Engineering in Youngstown, his birthplace.
There is mention of his great friend, Jimmie Peck (James Lincoln Holt
Peck), with brief information about him.

412. "U.S. Needs Ace Flyers, Peck Wants to Fly - But." *New York Amsterdam
News* (May 8, 1943): 5. Recounts the flying experience of James L. H.
Peck and his knowledge - the books and articles he has written for prominent journals - and his inablity to convince the U. S. Air Force to accept
him.

Chauncey E. Spencer

413. "Biplane Downed Near Sherwood." *Defiance Crescent News (Ohio)* (May
9, 1939). [The city of Defiance is twelve miles east of Sherwood, and the
newspaper was still being published in 1991]. Chauncey E. Spencer and
Dale White, both of Chicago, were forced to land on a farm because of a
broken crank shaft. They expect to resume their trip to Cleveland, Washington, and New York.

414. "Flyers Are Grounded by Motor Fault." *Chicago Defender* (May 13,
1939): 1, 4. Dale L. White and Chauncey E. Spencer en route to Cleveland, the first of ten stops, were forced down at Sherwood, Ohio, by a
broken crank shaft. White landed the plane without damage or injury.
Cornelius Coffey, president of the National Airmen's Association, will
come from Chicago to install a new shaft. Photograph of the three and
Longworth Quinn before they took off from Chicago.

415. "Intrepid Chicago Aviators Pilot 'Old Faithful' in Cross Country Goodwill
Tour." *Pittsburgh Courier* (May 20, 1939): 1. Chauncey "Clark Gable"
Spencer and Dale White are flying to eastern cities on behalf of an air
show to be held in Chicago in August. In Washington they will be

greeted by Edgar G. Brown, valiant crusader for racial rights, and government representatives.

416. Spencer, Chauncey E. "Prayer for Brotherhood." *AMC World (Wright-Patterson AFB, Ohio)* 2:8 (May 18, 1953): 3.

417. Spencer, Chauncey E. *Who is Chauncey Spencer?* Detroit, MI: Broadside Press, 1971. This is an autobiography of an aviator who played a pivotal role in establishing the right of blacks to enter aviation. He was a charter member of the National Airmen's Association (the certificate of incorporation is reproduced, Aug. 16, 1939), spoke to Sen. Truman to get Civilian Pilot Training, and flew with and knew just about all the black pilots of the thirties and forties. Unfortunately, there is no index. His mother was Anne Spencer, the poet and librarian.

418. "Two Chi Airmen Get Jobs as Technicians." (December 20, 194?). [Claude A. Barnett Papers, Chicago Historical Society]. Dale White and Chauncey Spencer were appointed as aeronautic technicians. This was "an indication that racial discrimination in national defense had taken a back seat." White and Spencer were former instructors at Harlem Airport and are members of the National Airmen's Association.They achieved fame a few years ago when they made a goodwill flight South.

419. "W-P Man Helped Break Race Barriers." *AMC World (Wright-Patterson AFB (Ohio)* 2:8 (May 18, 1953): 3. Chauncey E. Spencer, employee relations officer on the staff of Wright-Patterson's Inspector General, is featured in this biographical article. He is called "the one man most responsible for smashing aviation's color barrier." Mr. Spencer sees the integrated air force more as an example of what can be done, rather than a mission completed.

Other Individuals and Events

420. *Airplane Blues.* New York, August 3, 1935. This song was performed by Sleepy John Estes and was recorded on De-7354 and on Sw S-1219. The singer will fly his airplane all over town to find the woman he loves.

421. "Arkansas Airplane Pilot Gets License." *Pittsburgh Courier* (December 3, 1932): 5. The first Negro in Arkansas, authorized to be a private pilot, is

Pickens Black of Auverne in Jackson County. Black was required to have ten successful solo hours.

422. "Big Man in Biggest Building." *Ebony* (April 1963): 84, 86, 88, 90. Roy Kirklin Davenport was the first Negro to receive a pilot's license in South Carolina in the 1930's. He is now the highest-ranking (equal to that of a general) Negro civil servant at the Pentagon. An expert on personnel matters, Davenport was also a college professor.

423. "Boston Man Obtains Aviator's License." *Boston Chronicle* (November 22, 1930). Biographical information on John W. Greene Jr., the first Negro aviator in Massachusetts. Greene is a Hampton graduate.

424. Chadwick, Bruce. *When the Game Was Black and White: The Illustrated History of Baseball's Negro Leagues.* New York: Abbeville Press, 1992. Leroy "Satchel" Paige had his own airplanes so he could fly from game to game. Photograph of Paige leaning on his airplane, p. 125.

425. Collings, Kenneth B. "Black Hell in Ethiopia's Skies: Can Haile Selassie's Warriors Fight in the Air?" *Liberty* 12:46 (November 16, 1935): 36-37. A close-up of unpreparedness and apprehension behind the battle lines.

426. "Colored Birdman Tells Interesting Story of His Air Exploits." *New York Amsterdam News* (June 18, 1927). Samuel V.B. Sargusetsio (or Sauzereseteo, since both names are used in the article) claims flight from Moscow to Berlin on June 25, 1925 and other exploits. No biographical information.

427. Covington, Floyd C. "Ethiopia Spreads Her Wings." *Opportunity* 8:9 (September 1930): 276-277. Profile of Jay Howard Montgomery, a mining assayer for Guggenheim interests. Montgomery invented and patented a plane with wings modeled after those of the vulture. It is now being constructed by the Vortex Wing Company. Lockheed is also involved in the project.

428. "Died." *Crisis* 39:10 (October 1932): 329. Charles E. James, 30, manager of the James and Nelson Air Circus at Gary, Indiana when his plane crashed in flames. James was the first Negro to complete the course of training at Curtiss Field, NY.

429. "Few Colored Youths Entering Aviation." (September). [ANP release, no year, Claude A. Barnett Papers, Chicago Historical Society. Mentions recent flight of the Zeppelin]. Although applications are high for both white and black, very few qualify. Mentions three flyers: Dr. A. Porter Davis, and two flyers of Tulsa, Oklahoma [Allen and Banning?] All three learned to fly in Kansas and Oklahoma.

430. "First Aircraft Training For Negroes in South." ([November 1941]). [I was not able to locate this periodical. The article is in the Claude A. Barnett Papers, Chicago Historical Society]. As a result of a hard, nine-month fight by the Atlanta Urban League and the Atlanta Negro Defense Training Council, the first defense training program for Negroes aircraft workers in the deep South will start this week. The employer will be the Bell Aircraft Corporation. The article details the struggle.

431. "Haitian Passes U.S. Tests for License to Fly Plane." *New York Amsterdam News* (August 20, 1930): 11. Leon Paris received his private pilot's license after a year of study at the Institute of Aeronautics, 1780 Broadway. Paris emigrated from Haiti eight years ago.

432. "Hoosier Flyer Wings U.S. Air Mail." *Chicago Defender* [Claude A. Barnett Papers, Chicago Historical Society]. Photograph of Dr. Theodore Cable pictured before the plane he flew from Indianapolis to Greencastle in observance of National Air Mail week. Cable is a Harvard graduate, a dentist and a councilman, and has been flying for five years.

433. *Jesus is My Air-O-Plane*. Chicago, June 1930. Mother McCollough and her Sanctified Singers recorded this gospel song for Vocalion VO-1616.

434. Kisch, John, and Edward Mapp. *A Separate Cinema: Fifty Years of Black-Cast Posters*. New York: Farrar, Straus and Giroux, 1992. *The Flying Ace*, 1926, a silent film is described on p. 5. The stars were Lawrence Criner as Capt. Billy Stokes and Kathryn Boyd as Ruth Sawtell, "a female daredevil." A copy is held at the Black Film Center Archives, Indiana University at Bloomington (*Kaiser Index to Selected Black Resources*, vol. 3, p. 385).

435. "Lincoln Aircraft Institute Opens." *Kansas City Call* (April 25, 1941). The institute is the only school of its kind for Negroes in this section of the country. David S. Downing is the chief instructor, W. H. Oliver is the owner, and Dr. A. Porter Davis is on the advisory board.

436. "McEnheimer to Stage Air Show at Butler Airport October 30." *Pittsburgh Courier* (October 25, 1930). "Pittsburgh's brown-skinned Lindy," I. L. McEnheimer. Biographical information.

437. "Miss Harlem's Coming Flight." *New York Amsterdam News* (April 16, 1930). Student pilot Charles M. [*sic*] James , of Northport, L.I., will take delivery and fly his new plane "Miss Harlem" on May 14 at Westbury Airport. There will be other aerial events that day.

438. "Model Plane and Inventor." *New York Amsterdam News* (July 28, 1934). Photograph shows Clement J. Clarke working on a model of his airplane with wings which will flap like a bird's. His shop is at 2523 Seventh Avenue.

439. "Negro Fliers Open Field Here Jan. 1." *Washington Post* (December 15, 1933). The field, Hanson's Airport, will be the first for colored aviation enthusiasts. It will be near Forestville, Maryland. Jesse McCoy Hanson, a Negro pilot, has leased the space, and he will also operate a school of aviation. Mentions the Colored Junior Air Legion.

440. "Negro Inventor Explains the Clarke Ornithoptical Monoplane." *New World* (April 13, 1929). At a lecture held at St. Mark's Hall, Clement J. Clarke explained his invention which is "destined to revolutionize air travel."

441. *Oxford [Miss.] Eagle* (April 25, 1935). [Another citation, incomplete, refers to a similar event staged by William Faulkner and others: *Oxford Eagle*, October 31, 1935]. Willie Jones, the only Negro wing walker and parachute jumper in the world, will make a jump from four thousand feet Sunday afternoon.

442. "Photograph of Dr. A. Porter Davis. of Kansas City, with his own Airplane." *New York Amsterdam News* (April 2, 1930). Dr. Davis has been flying for two years, chiefly for pleasure.

443. Pickens, William. "Wings and Flight." *St. Louis Argus* (July 4, 1931). J. H. Montgomery of Los Angeles has invented "the most marvelous invention in aviation history," named the "Vortex Wing."

444. "Plane Accident Fatal to Two Negro Flyers." (October 27, 1929). [Gumby Collection, Columbia University, Scrapbook #1]. The dateline is Hamilton, Ohio. The flyers were Reuben Floyd and A.J. Miller.

445. "Plane Given Name of 'Miss Harlem'." *New York Amsterdam News* (May 7, 1930). One hundred aviation enthusiasts came to see Charles E. James' new plane christened by Mrs. Bessye J. Bearden.

446. Sampson, Henry T. *Blacks in Black and White: A Source Book on Black Films*. Metuchen, NJ: Scarecrow Press, 1977. Information about Maceo B. Sheffield, stuntman, actor, and a body guard for Cecil B. DeMille. Sheffield received a certificate in 1926 from the Roger School of Aeronautics, and later purchased two planes.

447. Schuyler, George S. "Views and Reviews." *Pittsburgh Courier* (April 24, 1937). [This appeared on the unnumbered editorial page]. Schuyler finds the second issue of *Craftsmen Aero-News* much better than the first. He berates the difficulty of getting "Young Black Joe" interested in aviation instead of learning the Suzy-Q. The address of the journal is 3408 Budlong Avenue in Los Angeles, and the eastern zone commander is Claud DeMond Lewis, an airplane designer.

448. "Sufi Abdul Hamid." *Goldsboro News-Argus* (August 30, 1935). Sufi Abdul Hamid is soliciting funds at churches in Goldsboro and Mt. Olive, North Carolina, to buy a Bellanca plane for 'Ace' Hawkins, a Negro pilot of Wilmington, North Carolina. The purpose is to send him to fight for Ethiopia.

449. *Terraplane Blues*. San Antonio, November 23, 1936. The performer is Robert Johnson and the song was recorded on ARC-7-03-56 and on Co CL-1654. Numerous *doubles entendres* concerning lost love and fidelity.

450. *Terraplane Blues*. Chicago, May 28, 1941. This song was performed by Frank Edwards and recorded on OK-06393 and on BC-6. The singer thinks his girl will return to him if he gets a terraplane and a V-Eight.

451. "Throng at Dedication of Airship." *New York Amsterdam News* (March 30, 1932): 3. Leon Paris's airplane was christened "Toussaint L'Ouverture" at New York Airport. Fox Movietone and Paramount Pix cameras filmed the ceremony. Paris will attempt to fly to Haiti next week, and John W. Green may accompany him. Another pilot in attendance was

Leon F. Desportes, president of the newly formed International Colored Aero Association.

452. "Training to Start Oct. 1." *Pittsburgh Courier* (September 15, 1939). Photographs of West Virginia State College, where a flying school will be established.

453. "Two Young Haitians Take to Air in Attempts to Earn Pilots' Licenses." *[NY Amsterdam News ?]* [Gumby Collection, Columbia University, Scrapbook #1]. Leon Paris and Leon Chipps are receiving flying lessons at Roosevelt Flying School in Mineola, L.I.

454. Williams, Paul. "Why Do They Crash?" *People's World* (June 4, 1938). Williams, a pilot and former lieutenant, j.g., in the U.S. Navy Air Corps, discusses reasons for air crashes. He discusses air safety in general, including social and economic conditions.

455. "Willie 'Suicide' Jones Sets U.S. Air Leap Record." *Chicago Defender* (May 13, 1939): 1. At Dixie Airport, Harvey, Illinois, Jones made a delayed parachute jump. He fell 23,668 feet before he activated his parachute. The previous record of 25,350 feet was held by a Russian. Jones "disdained jerking his rip cord until a scant 800 ft. from earth."

456. "Wings." *Crisis* 40 (May 1933): 111. Capitol Airport at Indianapolis plans to open its doors to colored students and proposed flyers. Article notes there are less than a score of Negroes trained in aviation.

World War II and After

The Tuskegee Airmen

457. "Air Aces Find Glory of War Deeds Fades Overnight." *Ebony* (January 1947): 8-10. Charles B. Hall, one of the first 27 pilots who went overseas with the 99th Pursuit Squadron, is now a restaurant manager at the Hotel Du Sable. Hall is credited as the first black pilot to down a Nazi plane. Hall wants to fly, but points out there isn't a single Negro pilot employed by a major airline in this country.

458. "Air Cadet Tells About English Troop Quarters." *Pittsburgh Courier* (December 12, 1942): 5. Cadet V. J. Richardson, from New York City, was sent to England before his application for flight training was approved. When the approval came through, he was sent to Tuskegee, where he is learning to solo.

459. "The Air Force Goes Interracial." *Ebony* (September 1949): 15-18. The Air Force has planned to eliminate segregation, and by January 1, 1950, the last vestiges of Jim Crow are to be grounded permanently. Negro officers will be able to command white units for the first time. Claude R. Platte is the first Negro to get through postwar advanced training. He was an instructor at Tuskegee.

460. "Air Force Stubbornly Resists Democracy." *Afro-American (Baltimore)* (January 9, 1943): 5. Most of the personnel assigned to air squadrons constitute labor battalions at Tuskegee.

461. "Air Pilots, But Segregated." *Crisis* 48 (February 1941): 39. [Roy Wilkins was the editor and may have been the writer]. An editorial which notes the War Department's announcement that an Army Air Corps Squadron with all-Negro personnel will be formed and trained at Tuskegee

Institute. It is called a step in the right direction, "but colored people want full integration." The squadron will consist of 27 pursuit planes, 33 pilots, and a ground force of 400.

462. "Air Show at Oshkosh is the World's Biggest." *New York Times* (August 2, 1992): 32. A photograph and the information that the 40th annual Experimental Aircraft Associatiion Fly-In Convention will honor World War II's Tuskegee Airmen, and their antique planes.

463. Aldridge, Madeline L. "Let's Look at the Record." *Opportunity* 23:1 (January-March 1945): 31-36. [Special issue on the Negro in the Armed Forces]. These pages deal with aviation. In effect, a capsule history of training at Tuskegee, and the pilots' activities in World War II. Other references are cited, and thirty-six pilots are mentioned by name. Included are excerpts from the citations accompanying the awards of the Distinguished Flying Cross to Benjamin O. Davis, Joseph D. Elsberry, Jack D. Holsclaw, and Clarence D. Lester.

464. Allen, Robert L. "Black Pioneers of the Air Force." *San Francisco Chronicle* (August 30, 1992): 8. [Book Review section]. A review of *Segregated Skies: All-Black Combat Squadrons of WW II*, by Stanley Sandler. Allen says the book is a carefully researched and engaging account, revealing that racial prejudice at home was sometimes a more serious threat to the black fliers than enemy fighters overseas.

465. "All-Negro Squadron Ready for Action." *Click* (September 1943). [This article has three pages. It was located on the VF fiche at the Schomburg Center for Research in Black Culture, NYPL. One page was on "U.S.-Army - Air Force" and two others were on "U.S.- Army - Air Force - 99th Pursuit Squadron."] This group, "tough, smart and rarin' to go," are at Oscoda AFB on Lake Huron, near Selfridge AFB. Their insignia shows a fire-spewing dragon. They are in training here for the final, critical and dangerous stage before combat. Pictured with informative captions are: George L. Knox, Elwood Driver, Wilmore B. Leonard, Robert Diez, Edward C. Gleed, Melvin T. Jackson, P.C. Verwayne, H.A Lawson, and Marion Cabble.

466. "An American in Vienna." *Ebony* (October 1950): 60-62, 65. Carl Johnson, a former 99th Pursuit Squadron pilot, works as a civilian auditor in Vienna. Johnson finds life in Austria has many cultural advantages.

467. "Archie Williams is Dead at 78; Won a Gold at Berlin Olympics." *New York Times* (June 26, 1993): 27. Williams won a gold medal for track in 1936. He died at Marin General Hospital in Greenbrae, California, on June 24. Although he had a degree in mechanical engineering he was unable to find work in that field. After he qualified for a pilot's license he joined the Army Air Corps in 1942, and trained pilots at Tuskegee Institute. In 1986 he retired as a lieutenant colonel. He became the co-owner of Blue Sky Advertising.

468. "Armour G. McDaniel." *New York Times* (November 16, 1989): B17. Armour G. McDaniel, a retired lieutenant colonel who was one of the first black pilots in the Army Air Force, died [11-12-89] in Indianapolis, where he lived. He was trained at Tuskegee, and flew over Italy and Germany.

469. "Army Air Corps Smoke Screen." *Crisis* 48 (April 1941): 103. [Roy Wilkins was the editor and may have been the writer]. Editorial comments that the official announcements of the War Department calling for Negro pilots, as detailed in the daily press, looks like a smoke screen to confuse and quiet Negro public opinion. Although calling for pilots, with only 33 Negroes out of 30,000 trainees a year, it appears very little actual training is taking place.

470. Ashe, Arthur R. *A Hard Road to Glory: A History of the African-American Athlete 1919-1945.* New York: Warner Books, 1988. There is biographical information on Wilmeth Sidat-Singh, who was killed while a Tuskegee Airman, and who played basketball and football for Syracuse University.

471. Austin, Manning. "The Negro is Flying." *Flying and Popular Aviation* (March 1941): 32-34, 74. [The article examined was incomplete]. A lengthy article about the aviation activities at Tuskegee Institute. "Airminded Negro youths have fought their way into aviation despite great odds. Theirs is a story of perseverance."

472. "Author Recalls Heroic Deed of Black Fighter Pilots." *Call and Post (Cleveland)* (January 25, 1990). Biographical information on William C. Ferguson, author of *Black Flyers in World War II*, and a former Tuskegee Airman.

473. "Aviation Ground Service Training for Negroes at Tuskegee." *Opportunity* 19:10 (October 1941): 313. Under the Works Project Administration, this project is designed to train airport mechanics. It is the first for Negroes in Alabama.

474. "Aviator Gilbert A. Cargill in Michigan Hall of Fame." *Jet* 77:6 (November 13, 1989): 30. Gilbert A. Cargill, the first black pilot examiner, was inducted into the Michigan Aviation Hall of Fame. Trained at Tuskegee , Cargill is now the chairman of the Michigan Aeronautics Commission.

475. "B-25 Bomber Students Make Good Progress." *Journal and Guide (Norfolk,VA)* (December 8, 1943): The first contingent of Negro flying officers who came to Mather Field, California, is becoming expert on the operation of B-52 bombers. Nearly all the men were trained at Tuskegee, and are qualified Army Air Force pilots.

476. Barnes, Bart. "Gen. Noel F.Parrish Dies; Trained Tuskegee Airmen." *Washington Post* (April 10, 1987): C-4. Parrish, the white commander of the all-black Tuskegee unit from 1942-1945, died on April 7. He managed to turn the unit into a well-functioning one despite indifference and hostility from high military officials. He later called for integration, which occured in the Air Force within months of Pres. Truman's 1948 order. Long full obituary.

477. Barnett, Elliott J. "Tuskegee A [?] Starts Seco [?]." *Atlanta World* (October 9, 1943). The division of aero-mechanics at Tuskegee Institute started its second year with increased enrollment and up-dated equipment. It is a two-year course of laboratory work and lectures, which ends with a license from the Civilian Aeronautics Authority.

478. Bernstein, James. "Orrin S. Watson, 31, Piloted Bombers." *Newsday* (April 11, 1981): n.p. Watson died in a car crash in Kansas, where he was training at McConnell AFB in Wichita. His father is Spann Watson, a former Tuskegee airman and retired lieut. colonel, who lives in Westbury. Biographical information.

479. "Black Airmen Draw Youths into Aviation." *Jet* 68:26 (September 9, 1985): 8. The Organization of Black Airline Pilots finances a summer program of flight training at Tuskegee for black youths. The group's founder, Benjamin Thomas, notes that there are according to the FAA

only 165 black pilots out of a total of 44,000. He hopes young people can aspire to aviation, as they now do to sports.

480. "Black Fliers to Take Oshkosh Spotlight." *USA Today* (July 30, 1992): 6. Diagramatic survey of the Tuskegee Airmen's actions in World War II.

481. "Blacks in the U.S. Army Air Force in World War II." *Folio (WBAI radio station)* (February 1987): 2. The story of the Tuskegee Airmen will be told on the program "Weaponry" night of Tuesday into Wednesday, February 10/11. Much information is given in this article and a photo of Charles Hall is featured.

482. "Body of Flyer Found in Lake after 49 Days." *Michigan Chronicle* (July 3, 1943). Wilmeth W. Sidat-Singh was killed on May 9, when he parachuted from his burning plane over Lake Huron, Michigan. Sidat-Singh, 25, had been a football star at Syracuse University, and with the 332nd Squadron at Tuskegee.

483. Booker, Simeon. "Ticker Tape U.S.A." *Jet* (December 15, 1977): 10. Announcement that famed Air Force pilot Elwood T. Driver will become the first black member of the National Transportation Safety Board.

484. Booker, Simeon. "Washington's Civil Rights Maverick." *Ebony* (May 1965): 140-145.An economist at the Department of Health, Education and Welfare, Julius Hobson has been a strong civil rights activist for two decades. Hobson was a pilot during the Allied invasion of Italy in World War II.

485. Bosch, Steven John. "Black History Month - Esquerre Pays Back." *Westbury Pennysaver (New York)* (February 4, 1989). A profile of Jean R. Esquerre, former director of the Grumman Corporation and a past president of the Tuskegee Airmen, Inc. Esquerre is active in raising scholarship money for those interested in aviation careers, and believes in helping others as he was once helped, "You don't forget where you came from." Before joining Grumman he worked for Republic Aviation. Esquerre mentions early flyers such as Eugene Bullard, Bessie Coleman, and Chauncey Spencer.

486. "Boy Scout Executive." *Ebony* (March 1971): 6. Now an executive with the Boy Scouts Of America in Newark, Joseph Merton was a fighter pilot in World War II.

487. Boyne, Walter J. *Air Force Eagles*. New York: Crown, 1992. [*Third in a series: Trophy for Eagles, Eagles at War*]. John Marshall, a former Tuskegee airman and master fighter pilot, is a major character in this novel. Marshall becomes a prisoner of war in Korea; the novel deals with the rebuilding of the Air Force, while recounting the story of the fight for civil rights in both civilian and military life.

488. Britt, Donna. "Pilots Who Broke the Barrier." *Washington Post* (August 12, 1989): C 1-3. A report of the Tuskegee Airmen's 18th anniversary convention, attended by 700. The article includes mention of the demonstration at Free[d]man Field in Indiana, and reminiscences of the pilots who were told they lacked the courage, skills, and brains to fly. They are: Phillip Brown, John Whitehead, Charles McGee, Harvey McDonald, Alexander Jefferson, Cornelius Gould, Daniel James, Benjamin O. Davis, and Walter McCreary. Some others who became well known are: Louis Stokes, Coleman Young, Percy Sutton, and Charles C. Diggs.

489. Brown, Roscoe C. Jr. "Are Black Officials 'Targets of Opportunity'?" *New York Amsterdam News* (February 29, 1992): 13, 37. [Dr. Brown was a Tuskegee airman and is now president of Bronx Community College]. The article is about politics, but Brown mentions his war service.

490. "Capt. Wendell Pruitt Killed in Plane Crash." *St.-Louis Post-Dispatch* (April 16, 1945). Pruitt was killed, along with his student, at Tuskegee where he was an instructor. Last December 12 was declared Wendell O. Pruitt Day by the mayor. Biographical information and list of survivors.

491. Carter, Elmer A. "The Negro Pilot." *Opprtunity* 18:9 (September 1940): 258. An editorial praising the editorial in the *Chicago Tribune* (August 8) which called for the War Department to include Negroes in its aviation programs.

492. Carter, Elmer A. "A Negro Pursuit Squadron." *Opportunity* 19:4 (April 1941): 98-99. Carter is gratified that the War Department has taken steps to organize and train a Negro aviation unit, but he is not satisfied. "Just why the Negro pilot must be trained at Tuskegee we are unable to say. Up to this point we have not learned of any special place where German, Italian, Jewish or Chinese Americans are being trained."

493. "Ceiling Unlimited; North Carolina's Only Negro Owned and Operated Airfield." *Our World* 3 (August 1948): 48-49. Edward Gibbs owns and

operates the Atlantic School of Aviation in Wilmington, North Carolina. He had been an instructor at Tuskegee and at a flying school on Long Island. One of the students is Marian Davis.

494. Chalk, Ocania. *Black College Sport*. New York: Dodd, Mead & Co., 1976. Biographical information on Wilmeth Sidat-Singh on pp.110-112, 188-189. Sidat-Singh played for Syracuse University and died in a plane crash while enrolled at Tuskegee.

495. Clanton, Stephan, and George Watson. "Black War Hero's Memory Kept Alive." *McGuire Airtides* (September 30, 1988): 2. The Hannibal M. "Killer" Cox Jr. Chapter of the Tuskegee Airmen Inc. at McGuire AFB is named for the colonel who fought in three wars. Biographical information provided about Cox, president of the Tuskegee Airmen for four years, and now active in community affairs in Miami. Thanks to this chapter, McGuire's First Street was renamed Tuskegee Airmen Avenue on June 18, 1988.

496. Cockerham, William. "Black Pilots Earned Their Wings and Respect of White Colleagues." *Hartford Courant* (September 28, 1992): 1, 4. Profile of retired Lt. Col. Bertram Wilson, a former Tuskegee Airman, who also fought in Korea and Vietnam. He recalls days at Tuskegee, and and anecdotes about Mac Ross, Herman Lawson, and Freeman Field in Indiana.

497. "Commercial Airline Pilot." *Ebony* (September 1951): 4. Biographical information on Fred Hutcherson. He was a Tuskegee Airman, operated a flying service in Haiti, served with the Royal Canadian Air Force, and has been working in Colombia since 1948.

498. "Congress Hears that Negro Airmen Leave for Combat." *Call and Post (Cleveland)* (May 1, 1943): 1, 9. Congressman Frances P. Bolten of Ohio informed Congress on April 15 that the squadrons trained at Tuskegee were soon to leave for combat. Her remarks were entered in the *Congressional Record*, and thousands of copies were printed for distribution.

499. "Conrad Johnson, 71, A Retired Architect." *New York Times* (July 23, 1991). Johnson and his partners designed many buildings in his native Harlem, including the state office building. He served in World War II as a pilot in the 100th Fighter Squadron which trained at Tuskegee Institute.

500. Corry, John. "'Unknown Soldier,' on Channel 13." *New York Times* (November 11, 1985): C17. The film reconstructs the lives of six men who died in World War II, and whose bodies were never identified. The black soldier is Alfonza Davis, a Tuskegee Airman who won a Distinguished Flying Cross and vanished over Yugoslavia. His widow is interviewed.

501. Crowley, Susan. "'On a Silver, Satin Road'." *AARP Bulletin* 32:3 (March 1991): 16. A profile of Louis Purnell, one of the original 450 Tuskegee Airmen. Now retired from his post as curator for the National Air and Space Museum, Purnell speaks of his days in World War II, discrimination, his jobs as a speech therapist, oceanographer, and of his present life.

502. Dade County Aviation Department. *Blacks in Aviation*. Miami, Florida: Miami International Airport, 1992. This brochure was written for the annual Blacks in Aviation reception, February 7, 1992. It contains an historical overview, and there is information on Benjamin O. Davis Jr., James O. Plinton, Spann Watson, C. Alfred Anderson, and Hannibal M. Cox. There is also information on black aviation organizations, and presidents of local chapters are featured: Carl Singletary of Negro Airmen International, Oscar Perry of Organization of Black Airline Pilots, and Sancta Watley of the National Black Coalition of Federal Aviation Employees. There is also note of Florida Memorial College which has a division of Airway and Computer Sciences.

503. Dade County Aviation Department. *Blacks in Aviation*. Miami, Florida: Miami International Airport, 1993. This is the brochure for the annual Blacks in Aviation reception. There is an historical overview and information on the guest speaker, Lt. Gen. Frank E. Petersen, retired, of the Marine Corps. Information is included on other honorees: Keith B. Jennings, Willie H. Fuller, and Charles J. Flowers. There is also information on black aviation organizations (see previous entry). The only change in local presidents is Ahmad M. Rafi of the Negro Airmen International. The local chapter president of the Tuskegee Airmen, Inc. is Leo R. Gray.

504. De Bow, Charles H. "I Got Wings." *American Magazine* (August 1942): 28-29, 104-106. [As told to William A. H. Birnie]. De Bow was one of the first five graduates at Tuskegee. He lists the others as Lem Custis, Ben Davis, George Roberts, and Mac Ross. The article consists of nearly equal parts of autobiography, patriotism, and experiences of first flights

and the rigorous training at Tuskegee. De Bow felt a double duty: to his country and to his race. He felt he was flying for the 12,000,000 Negroes in the U.S. The training at Tuskegee lasted five weeks, from 5:00 in the morning until 10:00 in the evening.

505. Dowling, Lyn. "Col. John D. Silvera: Gaining Rank Was Not Easy When the Ranks were All White." *Delegate* (1986): 156-157. [This periodical is an annual which chronicles meetings of black organizations]. Biographical information on Silvera, who was a Tuskegee Airman, an aide to Gov. Rockefeller, and is now a businessman in Florida. There is also information about the 15th annual convention to take place in Orlando, Florida, on August 5-10, 1986. Jean R. Esquerre is the president; other officers are listed.

506. "Drum Collecting Dental Surgeon." *Ebony* (September 1965): 44-46. [Part of the collection was exhibited at Watts Towers Museum in 1991]. Dr. Joseph Howard, an ex-World War II flight instuctor and dentist, collects drums from all over the world, lives in Los Angeles.

507. "Edges to Honor Famed Airmen." *New York Amsterdam News* (October 6, 1984): 6. The Edges Group, an organization of black professionals in industry and government, will hold their 12th annual luncheon on October 11th. They will salute black pilots of major airlines. Lee Archer Jr. is to receive an award. Two other Tuskegee Airmen will be present, as will thirty active pilots from fourteen airlines.

508. Edwards, Audrey. "Essencemen." *Essence* 8:5 (September 1977): 12. Biographical information on James O. Plinton, Eastern Airlines' first black vice president.

509. "Electron Beam Research Head." *Ebony* (June 1970): 6. Allen H. Turner now works at the Ford Motor Company in Dearborn, Michigan. He was an Air Force pilot and taught at Tuskegee.

510. "Elwood Driver, Safety Official, Tuskegee Airman, Dies at 70." *Washington Post* (April 1, 1992): D4. Obituary. Driver was a past president of the Tuskegee Airmen, Inc.

511. Erstein, Hap. "The Eagles Who Touched the Sky." *Insight* 7 (March 4, 1991): 53-55. The history of the pilots trained at Tuskegee has not been told properly. This situation is being remedied now with the production

of *Black Eagles* at Ford's Theater in Washington, D.C., and the publication of Benjamin O. Davis' autobiography. George Lucas has a film in production about the Tuskegee pilots, but Davis has refused to cooperate. The pilots who are interviewed are: Philip F. Lee, Washington; Woodrow W. Crockett, Annandale; Harry Sheppard, Arlington; and Elwood T. Driver, Reston. Driver comments on the play and remarks that the legacy of the Black Eagles was a giant step toward integration, not just in the military, but everywhere. Gen. Davis is featured in a separate box, "The Eagle who Soared the Highest." Davis believes the biggest problem facing the nation today is racism.

512. "Ex-GI Starts Haiti Airline." *Ebony* (February 1948): 28-30. James O. Plinton Jr., four years out of the Air Corps, started an airline and the first modern dry-cleaning plant in Port-au-Prince, Haiti. An instructor at Tuskegee, he could not enter commercial aviation after the war. Biographical information, and comments on Haitian-American relations.

513. Feather, Leonard. *Encyclopedia of Jazz.* New York: Horizon Press, 1960. Percy Heath, one of the most recorded bassists in jazz, was a fighter pilot in the Air Force for two and a half years, p. 249.

514. Ferguson, William C. *Black Flyers in World War II.* [Cleveland, Ohio]: [Ferguson's Publishing Co.], 1987. [Second Edition]. A personal account by a radio operator mechanic and gunner with the 617th Bombardment Squad. Illustrated with many photographs in sepia tone, the book includes lists of men, poetry, quotations, and history of the Tuskegee Airmen. In addition, there is an account of the incident at Freeman Field in Indiana, by Cornelius Gould, in April 1945, when black officers tried to use the all-white officers club. There is a photograph of Dorothy Arline Layne McIntyre.

515. Finucane, Martin. "Black Aviators Concerned About Decline in their Ranks." *Advocate (Connecticut)* (August 16, 1992): A16. The Tuskegee Airmen Inc. and the Organization of Black Airline Pilots held a joint annual convention in Boston. Elmore Kennedy of Detroit is president of the TAI, and M. Perry Jones is president of OBAP. Both groups urge that an aviation school be set up at a traditionally black college or university. Federal funding has been approved for a two-year, $1 million study. Jones said that only 600 of the nation's 72,000 pilots are black.

516. "First Negro Cadets Arrive at Texas Field." *Journal & Guide (Norfolk, VA)* (November 6, 1943): 1, 2. Thirty Negro cadets arrived at Hondo Army Air Field to be enrolled as navigator students. Biographical information on cadet Arnold W. Galimore of New York.

517. "First Negro Officers Commissioned in U.S. Air Corps." *Opportunity* 20:4 (April 1942): 120. On March 7 a group of Negro pilots became 2nd Lieutenants in the U.S. Army Air Corps, at Tuskegee, Alabama. They are B.O. Davis Jr., Mac Ross, George Spencer Roberts, Lemuel R. Custis, and Charles Henry De Bow. A photo includes some of the above and Frederick H. Moore, C. H. Flowers Jr., George Levi Knox, Lee Rayford, Sherman W. White Jr., and James B. Knighten. Biographical information on Davis and Roberts.

518. Fisher, Joseph. "His Scrapbooks Source of Memorable Material." *Asbury Park Press* (December 13, 1987): F8. An account of George Watson's life and his collection of scrapbooks, which he started in his youth. He used these scrapbooks to write the recently-published *Memorable Memoirs*, which details his experiences with the Tuskegee Unit during World War II.

519. "Flight Testing: New Opportunities in the Air." *Encore* 4 (March 17, 1975): 41-42, 45. Interview with Charles Sewall and Jean Esquerre, corporate director in charge of Grumman's EEO affirmative action program.

520. Flint, Jerry M. "Black Ex-Pilots Recall Bias in World War II." *New York Times* (August 14, 1972). Two hundred Tuskegee Airmen held a three-day reunion in Detroit. There are comments by Richard Macon, Coleman Young, Edward C. Gleed, Daniel James, Alex Jefferson, Ario Dixione, Ernest Browne, and Charles Hill.

521. "Flying Fire-Fighter." *Ebony* (April 1957): 148-150. Alvin E. Harrison is now a helicopter pilot for the U.S. Forestry Service in California. He was a former Captain in the 332nd Fighter Wing and served in Germany after World War II.

522. "Flying School." *Ebony* (January 1958): 26-32. Former bomber pilot Tuskegee airman (477th Bomber Group), Paul T. Anderson operates the B and A Air Service at Compton, CA. Ninety percent of the enrollees are white. Charles Foreman is an instructor at the school. Charles Gaines is a student. Connie Henry is the only Negro woman enrolled at the school.

Bernadette Anderson, his wife, is learning to fly. Danny Anderson, his nephew, is being trained to be a mechanic.

523. Francis, Charles E. *The Tuskegee Airmen: The Story of the Negro in the U.S. Air Force*. Boston: Bruce Humphries, Inc., 1955. [Second printing, 1968]. This history contains, in an appendix, lists of combat records, enemy aircraft shot down by Negro pilots, holders of the Distinguished Flying Cross, Letters of Commendation, and the Tuskegee Honor Roll (those killed while in service).

524. Francis, Charles E. *The Tuskegee Airmen: The Men who Changed a Nation*. Boston: Branden Publishing Company, 1988. "This author believes the story of these airmen has been so fragmentally told that the true story is still unknown. This book has been revised and enlarged in an attempt to tell as completely, accurately, and objectively as possible that story."

525. "From Computer Whiz to Karate Champ." *Grumman World* (February 12, 1988): 6. The article is about Debbie Pugh, but Jean Esquerre is quoted on the benefits of karate. Esquerre, a retired Grumman executive, is chief instructor and club founding president.

526. Gaskill, Gordon. "The Day the 99th Pursuit Squadron Defied a Command." *Negro Digest* (July 1961): 35-38. A Southerner's memory of the unselfish heroism of Negro pilots in Italy helped him to see the evil of segregation at home.

527. Gleed, Edward C. "The Story of America's Black Air Force." *Tony Brown's Journal* (January/March 1983): 4-7. [The entire issue is devoted to articles about the Tuskegee Airmen, to tie in with Tony Brown's four-part PBS television program, "The Black Eagles," to be shown in February. There are articles by Clarence D. Lester, p.5; Hannibal Cox, and Alexander Jefferson, p.15. All were pilots, and Jefferson was a German prisoner of war. There is also information on the Smithsonian's exhibition, "Black Wings: The American Black in Aviation," p.15. Many others are mentioned and pictured]. A historical account by a retired colonel in the Air Force.

528. Goldsmith, Benedict. "The True 'Hot' Pilots of WWII." *AARP Bulletin* 32:5 (May 1991): 15. [Letter to the Editor]. Response to article about Louis Purnell (March 1991). "I thought that I was a top-notch 'hot' pilot

until I examined the achievement charts... Those black cadets made us all look like fumblebums."

529. Guzman, Jessie Parkhurst. *Negro Yearbook: A Review of Events Affecting Negro Life, 1941-1946.* Tuskegee, Alabama: Tuskegee Institute, 1947. "The Negro in the Army Air Force," pp. 354-358, covers such subjects as discrimination, history, Tuskegee Army Air Field, the 99th Pursuit Squadron, the 332nd Fighter Squadron, the 447th Composite Group and statistics on 6,000 Negro technicians, mechanics, and pilots on August 31, 1945. Mentioned is the discrimination against Roderick Charles Williams, and William H. Hastie is quoted on another aspect of discrimination.

530. Hall, Debra M. "World War II Flying Aces." *Ebony Jr!* 10:8 (February 1983): 3. A brief description of the formation, training, and service of the Tuskegee Airmen. Definitions of words are included.

531. Halliburton, Warren J. *The Fighting Redtails: America's First Black Airmen.* New York: CPI, 1978. A children's book illustrated by Jon Gampert, and with photographs, on the history of the 332nd Fighter Group. A revised edition is forthcoming in 1993.

532. Harney, James. "Tuskegee Pilots: Men on a Mission." *USA Today* (July 30, 1992): 6. Interviews with a number of former Tuskegee Airmen, who will be honored at the world's largest air show to celebrate their 50th anniversary. There are now more than 30 Tuskegee Airmen chapters, with 1200 members, in the United States, Europe, and Japan. The men interviewed are: Herbert Carter, Roger Terry, Charles McGee, Robert Ashby, Lee Archer, Roscoe C. Brown, and Benjamin O. Davis.

533. Harper, Gena. "Tuskegee: Runway to Victory." *Soldiers* 39:2 (February 1984): 49-52. A history of the "Tuskegee Experiment." The Tuskegee Airmen had two enemies, one abroad and one at home. Their legacy was to smooth the route to integration for others.

534. Harris, Greg. "Black Pilot Shortage." *New York Amsterdam News* (October 7, 1989): 36. The scarcity of black pilots in both military and commercial aviation can't be attributed only to racism. The author says too few black youth concentrate on mathematics and physics in high school and college. Harris is himself a pilot and a Tuskegee Airman.

Included is a chart giving the numbers of black pilots and navigators in the U. S. Airforce as of March 31, 1989.

535. Harris, Lorenzo D. "All Guts, Little Glory: Black Aviators in WW II." *Airman* (February 1985): 27-31. A history of the 332nd Fighter Group, which includes interviews with members of the Greater Florida chapter of the Tuskegee Airmen, Inc. They are Samuel Wade Watts Jr., Hiram Mann, Channing Conway, and Charles McGee, the current president. Conway was involved in the incident at Freeman Field, Indiana.

536. Harris, Ruth Bates. *Harlem Princess: The Story of Harry Delaney's Daughter*. New York: Vantage Press, 1991. [There is no index. There are many photocopies of newspaper articles relating to Harris' work at NASA, and to her termination. They are not listed separately in the bibliography]. Harris was from October 1971 to October 1973 the first Director of Equal Employment Opportunity at NASA. At that time there were no women or minorities in the space program. She was rehired in August 1974 as Deputy Assistant Administrator for Public Affairs for Community and Human Relations, and she left in 1976. Chapter 17, pp. 253-281, covers this period. In addition, Harris was married to two Tuskegee airmen, Charles Foxx (chapters 7, 8, 9 and *passim*) and Alfred McKenzie (314-318, 334). The Tuskegee Experiment is recalled on pp.48-54, 61-65, 343-345. McKenzie writes of his pilot training at Tuskegee, and of the incident at Freeman Field, Indiana, which was sparked by the pilots' challenge to discrimination. In addition there is a moving tribute to Gen. B.O. Davis Jr. by Alan L. Gropman at a reunion of Tuskegee Airmen in 1989 on p. 344.

537. Hasdorff, James C. "Reflections on the Tuskegee Experiment: An Interview with Brig. Gen. Noel F. Parrish USAF (Ret.)" *Aerospace Historian* 25:3 (September 1977): 173-180. This discussion of Gen. Parrish's role in opening and commanding the flying school at Tuskegee is based on the author's oral history of Parrish, June 1974, at Trinity University in San Antonio, Texas.

538. "Hastie Condemns 'Unholy Alliance' Between Tuskegee and Air Forces." *Washington Tribune* (March 27, 1943). The Army Air Forces have announced a new program of college courses to be taught by 100 scholars. All the black cadets, mostly college graduates, will have to study at

Tuskegee, instead of at the prestigious colleges where the courses will be conducted.

539. Hastie, William H. *On Clipped Wings: The Story of Jim Crow in the Army Air Corps*. [New York]: [National Association for the Advancement of Colored People], [1943]. Hastie wrote this pamphlet after his resignation as Civilian Aide to the Secretary of War. This account reorganizes, rearranges, and in some cases, supplements his other writings about the reactionary policies and discriminatory practices of the Air Force. Sections are headed: Tuskegee - Jim Crow in Action, Pilot Training, and The Negro Specialist - Not Wanted. In the latter he presents the cases of experienced pilots such as Fred Hutcherson, who flies for Canada, James L. H. Peck, James W. Redders, Gilbert Cargill, Charles Ashe, and others.

540. Hatch, James V., and Leo Hamalian. *Artist and Influence 1989*. New York: Hatch-Billops Collection, 1989. In an interview with Ann Gibson, Ronald Joseph, a painter, speaks of his service in the Air Force at Tuskegee, pp. 69-70. Joseph was part of the ground crew. He speaks of the segregation there, and tells he did the lettering on the training planes.

541. Henderson, Edwin B. *The Black Athlete: Emergence and Arrival*. Cornwells Heights, Pa.: The Publishers Agency, Inc, 1976. Biographical information on Wilmeth Sidat-Singh on pp. 30, 47-49. Sidat-Singh was both a basketball and football star. He was a Tuskegee Airman.

542. "Hint 99th Pursuit Squadron on Duty." *Michigan Chronicle* (May 1, 1943). Mrs. Bolton lets cat out of the bag. Mrs. Bolton, a Republican representative from Ohio, announced to the Congress that the flyers who had been trained at Tuskegee were soon to go overseas.

543. Hochberg, Joshua E. "The Tuskegee Airmen: Courage on Two Fronts." *FAA Aviation News* (January-February 1993): 14-16. This history of the Tuskegee Airmen is preceded by a note from the Editor, to the effect that black aviation history has never been addressed in the magazine, aside from an article on Bessie Coleman in the January/ February 1983 issue. Clarence D. (Lucky) Lester's account of his three kills in July 1944 is included.

544. "Hold Military Rites for Aviator Killed in Crash." *Call and Post (Cleveland)* (May 29, 1943): 1. Lt. Jerome Tompkins Edwards was killed in an airplane crash at Oscoda Army Air Base, Michigan. He received

his wings at Tuskegee Nov. 10, 1942; other biographical information. His brother John Ellis Edwards is now a cadet at Tuskegee.

545. "Hollywood's Handsome Henry." *Ebony* (February 1959): 45-48. Henry Benjamin Scott acts, writes and directs. After 1943 Scott was a fighter pilot with the 332nd Fighter Squadron, and he won numerous medals for combat over Europe.

546. "Honoring Tuskegee Airmen." *New York Amsterdam News* (September 1, 1990): 20. A photograph taken at the Tuskegee Airmen's 19th National Convention in Los Angeles. Pictured are Nancy Leftenant-Colon, president of Tuskegee Airmen Inc. (TAI), Paul Lehman, and Lee Archer, among others.

547. Jablonski, Edward. *America in the Air War*. Alexandria, VA: Time-Life Books, 1982. "The Fifteenth's Red Tail Angels," pp.138-139. The 332nd Fighter Group was composed of the following four squadrons: the 99th, 100th, 301st and 302nd. They flew P-51 Mustangs whose tails were painted red. They escorted the Fifteenth Air Force. They damaged or destroyed 400 enemy aircraft, but never lost one of their own bombers. Those mentioned are Benjamin O. Davis, Armour G. McDaniel (photo), and Charles Hall.

548. Jakeman, Robert J. *The Divided Skies: Establishing Segregated Flight Training at Tuskegee, Alabama, 1934-1942*. Tuscaloosa, AL: University of Alabama Press, 1992. This scholarly work begins with Tuskegee's attempts to establish aviation courses in its curriculum, and ends with the graduation of the first class of black pilots. The author explores three main elements of the fierce campaign waged by blacks to open the Air Corps to them: tradition of military service by blacks, growing interest in aviation by the black public, and the emergence of civil rights as a national issue in the thirties. Highly readable, the book includes notes, bibliography, and an index.

549. Jasper, John. "Kimble Stuns Tuskegee." *Afro-American (Baltimore)* (January 9, 1943): 1, 2. Col. Frederick Kimble replaced Major Ellison, who treated the airmen at Tuskegee fairly. He ordered "Colored" and "White" signs put up over the mess and wash rooms. They were torn down. The unit was to have been all colored, but the staff of white instructors has increased.

550. "Jersey Men, Damon-Pythias at Tuskegee Flying School." *Pittsburgh Courier* (December 12, 1942): 8. Norman F. Prime and John L. Callaway, who have been friends since childhood, are now skilled technicians at Tuskegee.

551. "Jet Cameraman." *Ebony* (September 1952): 5. Lloyd "Scotty" Hathcock is a cameraman for the U.S. Air Force and has co-designed a high-speed camera and has helped perfect an escape mechanism. He was a Tuskegee-trained fighter pilot and a POW in Germany.

552. "Jet Pilot over Korea." *Ebony* (October 1950): 21-22, 24-26. James F. Harvey Jr. is one of an estimated 25 colored pilots integrated into air force units in Japan. Biographical information on Harvey as well as his comments on integration (feels the environment more to blame for prejudice than the individual). He was at Tuskegee from 1944-1949. Edward P. Drummond is the second black jet pilot.

553. Johnson, Ernest E. "Tries to Kill Self Over Army Jim Crow." (April 19, 1944). [ANP Release, Claude A. Barnett Papers, Chicago Historical Society]. Norman W. Spaulding, of Chicago, and a student at Howard University, slashed his wrists in a suicide pact he had with two other friends. He had studied at the Coffey School of Aeronautics, and at various fields, including Tuskegee.

554. Johnson, Hayden C. *The Fighting 99th Air Squadron, 1941-45*. New York: Vantage Press, 1987. A brief and bitter account of the origins and personality clashes of the squadrons at Tuskegee. Johnson disparages the personality and combat ability of Benjamin O. Davis, who "was extremely vindictive toward me because of my decision to practice law after the war rather than seek an army career with him." Many photographs and mention of other well-known pilots, but there is no index. There is a photograph of the author's brother, Capt. Maurice Johnson, "first Negro flight surgeon in the world." A photocopy of an obituary of George Spencer Roberts is included, but it lacks source and date.

555. Johnson, Maurice E. "The History and Development of Aviation Medicine." *Journal of the National Medical Association* 35:6 (November 1943): 194-199. Johnson, a doctor, gives a brief history, starting with a balloon flight in 1862 by a French physiologist. Johnson is a captain, flight examiner with the Air Corps Training Detachment at Tuskegee.

556. Johnston, Ernest. "Raymond Brown, A Lawyer's Lawyer for the Defense." *Black Enterprise* 9:12 (July 1979): 40. Famous as the defense lawyer in New Jersey's trial of Dr. X, Brown was trained to fly at Tuskegee.

557. "Jones Promoted to Lt. Col. at Pentagon Post." *Eagle & Swan* 2:6 (December 1979): 5. Reginald Jones was promoted on April 1, 1979. He graduated from Tuskegee Institute in 1963, and he has served in China, Utah, Vietnam, and Italy. Biographical information.

558. Jordan, John. "Daring Flyers Streamline Farm Work With Airplanes - No Less." [I was unable to locate the periodical or the date. From internal evidence it is after 1948]. Long article on Lawrence E. Anderson, a crop duster, and a former aviation instructor at Tuskegee Primary Air Base. Anderson is 28, a native of Greensburg, Pennsylvania. He received his private pilot's license in 1937, and his commercial pilot's license in 1939. he lives at 46 Manly Street in Portsmouth, Virginia. More biographical information.

559. "Joseph White, 68, Was Tuskegee Airman in War." *Asbury Park Press* (July 8, 1992). [Obituary, died July 6, 1992]. Joseph Ejaffa White of Freehold Township, NJ, was a probation officer, and had flown with the 332nd Fighter Group.

560. Kirsh, Diane. "Aviators Recall Struggle to Fly." *News and Advance* (August 29, 1991): B1, 7. Chauncey Spencer was unable to attend the Tuskegee Airmen's annual Convention in Detroit, so five members of the group visited him at home in Lynchburg, Virginia. Spencer and Dale White made a flight in 1939 to Washington, where they met Sen. Harry Truman by chance. He told them if they had the guts to fly the plane, he would have the guts to get their concerns into the congressional committee. This event led to the establishment of the training facilities at Tuskegee. The flyers who came to honor Spencer were: Robert Walker, Walter Robinson, Richard Jennings, William McClenick, and Wardell Polk. The men spoke of their desire to be Americans first. Spencer said, "We had to fight to get into the Army and then fight to get back into the country."

561. Lakeos, Nick. "Varoom! B-r-r-t Rat, Tat, Tat." *Washington Post* (August 20, 1977): B1, 2. Report of the annual convention of Tuskegee Airmen, held this year at Tuskegee. Despite the headline, the story is not so much about battles as it is about the pilots' experiences and qualities

necessary to be a fighter pilot. Prominently featured is Spann Watson. Others mentioned are Daniel James, Percy Sutton, and Curtis Robinson.

562. Lambert, Bruce. "Elwood Driver, 70, Wartime Pilot and Transportation Safety Expert." *New York Times* (April 4, 1992): 31. Elwood T. Driver, one of America's first black combat pilots died on March 26. He was a Tuskegee airman and shot down a German plane over Italy.

563. Lawson, Harry ed. *African Americans in Aviation in Arizona.* [Tucson], Arizona: Arizona Historical Society and Pima Community College, 1989. [Photocopy seen, 25 pp]. A report of the African American History Internship Project. Four interns were trained in oral history; cassettes of the interviews are at the AHS. The four people interviewed were involved with aviation before coming to Arizona. Interviews are with: Frances Archer, about her deceased husband, Fred, for whom the local Tuskegee Airmen's chapter is named; Janet Harmon Bragg (Waterford); Roy Comeaux; and Vernon Haywood. Unsuccessful attempts were made to interview Phillip Aaron, president of Golden Pacific Airline in Kingman.

564. Lee, Leslie. *Black Eagles.* New York: Samuel French, Inc., 1990. This play, about a reunion of the Tuskegee Airmen, was produced by the Manhattan Theatre Club in association with Crossroads Theatre Company on April 2, 1991.

565. "The Legend of Luther Smith." *Reporter (GE Aerospace Re-entry Systems, Philadelphia)* 2:4 (February 26, 1988): 2-5. [Cover story]. Luther Henry Smith has worked for General Motors for 37 years, and is now the Motivations Program Manager for the Re-entry Systems Department. He was a Tuskegee Airman, faced death four times on Friday, October 13, 1944, was a prisoner of war in Austria, and has received many medals. On his release from the prison camp he weighed 70 pounds. He is an engineer and the holder of six patents.

566. Leuthner, Stuart, and Oliver Jensen. *High Honor: Recollections by Men and Women of World War II Aviation.* Washington, D.C.: Smithsonian Institution Press, 1989. Roscoe Brown, "The Edge of Dignity," pp.238-247. Brown has been the president of Bronx Community College since 1977. He went on active duty in March 1943, immediately after college graduation. He recounts his days at Tuskegee, battle experiences, and he mentions his colleagues, C. Alfred Anderson, Noel Parrish, and

John Whitehead. The title refers to the necessity of giving up dignity, in the face of discrimination, to achieve a larger result. He learned to play the game but inch forward at the same time.

567. "Lieut. Sidat-Singh's Plane Found." *New York Amsterdam News* (May 15, 1943): 1. Wilmeth Sidat-Singh is still missing after his plane crashed in Michigan. The Harlemite was a football star at Syracuse University, and he graduated only two weeks ago from Tuskegee.

568. "Lt. Sidat-Singh Buried in Arlington Cemetery." *Call (Kansas City, MO)* (July 9, 1943). After a ceremony at Holy Redeemer Church in Washington, D.C. the 25-year old Lt. Wilmeth Sidat-Singh was buried with honors.

569. "Lt. Singh is Ready to Go." *Journal and Guide (Norfolk, VA)* (April 3, 1943): 12. Photo of Wilmeth Sidat-Singh in a fighter plane on the runway of Tuskegee Army Flying School. Biographical information.

570. LuTour, Lou. "Schenly Vice President Former Fighter Pilot." *Journal and Guide (Norfolk, VA)* (July 4, 1964): 10. Charles T. Williams was a Tuskegee Airman, won many medals and is a brother-in-law of Jackie Robinson.

571. "The Man who Runs an Airport." *Ebony* (September 1956): 108-110. Nathan Sams manages the Hatboro Airport near Muskogee, Oklahoma, and is the only Negro airport manager. He had been a student and an instructor at Tuskegee.

572. "Marchbanks, Gregory Are Lauded by Air Force Assn." *Jet* 69:6 (October 21, 1985): 16. At the Air Force Association's convention in Washington, Sen. Barry Goldwater awarded Ira Eaker Fellowships to Vance H. Marchbanks and Frederick D. Gregory. Marchbanks was the first black flight surgeon, and Gregory is an astronaut. Both are members of the Tuskegee Airmen, Inc. In 1983 Col. Fred V. Cherry was named an Eaker fellow; Cherry was held as a prisoner of war in Vietnam for more than seven years.

573. Marchbanks, Vance H. Jr. "The Black Physician and the USAF." *Journal of the National Medical Association* 64 (January 1972): 73-74. [Read at the NMA convention in Philadelphia in August 1971]. Marchbanks describes his early training and experiences as a doctor in the Air Force. He

mentions Maurice Johnson, the first black medical officer at Tuskegee, as well as many other doctors.

574. "Mayor White Proclaims 'Tuskegee Airmen Days' in Cleveland." *East Side News (Cleveland)* (January 16, 1990). The days proclaimed are from January 12th to 21st. The Smithsonian's exhibition, "Black Wings," is on display, as is the book written by William C. Ferguson Sr. Pictured are Ferguson, both today and during World War II, as well as Lewis Shepherd, Charles W. Ledbetter, Virgil A. Daniels, Louis Anderson, and Henry Fears.

575. McCollum, Berkley. "America's Black Air Force." *VFW (Veterans of Foreign Wars)* (November 1982): 40-41. [*VFW* is published in Kansas City, Missouri. The author notes (in a letter to the compiler) the magazine inserted erroneous information that B. O. Davis Jr. was a four-star general. He retired in 1970 with three stars]. A concise clear history of the all-black units in World War II: the 99th, the 100th, the 301st, and the 302nd fighter squadrons.

576. McCollum, Berkeley. "America's Forgotten Eagles." *Aviation Quarterly* 7:2 (1983): 148-171. [This was the final issue of *Aviation Quarterly*, a hard-cover publication, now scarce]. This detailed history of the Tuskegee Airmen, covers the events that led to their formation, and describes the battles and the men involved in them. Included are accounts of the actions of thirty-four men, as well as numerous photographs.

577. McGuire, Phillip. *He, Too, Spoke for Democracy: Judge Hastie, World War II, and the Black Soldier.* New York: Greenwood, 1988. The story of Wiliam H. Hastie's efforts to desegregate the Armed Forces. Hastie was Civilian Aide to the Secretary of War, 1940-1943. Information on the Tuskegee Air Base is on pp. 43-47, bibliography on pp. 131-148.

578. McGuire, Philip. "Judge Hastie, World War II, and the Army Air Corps." *Phylon* 42 (June 1981): 157-167. This article explores William Henry Hastie's impact on the Army Air Corps. Hastie, as Civilian Aide to Secretary of War Henry L. Stimson, from October 25, 1940 to January 31, 1943, fought vigorously to get the Army to modify or reverse its patterns of discrimination against blacks both in and out of uniform. Trainees at Tuskegee were relegated to menial tasks, instead of receiving training.

Biographical information, and there are many citations for further research.

579. Means, Howard. *Colin Powell: Soldier/Statesman, Statesman/ Soldier*. New York: Donald I. Fine Inc., 1992. General Powell addressed the twentieth annual convention of the Tuskegee Airmen in August 1991, in Detroit. The text of his address is given, pp. 101-103, including a poem he recited. It is called "These Are Our Finest" and was written by John H. Young III. Young was an instructor at Tuskegee.

580. Millican, Anthony. "Spreading Their Wings: Black WW II Airmen's New Mission is to Inspire and Motivate Youths." *Los Angeles Times* (July 12, 1992): B1, 5. Interviews with members of the Los Angeles chapter of the Tuskegee Airmen, Inc., on their fiftieth anniversary. They now give speeches at schools and universities, and to civic groups. The veterans give dramatic descriptions of their service fifty years ago and recount historical events. Featured are O. Oliver Goodall, Mitch Higginbotham, Roger C. (Bill) Terry, Rusty Burns, Charles M. Bussey, and William Ellis.

581. "Mini-Railroader." *Ebony* (December 1968): 92-94, 96, 98. [Another article, *Ebony* (April 1954) 38, 41-44]. Frank Mann has built and operates a miniature railroad line in his back yard in Pacoima, California. When he was 12, ca.1930, he designed, built and flew his own monoplane airplane. He later became a stunt pilot, and was a 1st Lieutenant in the 99th Fighter Squadron in World War II.

582. Moore, James. "A Pilot Rolls his Point." *Negro Digest* 9 (July 1951): 88-92. Story of 2nd Lieut. Howard Jefferson who landed his plane against the odds of low fuel and driving rain over Lunken Airport in Cincinnati, in the fall of 1942. Jefferson was in the 99th Fighter Squadron.

583. "Mother and Fiancee See Pilot Get Wings." *Journal and Guide (Norfolk, VA)* (April 3, 1943): 20. The pilot is Wilmeth Sidat-Singh.

584. Motley, Mary. *The Invisible Soldier*. Detroit: Wayne State University, 1975. Motley taped interviews with black servicemen in 1971-72. These oral histories of veterans of World War II were assisted by the diaries and letters kept by the men. The statements are personal, frank, and vivid. They cover training and battle experience. There is always the overlay of discrimination. "The unceasing prejudice was a nauseating and angering

mixture." Chapter 4 is entitled "The 'Spookwaffe': Airmen of the 332nd Fighter Group," pp. 194-257. 'Spookwaffe' was a name "we hung on ourselves" to the displeasure of the Air Force. The men even had yellow scarves embroidered with the name. The men interviewed mention many others such as Mac Ross and Wendell Pruitt ("a gem, a champ") who died, and their experiences in Italy, Europe, and Africa. Those interviewed are: Gilbert Cargill, Ralph Jones, Robert Pitts, Walter Downs, Samuel Fuller, Alexander Jefferson, who was a prisoner of war in Germany, Henry Peoples, Charles A. Hill Jr., Herbert Barland, Earl Kennedy, Ambrose B. Nutt, and Warren Bryant. Bryant was the only one who served in Africa for an extended time, and he comments on multicultural encounters other than between black and white.

585. "'Mr. Death': Flying Ace." *Ebony* (January 1951): 28-30, 32-34. [Cover story]. John L. Whitehead has a remarkable record instructing student pilots to fly 600-miles-an hour jets. He is an engineer and a much-decorated flying ace for service over Italy. He is called Mr. Death because he is 5 ft. 6 in. and weighs 121 lbs.

586. "Mrs. Bolton Reveals First Negro Flyers are 'Ready for Action'." *Call and Post (Cleveland)* (May 1, 1943): 2. [Second section]. Cleveland Congresswoman praised Tuskegee's flying program on the floor of the House. She stated that criticism of the segregated aviation school was ill-advised. Instead she hit the jim-crow system that gave birth to the 99th Pursuit Squadron. Mrs. Bolton said that education for the Negro must be improved.

587. Mullen, Sharon. "Soaring with History." *Asbury Park Press* (November 18, 1991): 1, 6. Nineteeen "Ebony Eagles" from the 18th Airlift Squadron at McGuire AFB set out on a six-day flight to Europe and Saudi Arabia to honor the Tuskegee Airmen. George Watson Sr., a Tuskegee Airman and chapter historian, will accompany them on the first leg of their mission.Some of the fliers are Jepheth White and Derek P. Green. Maj. Gen. Albert J. Edmonds was the guest speaker at the ceremonies.

588. Nalty, Bernard C. *Strength for the Fight: A History of Black Americans in the Military*. New York: Free Press, 1986. Besides Ch. 10, "The Army's Black Eagles," pp.143-161, there are other references to black aviators, easily found through the index. Largely based on the author's previous

work, a thirteen-volume collection of documents relating to blacks in the armed forces, this is both readable and scholarly.

589. "Negro Air Cadets Greeted at City Hall by the Mayor." *New York Times* (February 19, 1944). Photograph of Mayor LaGuardia of New York with about twenty cadets who will be commissioned at Hondo Field, TX, on February 26.

590. "Negro Gets Medal for Saving Flyer." *PM (New York)* (May 7, 1944). R. C. McDaniel of Tuskegee, Alabama, was awarded a bronze medal by the Carnegie Hero Fund Commission. He rescued Andrew H. Doswell from his burning plane after it had crashed. Doswell, a fighter pilot trainee, recovered.

591. "Negro Pilots Get Wings." *Life* (March 23, 1942): 30-31. Article, in brief text and seven photos, notes that five young Negro lieutenants recieved their wings on March 7, as the "first graduating class of the Army's first Negro air school." The article continues, "White instructors ... agree that their charges, by virtue of exceptional eyesight, courage and coordination, will prove crack pilots. Upon their performance and promise hang the hopes of additional thousands of aspiring Negro fliers throughout the land." Benjamin O. Davis Jr. is the only one named.

592. "99th." *Time* (September 15, 1941): 32, 34. The airfield at Tuskegee is described as "something new in the world." That is, all the pilots and other personnel are Negroes and the facility, which cost $2,000,000, was built by Negro contractors. Of the twelve cadets in the first class, eleven are college graduates and five have private pilots' licenses. In addition, the Army is training 278 Negro mechanics at Chanute Field to service the 99th's planes, guns, and instruments. Only the "tea-colored Ben Davis" is named.

593. "99th Veteran in Capital." *Journal and Guide (Norfolk, VA)* (June 10, 1944). Photograph of 25-year-old Major George S. Roberts, ex-commanding officer of the 99th Fighter Squadron in Italy, in a conference room at the Pentagon. Some biographical information.

594. "NYC to Get Glimpse of Crack Negro Flyers." *New York Amsterdam News* (July 31, 1948): 3. The 332nd Fighter Group will be in opening day ceremonies of the International Air Exposition at Idlewild Airport. President Truman will be among the spectators.

595. "Obituary." *New York Times* (June 11,1983). George Leward Washington, who helped establish an Air Force training program for black pilots at Tuskegee Institute, died at the age of 80. Biographical information.

596. O'Grady, Dan. "Black Pilots Fought a War on Bias, Too." *Daily News* (February 18, 1984): 1, 3. Percy Sutton and Roscoe Brown Jr. and other veterans will meet in Manhattan to observe the 42nd anniversary of the formation of their World War II squadrons at Tuskegee. Their toughest battle was for the right to fight, and perhaps die, for their country. There is biographical information on Brown.

597. "Only Negro Commanding Pursuit Squadron Visits Wife, Daughter, Sisters in City." *People's Voice* (February 14, 1942): 10. Alonzo S. Ward, of New York City, commands the 99th Pursuit Squadron at Tuskegee. Biographical information.

598. Owen, Chandler. *Negroes and the War*. Washington, D.C.: U.S. Office of War Information, 1945. Words and many pictures show Negroes in agriculture, industry, and the armed services. Pictures include an aircraft worker, a woman working in the parachute factory owned by Eddie Anderson and three views of students at Tuskegee Flying School.

599. Paszek, Lawrence J. "Separate But Equal? The Story of the 99th Fighter Squadron." *Aerospace Historian* (September 1977): 135-145. A lengthy and important article by a historian.

600. Peck, Phillips J. "Black Aces of the AAF." *Negro Digest* (November 1945): 72-74. [Condensed from *Flying* (June 1945)]. A description of the war record of the 332nd Fighter Group that answers doubters of the Negro's ability to fly. In less than a year they destroyed 75 enemy planes in the air and 150 on the ground. Peck quotes B.O. Davis and George S. Roberts on the Tuskegee experiment, Noel Parrish's words at the first graduation in 1942: "Flying is an individual proposition. There is no colored way to fly."

601. "Photo." *Call and Post (Cleveland)* (July 10, 1943): 1. Second Lieutenant William F. Williams, a native of Cleveland, is shown preparing to enter his fighter plane. He was commissioned at Tuskegee. Biographical information.

602. "[Photo of seven New York bombadiers]." *Crisis* 52:2 (February 1945). [Cover photo]. Description of cover photo: Seven New York men who graduated in January as full-fledged bombadiers shown at Midland Army Air Field, Texas. They are Clarence Conway, James E. Wolfe, Robert L. Mason, Albert Holland, Marcel Clyne, Edward Tabbanor, and Edward W. Woodward.

603. "[Photograph]." *Tri-Town News [Lakewood-Howell-Jackson, NJ]* 4: 18 (November 14, 1991): 1. George Watson Sr. is one of three of Lakewood's distinguished war veterans raising the flag in front of the municipal building to celebrate Veterans' Day. Watson was part of the ground crew at Tuskegee.

604. Pierce, Fred. "Tuskegee Airman, Parnell [*sic*], Speaks at College Park." *Atlantic Flyer* 8:1 (March 1993): B20-22. On February 6, Louis R. Purnell, spoke about his war experiences, including why he chose a second tour of duty after completing fifty missions. The "relative safety and dignity" of combat was preferable to being refused entry to restaurants and other forms of harassment. Information about the planes Purnell flew, and background information about the Tuskegee Airmen.

605. "Pilots for 99th Pursuit Squadron Begin Training at Tuskegee." *Opportunity* 19:8 (August 1941): 247-248. Ten young men began pilot training on July 19. They are Charles Dudley Brown, Lemuel Rodney Custis, Frederick Henry Moore, John Corrie Anderson Jr., Charles Henry De Bow, George Spencer Roberts, William Arthur Buckner, Theodore E. Brown, Roderick C. Williams, and Ulysses S. Pannell. An air base is being constructed at Tuskegee, Alabama for the squadron by a colored architect and a colored construction concern.

606. "Pioneer Black Army Air Force Pilot Dies at 73." *Jet* 77:9 (December 4, 1989): 40. Armour G. McDaniel, one of the first black Air Force pilots, died in Indianapolis. He was trained at Tuskegee, and had been a prisoner of war. Biographical information.

607. Porter, Dorothy B. "Negro Women in Our Wars." *Negro History Bulletin* 7:9 (June 1944): 195-196, 215. Cecilia Dixon of Columbia, South Carolina, is probably the first Negro woman aircraft dispatcher (Tuskegee Air Field).

608. Purnell, Louis R. "The Flight of the Bumblebee." *Air & Space* (October/November 1989): 32-33, 35-37, 39-40. A member of the first squadron of black pilots in World War II tells his story. Purnell recalls "the theory that because of wingspan-to-weight ratio, the bumblebee shouldn't be able to fly. But the bee, unaware of this, flies anyhow. The same was true of us." Purnell's inspiration was Hubert F. Julian, about whom he tells some anecdotes.

609. "Races: The 99th Squadron." *Time* (August 3, 1942): 17. The 99th Pursuit Squadron is "training in circumstances that might have exasperated Job." The Negroes faced two problems: 1) learning to fly, and 2) learning to become aggressive, when every tradition had taught them submissiveness. The article also mentions threats from white planters, which were handled by the commanding officer Noel F. Parrish. There is strong criticism of the Negro press for calling these trainees "Uncle Toms" for being willing to serve in this segregated unit.

610. Rankin, Allen C. "How a Man Gets His Wings at Tuskegee." [No source, Schomburg Center for Research in Black Culture, NYPL, Clipping file, U.S. Army-Air Force-99th Pursuit Squadron, "undated material." No date, but the article is a report on "the Army's first flying school for Negroes since it opened in Alabama one year ago." That would date the article 1942]. The author, a 1st Lt. in the Air Force, gives a detailed and dramatic account of Tuskegee's aviation school's beginnings: "Last year the site of the airdrome was a jutting hill spiked with the headstones of a neglected graveyard, and a low bog hole full of snakes and terrapins." He comments that everyone there is Negro: mechanics, doctors, photographers. He describes in detail the "famously tough and disheartening course ... . To start with, they must be physically perfect." Anecdotes about Mac Ross and Benjamin O. Davis.

611. Reininger, Stuart. "Black History Month: Education Helps Fight Bigotry." *Ocean County Observer* (February 12, 1990): A8. Profiles George Watson Sr., George Watson Jr. and Lillie Shelton, who all believe both blacks and whites need to learn black history. The elder Watson is a historian of the Tuskegee Airmen and was instrumental in opening membership to interested civilians, black and white. Watson states he has become more militant over the years, but having experienced bigotry himself, he would not show it to anyone else.

612. Rich, Frank. "'Black Eagles', a World War II Fighter Squadron." *New York Times* (April 22, 1991): C13. [Play review]. Unfavorable review of a play by Leslie Lee, about the Army Air Force's 99th Fighter Squadron.

613. "Rites Held in D.C. for WW II Ace 'Lucky' Lester." *Jet* 70:4 (April 14, 1986): 18. Clarence Lester shot down three German aircraft in five minutes, a feat no other pilot had accomplished. He was trained at Tuskegee, and he retired as a full colonel. He also served in Korea. Biographical information.

614. Robinson, Theodore W. "The Tuskegee Experience." *Air & Space* (October/November 1989): 38. Robinson, both a pilot and historian, describes conditions that led to the Tuskegee experiment and their record in war.

615. Rose, Robert A. "Art and the Airman." *Journal, American Aviation Historical Society* 199:3 (Fall 1974): 222-225. An unusual and humorous article depicting the artwork that appeared on the planes flown by black pilots. It also describes the distinctive markings and colors of the squadrons. The men with their planes who are featured are: Herman Lawson, Charles Bailey, L. E. Johnson, John Briggs, Jack Holsclaw, Lowell Steward, Robert Nelson, Fred Hutchins, James Johnson, Charles White, and Ed Toppins.

616. Rose, Robert. "Lonely Eagles." *Journal, American Aviation Historical Society* 20:2 (Summer 1975): 118-127. [The second part of the article is in vol. 20, no. 4, pp. 240-252]. These two articles may have formed the basis for Rose's book of the same title.

617. Rose, Robert A. *Lonely Eagles: The Story of America's Black Air Force in World War II.* Los Angeles: Tuskegee Airmen Inc., 1976. [Second printing, 1980]. This is a history of the "Tuskegee Experiment" and after, copiously illustrated with photographs. Rose is the historian of the Tuskegee Airmen Inc., Western Region. He was also a book reviewer and associate editor of the *Journal* of the American Aviation Historical Society.

618. Rowan, Carl. "Indomitable Tuskegee Flyers Taught America a Key Lesson." *Atlanta Constitution* (October 30, 1989): The lesson is that blacks are able to fly.

619. Sandler, Stanley. *Segregated Skies: All-Black Combat Squadrons of WW II*. Washington, D.C.: Smithsonian Institution, 1992. Sandler examines the operational and combat history of the four fighter squadrons, the Tuskegee Airmen, from their early training to aerial combat in Europe. Well-researched (oral histories, archives of the federal government, the Army and Army Air Forces), this is an important addition to the history of blacks in aviation in particular, and to race relations in the United States in general.

620. Schiesel, Seth. "Black Airmen Gather to Pay Tribute." *Boston Sunday Globe* (August 16, 1992): 26. For the second year the Tuskegee Airmen held a joint convention with the Organization of Black Airline Pilots. Both organizations are concerned with fostering interest in aviation among black youth, because there are only 600 black civilian pilots out of 70,000 pilots in the industry. This was the fiftieth anniversary of the graduation of the first pilots at Tuskegee. Those quoted are M. Perry Jones, William R. Norwood, and George Taylor.

621. "Segregated Skies: All-Black Combat Squadrons of World War II." *Publishers Weekly* (May 11, 1992): 61. [Book review]. Published by the Smithsonian Institution and written by Stanley Sandler, this is a history of the 332nd Fighter Group and the 477th Medium Bomber Group. Based on interviews and important documents, the author reveals how painfully aware the pilots and ground crew were of having to "prove" themselves as no white squadron had to.

622. Shaw, Irwin. "Graphic Story of Tuskegee Flyers and P-40's in Action." *Michigan Chronicle* (August 21, 1942). [The article originally appeared in *Yank*, n.d.]. Description of a battle fought in the Mediterrean Theater. The pilots named are: G.W. Dryden [Charles W. Dryden], Leo [Lee] Rayford, Willie Ashley, Spann Watson, S.P. Brooks, and Leon Roberts.

623. Smith, Milton. "Capt. Charles W. Dryden, Flying Sensation of Two Wars: "I Forgot He Was Colored..."." *Journal and Guide [Norfolk, VA]* (December 2, 1950): 1-2. Charles Dryden is now special services officer at Yokota AFB, Japan. Smith provides biographical information on New Yorker Dryden, and on life in the Air Force, now that it has been totally integrated.

624. "Space Doctor for the Astronauts." *Ebony* (April 1962): 35-36, 38-40, 42. Biographical and scientific information on Col. Vance H. Marchbanks Jr., who monitored John Glenn's medical condition during Project Mercury. He worked from the tracking station in Kano, Nigeria. He joined the Army Air Corps at Tuskegee in 1941, and won a Bronze Star for service in Italy.

625. "Spunky Widow Runs Modern Pilot School." *Ebony* 22 (October 1967): 38-40, 42-44. Edith Smith, of Westchester, took over her husband's flying school when he died last December. It is called Warhawk Aviation Service, Inc. The chief pilot is Henry Lopez. Biographical information on Archie Smith, who formerly taught at Tuskegee.

626. Strickland, Patricia. *The Putt-Putt Airforce: The Story of the Civilian Pilot Training Program and the War Training Service (1939-1944)*. Washington, D.C.: U.S. Federal Aviation Administration, 1970. Chapter IX, "Negro Fliers," pp. 39-47. Photograph of Dorothy Layne, now McIntyre.

627. "Stunt Flyer." *Ebony* (May 1950): 40-43. Charles R. Foxx, a former instructor at Tuskegee, is now a stunt flyer, or barnstormer, and operates a pilot training school in Norfolk, Virginia. C. Alfred Anderson was his teacher.

628. Sulaiman, Madeline. "The Black Eagles: Story of the Tuskegee Airmen." *about...time* 11:2 (February 1983): 14-17. "Much of the history of major black contributions to the building of America has slipped away from us as easily as water slips from a cupped hand." But the story of the Tuskegee Airmen will be told in four parts on TV, *Tony Brown's Journal*. Known as the Tuskegee, or Noble, Experiment, 10,000 men and women participated.

629. Sykes-Kennedy, Janie ed. *Excel 1984*. New York: Schenly Affiliated Brands, 1984. [Excellence in Black Organizations and Black Achievers]. The Tuskegee Airmen, pp. 12-13.

630. Taylor, Woody L. "'No Noise' When You Speed Through Air, Says Jet Pilot." *Afro-American (Baltimore)* (July 1, 1950): 3. [Magazine section]. Laurel C. Prince 3rd, a second lieutenant, is the only black jet pilot at Selfridge Air Force Base, Michigan. Information about flying the new jet planes, as well as biographical information. Prince's best friend was Jesse L. Brown who became a pilot for the Navy. Prince's older brother,

Joseph, had been a pilot at Tuskegee. When Prince arrived at Selfridge AFB in 1949, there were two other colored pilots: Calvin E. Peterson and Thomas Sims.

631. Terkel, Studs. "Lonely Eagles." *Newsday* (October 4, 1984): 3. [Part II]. An excerpt from Terkel's oral history, *The Good War*. Lowell Steward, a Tuskegee Airman, tells what the war was like for the black soldier. Terkel interviewed him in his home in Los Angeles. There are also comments by his friend Col. Edward Gleed, who was visiting.

632. Terrell, Angela Brown. "The Tuskegee Airmen." *Atlanta Journal* (July 14, 1982): 1B, 11B. Profile of the Atlanta chapter of the Tuskegee Airmen. Recollections of the pilots of their comprehensive training and the Army's disinclination to use them in combat. Featured are Charles Dryden, Ron Eley, Charles Schaffer, Huey Charlton, and Fred E. Hutchins.

633. "They Came from Haiti to Learn to Fly the American Way." *Journal and Guide (Norfolk, VA)* (April 10, 1943): 1. Photograph of three Haitians at Tuskegee: Raymond Cassagnol, Phillippe Celestin, and Alix Pasquet.

634. "They're Earning Their Wings in Army to Battle for a Better World." *PM (New York)* (April 19, 1943). Photograph of Marjorie Dosey, a mechanic, and Cornelius G. Rogers, a pilot, at Tuskegee.

635. "Time Says Army Not Satisfied with the 99th." *Atlanta World* (September 25, 1943): 1-2. An article in *Time* magazine states that the high command of the Air Force is not pleased with the work of the squadron despite glowing reports. Few commanders abroad want Negro troops. They take them only in small numbers, as engineers or laborers, not as combat troops.

636. "Tiny High Flyer." *Ebony* (May 1958): 33-36. Bennita Farmer, the three-year old daughter of Sgt. Bennie Farmer of the Air Force, is the subject of this article. Biographical information on her father, who served in the 447th Bomber Group, learned to fly in 1935, and founded the Luke Aero Club in 1952, at Luke AFB near Phoenix, Arizona. His son Robert, 14, is a cadet in the Civilian Air Patrol.

637. "Tower Man." *Ebony* (May 1956): 127-131. Alexander Boudreaux is an air traffic controller at Port Columbus, Ohio. He studied at Tuskegee and was a flight officer.

638. "Tuskegee Airman Heads Chicago Air Crash Probe." *Jet* (June 14, 1979):
5. Elwood T. Driver, vice chairman of the National Transportation Safety
Board, rushed to Chicago to determine the cause of the disaster which
took 275 lives. Driver discovered that a tiny bolt had snapped, causing a
wing engine to break away. Biographical information.

639. "Tuskegee Airmen." *Stars and Stripes* (April 20-26, 1992): [1]. A photograph of ten Tuskegee Airmen who met in Chicago in February. None is
identified.

640. "Tuskegee Airmen Honor Lena Horne with an Award." *Jet* 63 (January 3,
1983): 31. Lena Horne received a Distinguished Achievement Award
from the Tuskegee Airmen Inc. at a recent meeting in Beverly Hills. Article gives history of the group, and the president, Jean Esquerre, is pictured with Ms. Horne.

641. "Tuskegee Airmen, Inc." *Delegate* (1982): 246-247, 302-303. [This periodical is an annual which chronicles meetings of black organizations].
Some biographical information on Jean R. Esquerre, president of TAI,
and formerly of Grumman Aerospace Corporation. TAI will hold their
annual meeting in St. Louis, Missouri, on October 15-18, 1982.

642. "Tuskegee Airmen Inc. Holds Annual Meet in St. Louis." *Jet* 63
(December 13, 1982): 24. Guion S. Bluford was a featured speaker. Also
mentioned are Lewis J. Lynch, president of the St. Louis chapter and
Jean Esquerre, president of the group.

643. "Tuskegee Airmen Keep On Flying." *Newsweek* (August 9, 1982): 10. Interviews with Tuskegee Airmen who became prominent: Benjamin O.
Davis Jr., Coleman Young, Percy Sutton, and William T. Coleman. Davis and Sutton recall discriminatory treatment. Davis gives this advice,
"Keep your sense of humor and don't get beaten down. The important
objective is to prove our abilities. Once we do that, everything else will
fall into place." The group of 1,400 members will meet in St. Louis "later this month."

644. "Tuskegee Airmen Scholarship." *Eagle & Swan* 2:2 (May 1979): 9. Lowell Steward, president of the L.A. chapter of the Tuskegee Airmen, Inc.,
announced a goal of $1,000,000 to provide fifty scholarships a year to
young men and women who want careers in aviation and aerospace. "Our

country's future air strength depends on every talented person - black, white, red, yellow, or brown, male or female."

645. "Tuskegee Airmen Scholarship Fund." *Bay State Banner* (September 23, 1981): 2. Fifteen awards of $1,000 each were made to high school graduates without regard to race, creed, color, or national origin. The awards are made to those of modest income and with an interest in a career in aeronautics or aerospace.

646. "The Tuskegee Airmen—The Black Air Force Unit of World War II—Fought Battles in the Air and on the Ground." *National Black Review* 4:3 (May/June 1991): 7-10. A general history, mentioning John L. Hamilton, the first member of the 99th to receive a Purple Heart, and stating that the scholarship fund of the Tuskegee Airmen, Inc. (TAI) has awarded more than $350,000 to young Americans without regard to race, religion, sex, or creed.

647. "Tuskegee Engineers Wage Successful War Against Malaria." *Pittsburgh Courier* (December 12, 1942): 8. The post engineer and the post surgeon joined forces a year ago to eradicate the malaria-carrying mosquitoes around the Tuskegee base. Construction problems included snakes and beavers, which had to be cleared away.

648. "Tuskegee Experiment Leads to Integration." *New York Amsterdam News* (February 26, 1983): 4. [Part IV]. This is a resume of the four-part series, "The Black Eagles," on the television program, Tony Brown's Journal.

649. "Tuskegee Trainee is Star." *Call (Kansas City, MO)* (December 10, 1943). Cadet Othel Dickson became the top-ranking aerial gunner among Eastern Flying Training Command Cadets. Eleven schools sent their top marksmen. Dickson is from Coffeyville, Kansas.

650. "Two Killed in a Plane Crash at Tuskegee." *New York Amsterdam News* (May 15, 1943): 1. James E. Brothers of Chicago and Ross C. Stewart of Baltimore died in a training accident; Brothers was the pilot.

651. Walker, Kenneth. "Black Pilots Recall War's Woes, Glory." *Washington Star-News* (August 12, 1973): B2. [Metro section]. Report of the third annual convention of the Tuskegee Airmen. Quoted or pictured are Louis Purnell, Elwood T. Driver, and Benjamin O. Davis Jr.

652. Walker, Sidney. "'Hate Rule' at Tuskegee Air Base Charged to Col. Kimble." *Pittsburgh Courier* (January 2, 1943): 1, 4. "Negro fighting pilots are being trained in a hell-hole of racial discrimination." The silence of the Negro press and Negro leadership because it would help "their boys" make good as airmen for Uncle Sam. Blame for the bad conditions is placed on Col. Frederick Kimble, the commanding officer, and on Lt. Col. Hazard, the executive officer.

653. "War Department Enlists Negro Recruits for Air Corps." *Opportunity* 19:4 (April 1941): 119. The War Department will create a Negro unit of the Air Corps. The plan is to train 276 Negroes at Chanute Field, Illinois, and later transfer them to Tuskegee, where a Pursuit Squadron of the air will be formed.

654. Ward, Francis. "Jim Plinton's Flight to Corporate Success." *Black Enterprise* 10:12 (September 1979): 59-60. Jim Plinton retired as vice president for marketing development at Eastern, bringing to a close 40 years in aviation. He had been a pilot, flight instructor, entrepreneur, and airline executive. Biographical information and his philosophy of life.

655. Watson, George Sr. *Memorable Memoirs*. New York: Carlton Press, 1987. Watson's memoir concerns the 332nd Fighter Group which consisted of the 99th, 100th, 301st, and 302nd squadrons, all trained at Tuskegee. For every black pilot there were ten men and women serving as ground support. Watson was one of them and tells the story from that viewpoint. He is now the historian for the Tuskegee Airmen, Inc. at McGuire AFB in New Jersey.

656. "West Point Graduate to Selfridge Field." *Call (Kansas City, MO)* (May 28, 1943). Robert Bernard Tresville Jr., the first Negro to graduate from the United States Military Academy as an Air Corps officer, has reported to Selfridge Field. He trained at Tuskegee from June-December 1942.

657. Williams, Carol Gorga. "Tuskegee Airman Flies Again." *Asbury Park Press* (November 17, 1991): 1, 17. George Watson Sr., a Tuskegee Airman, will be the only civilian aboard today when the Ebony Eagles, a group at McGuire AFB, begin a week-long flight to commemorate 50 years of Air Force service by blacks. The flight will go halfway around the world. The article includes history of the Tuskegee Airmen, and

Watson discusses racism. The pilot is Capt. Monica Smith. J. Bruce Bennett, another Tuskegee Airman, will join the group later.

658. Williams, James D., and Kip Branch. "Tuskegee Airmen." *Crisis* 98:6 (July 1991): 46-49, 64, 70. A history of the Tuskegee Airmen on the occasion of its 50th anniversary. Mentioned is the National Museum of the Tuskegee Airmen Fort Wayne, Detroit, Michigan. It was founded in 1987. The telephone number is (313) 297-9360.

659. "Wings Above Tuskegee." (October 1940): [Brochure No.4, Bureau of Public Relations (Tuskegee Institute)]. Information about the airfield-to-be. At first the students had to travel eighty miles to the airport at Montgomery for training. The brochure was written one year after Tuskegee had been approved for participation in the Civilian Pilot Training Program (CPTP). George L. Washington was the director.

660. Witkin, Richard. "First Negro Airlines Pilot Hired; He Will Fly Helicopters Here." *New York Times* (December 14, 1956). New York Airways broke the color line when they hired Perry H. Young. He was one of the Tuskegee Airmen. Young had been trying to land a job with a commercial airliner since 1945, when the war ended.

661. Wylie, James. *The Homestead Grays.* London: New English Library, 1978. [Published by G.P. Putnam's Sons in 1977]. Based on the story of the black air squadrons of World War II, this novel deals with battles with the enemy as well as with the inner battles of the men themselves. The group is named after a baseball team in the Negro Leagues.

662. "Yesterday in Negro History." *Jet* (March 8, 1962): 11. On March 7, 1942 the following completed flight training at Tuskegee and became the first Negroes to win their wings in the U.S. Army Air Force: Benjamin O. Davis, Mac Ross, George S. Roberts, Lemuel Custis, and Charles De Bow.

663. "Yesterday in Negro History." *Jet* (December 17, 1964): 11. On December 17, 1956 Perry H. Young Jr. became the first Negro hired as a flight crewman by any U.S. scheduled passenger airline. He was hired by New York Airways, a helicopter line. Young had been an instructor at Tuskegee.

Benjamin O. Davis Jr.

664. Adams, Russell L. *Great Negroes Past and Present*. Chicago: Afro-Am Publishing Co., 1976. [This is the third edition; originally published 1969]. Biographical information on Benjamin O. Davis Jr. in "Leader Aloft," p.113. Additional references are cited.

665. "Air Force's Gen. Davis Nominated for 4th Star." *Evening Star (Washington, D.C.)* (May 16, 1967). President Johnson named Lt. Gen. Benjamin O. Davis Jr. for promotion to full general and assignment August 1 as commander of the 13th Air Force at Clark Field in the Phillipines.

666. Bardolph, Richard. *The Negro Vanguard*. New York: Rinehart and Co., 1959. [Pp. 332-333]. Information about Benjamin O. Davis Sr. and Benjamin O. Davis Jr. There is also a brief description of integration in the armed forces, by "swift, massive action of the president [Harry S. Truman] and vigorously prosecuted by him." Bardolph notes the Air Force made the changeover in mere months, and he considers this event the most important in American racial patterns since Emancipation.

667. "Benjamin O. Davis, Jr.: American." *National Black Review* 4:3 (May/June 1991): 11-12. Book review summarizes above title.

668. Black, Ermetra. "Why General Davis Quit Cleveland Police Force: Blames Lack of Support, but Mayor Points to Selfish Motive." *Jet* (August 13, 1970): 14-19. Benjamin O. Davis Jr. left the position of Public Safety Director after six months. Mayor Carl Stokes claims Davis was overzealous in his crackdown on black militants.

669. Blume. Howard. "Getting a General Education." *Los Angeles Times* (January 22, 1993): B1, 8. Gen. Benjamin O. Davis visited the middle school in Compton named for him. Biographical information on Davis, and a report of the interactions between the general and the 1,000 children who attended the event. He advised the children to minimize their use of television, maximize their use of books, and to discontinue the purchase of expensive faddish clothing.

670. Bontemps, Arna W. *We Have Tomorrow*. Boston: Houghton Mifflin, 1945. [Chapter 12, "Wings on His Shoulders: Benjamin Davis Jr.,"

pp.118-131]. Written for young people, this is an excellent account of Davis' early life, before, at, and after, West Point.

671. Britton, John H. "Davis May Earn Fourth Star as Civilian Police Reformer." *Jet* (March 19, 1970): 14-20. [Cover story]. Carl Stokes, Mayor of Cleveland, convinced retired general Benjamin O. Davis Jr. to become the city's Public Safety Director. Biographical information, and description of the demanding job, including a militant sit-in in his office during the first week on the job.

672. "Col. Davis Takes Over Head of 332nd Group." *Michigan Chronicle* (October 16, 1943). When Col. Benjamin O. Davis Jr. assumed command of the 332nd Fighter Group at Selfridge Field, he became the first Negro commander of this group.

673. *Current Biography*. New York: Wilson Compnay, 1955. Benjamin O. Davis Jr., pp. 150-152.

674. Davis, Benjamin O. Jr. *Benjamin O. Davis, Jr.: American*. Washington, D.C.: Smithsonian Institution, 1991. Davis has written his autobiography in a compelling and riveting way. His success over entrenched forces of discrimination in all aspects of American society is told with frankness. He has led a remarkable life and this is a full account of it.

675. "Davis Becomes First Negro Major General." *Washington Post & Times Herald* (July 1, 1959). Yesterday the Senate approved the promotion of Brig. Gen. Benjamin O. Davis Jr. to the temporary rank of major general. Davis is the first of his race to achieve that rank.

676. Dreyer, Martin. *Black Is*. N.p.: Lawrence Field & Associates, 1971. Brief biographical sketch of Gen. Benjamin O. Davis Jr., with pictures of him at home.

677. Flynn, James J. *Negroes of Achievement in Modern America*. New York: Dodd, Mead and Co., 1970. In a chapter on the father and son Generals Benjamin Davis, pp.18-37, Flynn provides a great deal of family background, and shows how close they were to each other.

678. Frisbee, John L. *Makers of the United States Air Force*. Washington, D.C.: Pergamon-Brassey's, with the Aerospace Education Foundation, Air Force Association, 1989. Ch. 10, pp.229-255. Gropman, Alan L.

"Benjamin O. Davis, Jr.: History on Two Fronts." Gropman gives an account of Davis' life before, during, and after World War II. Insults were answered his way, with articulate silence and the demonstrated ability to fly and fight.

679. Gropman, Alan L. "Against All Foes." *Airman* (September 1985): 44-48. An important lengthy article about Benjamin O. Davis, by a historian of integration in the Air Force. "Benjamin O. Davis Jr. fought the bonds of segregation to prove his black airmen could fly and fight as well as white pilots."

680. "Historic Show on Black Aviators at Smithsonian." *Jet* 63 (October 11, 1982): 39. The exhibition "Black Wings: The American Black in Aviation," includes photographs and a film narrated by Benjamin O. Davis Jr.

681. Hornett, Garnett D. "Gen. Davis Named Head of Anti-Hijacking Battle." *Washington Star* (September 21, 1970). Davis was appointed Director of civil aviation security to halt increasing acts of air piracy.

682. Hughes, Langston. *Famous Negro Heroes of America*. New York: Dodd, Mead & Co., 1958. In the chapter "Benjamin O. Davis, Jr.: General of the Air Force," pp.188-198, Hughes recounts the story of Davis' life and achievements. He quotes from Arna Bontemps' *We Have Tomorrow*, from Roi Ottley's 1944 battlefront reports, and from Col. Noel Parrish, who praised Davis' abilities as a commanding officer.

683. "In Father's Footsteps: First Negro Named General of Air Force by President." *Herald Tribune* (October 28, 1954). [The same article appeared in the *New York Times* the same day]. Biographical information on Benjamin O. Davis Jr.

684. Johnson, Ernest E. "Stimson Lauds 99th Flyers on Return to America." *Michigan Chronicle* (August 14, 1943). Secretary of War Henry L. Stimson warmly praised Negro units for their role in the invasion of Sicily. He also inspected troops in England and found "an interesting situation" - the men were all getting along well together. He also met Benjamin O. Davis, commander of the 99th Pursuit Squadron in Italy.

685. Johnson, Jesse J. "Profile of Lt. Gen. Benjamin O. Davis Jr.: A Keen Mind Leads to Success." *Eagle & Swan* 2:1 (February/March 1979): 48. A biographical sketch by a military historian.

686. Johnson, Robert E. "Silent Treatment Meted to Black Cadet 41 Years Ago Haunts White Cadet." *Jet* 44 (June 28, 1973): 12-13. A recent white graduate of West Point, J.J. Pelosi, called for the abolition of the Silent Treatment after having undergone it. This incident recalls the similar treatment given to Benjamin O. Davis from 1932-1936, because he was black, not because of any wrongdoing. Davis survived because he knew 56 years before West Point's first black graduate, Henry O. Flipper, endured the same ostracism, and because of Davis' close relationship with his father. "... he could survive on intelligence rather than perish on anger."

687. Lee, Irvin H. *Negro Medal of Honor Men*. New York: Dodd, Mead and Co., 1969. [Third edition, new and enlarged]. Besides including a list of winners of the Medal of Honor, by war, the author provides a narrative about the role of blacks in the country's wars. Information on Benjamin O. Davis Jr is on pp. 111-115. Sgt. Lee is in the Air Force.

688. "Lt. Gen. Benjamin O. Davis Jr." *Ebony* (August 1968): 56-58. Biographical information and full-page portrait.

689. "Lt. Gen. B.O.Davis Jr is Praised, Cited at Ceremony." *Jet* (February 19, 1970): 5. Lt. Gen. Davis accepted the Distinguished Service Medal as he retired from the Air Force after more than 37 years of service. The ceremonies were at MacDill AFB, Florida.

690. Mason, B. J. "Grounding the Skyjacker: Gen. B.O. Davis Jr. Tightens Security on U.S. Airlines." *Ebony* (November 1972): 48-50, 52, 55, 57. Davis was recruited to stop the increase in highjacking incidents.

691. Mitgang, Herbert. "A Black Military Hero Tells His Story." *New York Times* (February 20, 1991): C15. A generally favorable review of *Benjamin O. Davis Jr., American*, with a great deal of information about Davis' life and contribution. "Now, in his autobiography, ... he breaks the silence he maintained while in uniform, and for years afterward .... His personal story should come as a revelation to many readers... ."

692. "Negro Colonel Gets Command of Air Group." *Herald Tribune* (June 22, 1945). Colonel Benjamin O. Davis Jr., crack Negro flyer, today took command of the 477th Composite Group at Godman Field, Kentucky, replacing Col. Robert R. Selway Jr., who was the center of a recent racial controversy at Freeman Field, Indiana. Describes the dispute.

693. "Negro Flyers in Africa Win Army Officers' Praise." *Call and Post (Cleveland)* (July 10, 1943): 9. [Second section]. The squadron's ground crews, as well as the pilots, were praised for their discipline and pride. Lt. Col. Benjamin O. Davis, the commanding officer, is quoted.

694. "Negro Pilot Gets Silver Star." (June 20, 1945). [Library, National Air and Space Museum, Washington, D. C.]. Col. Benjamin O. Davis Jr. received the Silver Star for gallantry in action on April 15, when he led a strafing attack on rail targets in Austria. It was the first time a Negro pilot had won this award.

695. Park, Edwards. "Around the Mall and Beyond." *Smithsonian* 21 (March 1991): 18, 20, 22. The author, a former pilot, interviews Gen. Benjamin O. Davis on the publication of his autobiography. There is biographical information and also a great deal about the types of planes used in World War II. Gen. Davis comments on discrimination in the United States which forced black pilots to fight two wars: one against Hitler and one against the Air Force.

696. Reasons, George, and Sam Patrick. *They Had a Dream*. Los Angeles: Los Angeles Times Syndicate, 1969, 1971. Brief biographical information and a drawing of Benjamin O. Davis Jr., vol.1, p.21 and of Daniel James Jr., vol.3, p. 35.

697. Richardson, Ben. *Great American Negroes*. New York: Thomas Y. Crowell, 1956. Information on Benjamin O. Davis Jr. on pp. 326-330. The drawing on p. 325 is, however, of his father, although it is identified as Davis Jr.

698. Robinson, Wilhelmina S. *Historical Afro-American Biographies*. Crown Heights, PA: The Publishers Agency [with] the Association for the Study of Afro-American Life and History, 1976. This book for older children or adults has biographical information on Benjamin O. Davis Jr., pp.178-179, and on William H. Hastie, pp. 199-200.

699. "Scholarship." *Opportunity* 14:7 (July 1936): 217. Photograph shows B. O. Davis Jr. receiving his diploma from General John J. Pershing, as he was graduated from the United States Military Academy at West Point.

700. "Son of Brigadier General B.O. Davis made a Lieutenant Colonel." *Opportunity* 20:6 (June 1942): 186. Capt. Davis was promoted to Major on March 1. It was later announced that as of March 1 [*sic*] he was Lieutenant Colonel Davis. Other biographical information.

701. Stratton, Madeline R. *Negroes Who Helped Build America.* Boston: Ginn and Co., 1965. "Benjamin Oliver Davis: Air Commander," pp. 26-33. This brief biography of Davis brings his life up to date, including tours of duty in Japan, Taiwan, and Germany. Letters written by Mrs. Davis, while in those countries, are cited.

702. Toppin, Edgar A. *A Biographical History of Blacks in America Since 1528.* New York: David McKay Co., 1971. Benjamin O. Davis Jr., pp. 275-276; William H. Hastie, pp. 313-315.

703. Van Riper, Frank, and Jeffrey Antevil. "Ex-General Heads Sky Marshals." *Daily News (New York)* (September 22, 1970). President Nixon created the force of sky marshalls only eleven days earlier, after the wave of air piracy by Palestinian guerrillas. He named Benjamin O. Davis Jr. as director of the new force. This article provides a good deal of information, including the opposition to funding.

704. Wolff, C. A. "The 'Black Baron' - Great American Airman." [n.s., n.d.] Biographical information on Benjamin O. Davis Jr., and the 99th Fighter Squadron.

705. Yancey, Matt. "Black Pilots Honored in Smithsonian Exhibition." *Staten Island Advance* (September 23, 1982). [Article also is in the *Atlanta Journal*, September 26, 1982, p. 25]. Benjamin O. Davis and Clarence D. "Lucky" Lester are interviewed at the opening of "Black Wings: The American Black in Aviation" in Washington, D. C.

Daniel James Jr.

706. "Air Force Jet Stunt Pilot Credits 'Chappie' James for Success in Service." *Jet* 58:23 (August 21, 1980): 24. Joseph Peterson is the only black

member of the jet stunt team, the Thunderbirds. When Peterson was a child he met Daniel James at Tuskegee, and he was inspired by him to become a pilot.

707. Alotta, Robert I. "Biography Traces Heroic Career of Black General." *Atlanta Constitution* (August 25, 1985). A favorable review of *Black Eagle: General Daniel ("Chappie") James Jr.* by James R. Mc Govern.

708. "Art." *Eagle and Swan* 1:4 (1978): 56-57. Roy La Grone is a designer, illustrator, and painter who has worked for the Air Force Art Program. He now works at Columbia House in New York. Four of his paintings are shown, two of them are of Daniel James Jr.

709. "Big Man with a Big Message." *Sepia* 17:4 (April 1966): 64-66. Col. Daniel James addressed an Air Force Association banquet at Carswell AFB in Fort Worth, Texas. He voiced his support for America and the conduct of the war in Vietnam.

710. "A Black 4-Star General Named." *New York Times* (July 3, 1975). Brief biographical article on Daniel James Jr.

711. "Black Armed Forces Brass." *Crisis* 80:10 (December 1973): 341-346. Biographical information. Those in the Air Force are: Thomas E. Clifford, James Frank Hamlet, Daniel James Jr., Roscoe Robinson Jr., and Charles Calvin Rogers. [Robinson's obituary - *The New York Times* (July 23, 1993) 19].

712. "The Career of 'Chappie' James." *Washington Post* (January 23, 1978). [Editorial ?]. Assesses Daniel James and his career.

713. "Chappie Center." *New York Amsterdam News* (October 16, 1982). President Reagan signed a bill to appropriate $9 million for the General Daniel "Chappie" James Center for Aerospace Science and Health Education at Tuskegee Institute.

714. "Chappie James Confirmed as Four-Star General." *Jet* (August 14, 1975): 40. Daniel James was unanimously confirmed by the Senate, and he will become the highest-ranking black officer in military history.The ceremony is to take place at Scott AFB in Illinois. On the same page is a brief article, "Chappie is a Mason," showing him being inducted into the Prince Hall Masons of Illinois.

715. Crawford, Marc. "From the Editor's Desk." *Eagle & Swan* 1:2 (March 1978): 6. [Another tribute and a painting of James appear on pp. 8-9]. A memorial tribute to Daniel "Chappie" James Jr., who died on February 25, 1978.

716. Crawford, Marc. "The Importance of Being Chappie." *Eagle & Swan* 1:2 (March 1978): 18-20, 22-23. Biographical information on Daniel James Jr.

717. *Current Biography*. New York: Wilson Company, 1976. Daniel James Jr., pp. 196-198.

718. "Daniel 'Chappie' James Jr." *Washington Post* (March 1, 1978). [Editorial ?].

719. "Daniel James." *Jet* (December 23, 1976): 20. General Daniel James Jr. was awarded the 1976 "Horatio Alger Award" by the American Schools & Colleges Association.

720. "Daring Pilot From Florida [?]." *Pittsburgh Courier* (January 27, 1951). Describes the activities of Captain Daniel James as he flies an unarmed plane over Korea so that a photographer can take pictures of air strikes against enemy ground forces. Article describes his personality and hair-raising incidents in his career.

721. "Died." *Newsweek* (March 6, 1978). Obituary of Gen. Daniel James Jr.

722. "Died." *Time* (March 6, 1978). Obituary of Gen. Daniel James Jr.

723. Du Bose, Carolyn. "'Chappie' James: A New Role for an Old Warrior." *Ebony* (October 1970): 152-154, 156. The highest-ranking black man in the Air Force, Brig. Gen. Daniel James is now the spokesman for the Pentagon. Biographical information and his frank comments on civil rights. His daughter, Danice, graduated from TWA's airline hostess school in 1965, and his son, Lt. Daniel (Spike) James III, is an Air Force pilot.

724. Dunson, Lynn. "'Chappie' James, 1st Black 4-Star General, Dies." *Washington Star* (February 26, 1978): A1, 7. Obituary.

725. Ebony. *The Ebony Success Library: Volume II, Famous Blacks Give Secrets of Success.* Chicago: Johnson Publishing Company, 1973. Major General Daniel James Jr., pp.122-125. General James credits his success to commitment, determination, and will.

726. Ellington, Charles G. ""Thank You, Jesus, I'll Take Over Now."." *Crisis* (March 1983): 26. Author's brief account of meeting "many years ago" Daniel James after his first trip through the sound barrier. The title was James' comment.

727. "Four-Star Black Pioneer." *New York Times* (May 11, 1987). Brief biographical information on Daniel James Jr. President Reagan dedicated an aerospace and science center at Tuskegee University yesterday to honor General James.

728. "'Freedom - My Heritage, My Responsibility'." *Air Force Magazine* 51:4 (April 1968): 178-179. At the Freedoms Foundation's nineteenth annual National and School Awards program , three USAF officers were among the top ten winners in the "Letters" category on the title theme. Col Daniel James Jr.'s winning letter is published in full. Biographical information.

729. Garnett, Bernard. "Vietnam War Pilot May Be Named Third Negro General." *Jet* (February 1, 1968): 22-26. [Cover story]. Biographical information on Daniel (Chappie) James.

730. "Gen. Daniel James Dies." *Air Force Times* (March 13, 1978): 20.

731. "Gen. James' Retirement, Health Status Clouded." *Jet* (December 15, 1977): 4. Gen. James suffered a mild heart attack last month. The article questions if he is being forced out because of a letter he wrote protesting a re-organization plan.

732. "General James Gets 4th Star at Air Force Ceremonies." *Jet* (September 18, 1975): 24-26. The ceremony was held at Peterson Field in Colorado. Gen. Daniel James is to replace retiring Gen. Lucius D. Clay Jr. of NORAD. Biographical and family information. His sons and son-in-law are in the Air Force.

733. "Goldwater Favors Voting Act, Memorial for General James." *Jet* 60:18 (July 16, 1981): 12. Sen. Barry Goldwater was a close friend of General

Daniel James and he maintains contact with the family to plan for a memorial to James at Tuskegee.

734. Grieder, William. "An American Success Story." *Washington Post* (July 21, 1975): A1, 16. "James is a complicated man." In his interview with the author James talked freely about his past, his family and his upbringing. A lively article, filled with James' statements.

735. Horton, Benjamin. "General Daniel 'Chappie' James - A Legend in His Own Time." *Educating in Faith* 59:2 (March-April 1978): 16-29. [Cover story. Published by the Catholic Negro-American Mission Board (NY)]. Biographical information on Daniel James Jr.

736. Huey, John. "Guarding the Skies: Black 4-Star General is a Man Accustomed to Tough Assignments." *Wall Street Journal* (November 23, 1976): 1, 34. A long feature article on General Daniel James, commander of the North American Air Defense Command. He is responsible for a $1.6 billion budget and 58,000 employees around the world. James is "the only U. S. military officer with authority to deploy nuclear weapons without presidential approval."

737. "'It Makes No Difference, As Long As He's a Negro'." *Jet* (February 26, 1970): 5. Daniel (Chappie) James, the highest ranked black in the U.S. Air Force was recently barred from the Torch Lounge in his home town of Pensacola, Florida. The owner used the words in the title. James was in town to receive the 'Man of the Year' award from the local Kiwanis Club.

738. James, Daniel Jr. "We Americans, All of Us, Must Make the System Work." *Eagle & Swan* 1:1 (December 1977-March 1978): 5. In a guest editorial for the premiere issue, General James stresses the need for all Americans to work together, and he lauds the record of the Defense Department in the progress of equal opportunity for all.

739. Johnson, Herschel. "Stand-In for the Enemy." *Ebony* (February 1978): 87-90, 92. Capt. Daniel (Spike) James III follows in his famed father's footsteps. He is instructor pilot of the elite 'Red' Aggressors at Nellis AFB, Nevada. Lloyd (Fig) Newton is also mentioned.

740. Johnson, Ralph. "America's First Black Four-Star General vs. his Militant Critics." *Sepia* 25:2 (February 1976): 34-41. Biographical information.

"Berated as 'super nigger' in new Air Force post as commander of North American air defenses, Gen. James speaks out sharply and coolly on critical race issues in *Sepia* interview."

741. Killen, Patrick J. "Four Stars, the Hard Way." *Long Island Press* (August 24, 1975). Biographical information on Daniel James Jr.

742. "Ladies Home Journal Looks at a Negro Family." *Daily Worker* (February 21, 1957). While deploring the emphasis placed on material values in the magazine, the writer of this article does allow that the family of Lt. Col. Daniel James is composed of capable and attractive human beings whose way has not been smooth.

743. Lang, John S. "Man in the News. General Daniel James Jr.: The First Four Stars." *New York Post* (August 16, 1975). A lengthy biographical article of two pages.

744. "Legacies of Leadership." *Ebony* 48:1 (November 1992): 87. [Advertisement for the Air Force]. General Daniel "Chappie" James is shown in a recruitment effort.

745. MacGregor, Morris J. "Airman for a New Age." *Washington Post* (September 23, 1985). Book review of *Black Eagle: General Daniel 'Chappie' James* by James R. McGovern. "... accurate and generally perceptive study. Depending on the best secondary sources and a host of interviews, he draws a portrait of a complex man whose outsized zest for life and friendship was matched by a consuming and lonely ambition to succeed."

746. "Mass Set for AF Gen. 'Chappie' James." *Washington Post* (March 1, 1978). A mass will be held for Daniel James tonight at the National Shrine of the Immaculate Conception. Burial is tomorrow at Arlington National Cemetery.

747. McGee, Frank. "Interview." *Encore* (October 1972): 13. Frank McGee interviewed General Daniel C. James on the "Today" show, NBC-TV, August 18, 1972. The discussion centered on prisoners of war held by the Vietnamese.

748. McGovern, James R. *Black Eagle: General Daniel "Chappie" James, Jr.* University, AL: University of Alabama Press, 1985. Biography of James

with photographs, notes, and index. The bibliography, pp. 187-194, includes books, unpublished material, articles, pamphlets, government documents, unit histories, interviews conducted by the author, interviews with James and others, speeches by James and letters to the author.

749. "Military's Black Generals get Pentagon Duty." *Jet* (April 16, 1970): 3. Brig. Gen. Daniel James Jr. sworn in as Deputy Assistant Secretary of Defense for Public Affairs for the Air Force. General James will handle public relations projects.

750. "Names in the News." *Black Enterprise* 3:11 (June 1973): 14. Maj. Gen. Daniel James will be promoted to Principal Deputy Assistant Secretary of Defense. With this promotion, James will become the first black ever to obtain the rank of three-star general.

751. "Nix Plan for Pilot to Debate Carmichael." *Jet* (October 26, 1967): 3. Col. Daniel (Chappie) James will not debate former SNCC chairman Stokely Carmichael as advocated by some congressmen. They were to have debated the merits of Negro youth serving in the military in Vietnam.

752. Novak, Ralph. "Gen. Chappie James is the Boss of America's 'Defense Business' and its Four-Star Salesman." *People* (July 18, 1977): 78-80, 85. Personal and biographical information about General Daniel James, now in charge of North American Air Defense Command (NORAD). NORAD is a joint U.S.-Canadian system with a staff of 55, 000.

753. Olert, Chris. "A General Agreement." *Staten Island Advance* (December 6, 1977). General James will retire next year after 35 years in military service. He does not plan to run for public office. He had a mild heart attack on September 20.

754. "1,500 Pay Final Tribute to a 'Fighter for Peace'." *Evening Star (Washington, D.C.)* (March 2, 1978). Funeral service for Gen. Daniel James Jr.

755. Phelps, J. Alfred. *Chappie: America's First Black Star General, The Life and Times of Daniel James, Jr.* Novato, CA: Presidio Press, 1991. [Phelps was a master sergeant in the U.S. Air Force]. This biography of James includes many available sources, including letters to, and interviews with, the author, photographs, notes and a bibliography, pp.353-358.

756. "Pilot Urges Continued Bombing in Vietnam." *Jet* (December 28, 1967): 24. Col. James, in a debriefing session with President Johnson, discussed the air campaign in Vietnam, the pilots' morale, equipment, and urged continued bombing. James has flown 78 combat missions over Vietnam and 191 over Korea.

757. Poinsett, Alex. "Gen. Daniel (Chappie) James Jr.: New Boss of the Nation's Air Defense." *Ebony* (December 1975): 48-51, 54, 58-59, 62. Biographical and scientific information.

758. "Portrait of a Warrior." *Daily News (NY)* (February 24, 1980). [New Jersey edition]. Photograph of Don Miller, an artist in Montclair, New Jersey, standing beside his portrait of General Daniel James. It was commissioned by the Tuskegee Airmen, Inc. and unveiled at the Officers' Club at Andrews AFB.

759. Reasons, George, and Sam Patrick. "Gen. James - Top U.S. Fighter Pilot." *Evening Star (Washington, D.C.)* (February 27, 1971). [Reasons and Patrick are the authors of a series of biographical sketches of African Americans, under the title of *They Had a Dream]*. Lengthy quotations by James.

760. Scharff, Ned. "Q and A: Black General Hopes to See Last of 'Firsts'." *Washington Star* (May 10, 1976): A1, D15. In an interview Gen. James states that the military has made more progress in solving the ills of unequal opportunity than any other segment of society. James quotes his mother, who hoped for the day that black people will do so many notewothy things, that they would no longer be newsworthy, as in 'first' or 'only.'

761. "School Named to Honor 'Chappie'." *Eagle & Swan* 2:1 (February/March 1979): 9. P.S. 183, Brooklyn, has become the General Daniel "Chappie" James Jr. School.

762. Smith, J. Y. "Mourners at James Burial." *Washington Post* (March 3, 1978). Description of the funeral service for General Daniel James Jr.

763. Smith, J. Y. "Tribute Paid to Gen. James." *Washington Post* (March 2, 1978): C1, 9. Description of funeral rites for Daniel James, with remarks from friends and strangers whose lives he touched.

764. "Squadron Commander." *Look* 8:21 (October 19, 1954): 129-135. In May 1953 Major Daniel James Jr. took command of the 437th Fighter Squadron, which is responsible for the defense of New York, Boston, and Washington, D.C. "On 24-hour alert against enemy attack, he's the "Old Man" to 400 men; neither he nor they take time to worry about the color of his skin." Article describes typical activities and includes numerous examples of his philosophy of Americanism and his personal 11th commandment, "Thou shalt not quit."

765. "A Study in Success." *Challenge* (1970): 36-40. [From internal evidence this article may have a date of 1970. It refers to James' recent promotion to Brigadier General (July 1, 1970) and "looking back over his first fifty years" (James was born in 1920)]. An interview, with many lengthy quotations from James.

766. Tatz, Vicki. "Only Black 4-Star General Retires." *News World* (January 26, 1978): 1, 8. Biographical information on Daniel James. His advice to minority youth is to get an education and skills, ignore the hatred, and remember your responsibility to your country.

767. "Texang Recruits 'Chappie''s Son." *Eagle & Swan* 2:1 (February/ March 1979): 20. Capt. Daniel James III has been assigned to the 182nd Tactical Fighter Squadron at Kelly AFB, Texas. He was sworn into the Texas Air National Guard (Texang). Biographical information.

768. Thimmesch, Nick. "To The Top: Super-Patriot 'Chappie' James Earns an Unprecedented Fourth Star." *People* (July 28, 1975): 24-25. Personal and biographical information on Daniel James.

769. Thorne, Bliss K. "A Ride Through the Sound Barrier." *Reader's Digest* (January 1954): 115-117. [Condensed from the *New York Times*, October 11, 1953]. The pilot for this ride was Major Daniel James. There is no mention that he is black.

770. Treaster, Joseph B. "Gen. Daniel James Jr. Dies at 58; Black Led American Air Defense." *New York Times* (February 26, 1978). [Obituary, died February 25, 1978]. Biographical information, including many quotations by James.

771. Trescott, Jacqueline. "The Law and Gen. James." *Washington Post* (May 11, 1976): B1, 3. Recounts the story of how James, a young air force

officer, was charged with mutiny in 1945. He was part of a group that tried to integrate an officers club in Kentucky. The young law clerk who helped Thurgood Marshall prepare his case was William T. Coleman, now Secretary of Transportation. Both were honored at an NAACP benefit dinner last night.

772. Turner, Glennette Tilly. *Take a Walk in their Shoes.* New York: Dutton, 1989. [Illus. by Elton Fax]. A children's book. A biographical sketch of Gen. Daniel James Jr., pp. 80-87; a dramatic skit, "The Eagles Return to the Nest" on pp. 88-91.

773. Ulman, William. "Chappie James Has Twenty Minutes." *Argosy* (December 1954): 33+. The 437th Fighter Squadron is as good as they come. It is one of the few virtually all-white outfits in the Air Force that is commanded by a Negro. Long article describes James' work and family.

774. Vroman, Mary Elizabeth, and Nelle Keys Perry. "Demonstrated Ability." *Ladies Home Journal* (February 1957): 149-157. Part of the series "How America Lives," this article gives personal details of the life of the Daniel James family. There is information about their families, courtship, religion, children, monthly expenses ($925.00), and other aspects of their lives.

775. "Wallace & Wallace Enterprises Salutes Black Heritage." *Eagle & Swan* 1:December 1977-March 1978 (1): 2. An advertisement for a company that is financing the construction and development of the General Daniel "Chappie" James Jr. Airmen and Industrial Museum, at Tuskegee, Alabama. The groundbreaking was held on August 19, 1977. A painting of James is reproduced. The artist is Hiram E. Jackson Jr.

776. Wilkins, Roy. "The Fourth Star." *New York Post* (September 13, 1975). Biographical information on Daniel James Jr.

777. Wilson, George C. "Gen. Daniel (Chappie) James, Former NORAD Chief, Dies." *Washington Post* (February 26, 1978): B7. A lengthy obituary, revealing incidents of his life, including comments made by General James.

778. Wolff, C. A. "Thumbs Up to 'Chappie' James." *Golden Eagle (California)* (February 21, 1986). Biographical information and personal

reminiscences by Wolff, retired Navy Avionics Chief, who serviced James' airplane.

779. "World's Biggest Jet Pilot." *Ebony* (May 1954): 80-82, 85-88. Major Daniel James is the only Negro to command a fighter squadron, the 437th at Otis AFB, Massachusetts. Biographical information and emphasis on his leadership qualities.

World War II

780. "African-American Airmen." *The African* 2:7 (October 1943): 10-11. More an editorial than an article, this piece notes the irony of something good (black youth soaring on wings of aluminum and steel) coming out of the blood bath now drenching the world. There is mention of early fliers who "braved the disbelief of their fellow men and the sneers of whites to learn to fly."

781. "Aircraft Institute Established to Train Negro Youth for Jobs." *Opportunity* 19:4 (April 1941): 120. Lincoln Aircraft Institute has been established in Kansas City, Missouri, to turn out qualified Negro workers for all activities affecting national defense.

782. "American Negro Airman Downs Nazi Plane." *Call and Post (Cleveland)* (July 10, 1943): 1, 3. Charles B. Hall claimed the first Axis plane to be shot down by the colored fighter squadron. Hall describes the battle, which took place over Sicily.

783. "Archer Leads All U.S. Negro Airmen." *New York Sun* (January 29, 1945). "Ten kills - four in the air and six on the ground - make Lieut. Lee A. Archer Jr. of New York city the nation's No. 1 Negro fighter pilot." Archer recounts some of his flights over Italy, and mentions his companion pilot, Wendell Pruitt.

784. De Vries, Hilary. "Theater's Godfather Reaches Entr'acte." *New York Times* (June 30. 1991): Sect. 2, 1, 5. Lloyd Richards, Director of the Yale

Repertory Theater and dean of the Yale School of Drama, served as a pilot in World War II.

785. "Downed Nazi." *Pittsburgh Courier* (July 10, 1943): 1. First Lt. Charles B. Hall is the first colored airman to get an enemy plane in combat. It occured over Sicily.

786. "Hero's Dismissal Brings AF Security Setup Under Attack." *New York Post* (April 19, 1955). Air Force S/Sgt. Willie Davis of Detroit was ordered discharged after a landlord with whom he had an argument in 1950, accused him of being a communist. Rep. Diggs is investigating. Davis was a gunner in World War II and won a Bronze Star.

787. Jaggi, Maya. "Four Rum Jamaicans." *Times Literary Supplement* (April 19, 1991): 19. Review of a play by Fred D' Aguiar, *A Jamaican Airman Foresees His Death*. Through an episodic, exuberant juxtaposition of dialogue, verse and song, D' Aguiar transfers the poem's (after Yeats) ambivalence about fighting another country's battles to the experience of Jamaican recruits in the Second World War.

788. Knickerbocker, H. R. "Few Squadrons Fight Harder Than the 99th." *PM (New York)* (February 17, 1944): 13. [*PM*'s Daily Picture Magazine. See also another article by Knickerbocker]. This is the second of two articles about the 99th in Italy. The article lists the following men and the number of missions they flew: James T. Wiley, 77; Wilson V. Eagleson, 14, downing two planes; Elwood T. Driver, 43; Leonard M. Jackson, 30; Charles P. Bailey, 30; Leon C. Roberts, 71; Edward J. Toppins, 50; Howard L. Baugh, 46; Willie Ashley, 57; Clarence Allen, 42; Clinton Mills, 30; George S. Roberts, the commanding officer, 30; and Lemuel Custis, 49. Twenty-one other men are listed with their home towns. Knickerbocker notes one "odd item" : although the men are offered two ounces of whiskey by medicos after every mission, only half of the 99th take it, while almost all white pilots do.

789. Knickerbocker, H. R. "Negro Fliers Bat Down 16 Planes at Beachhead." *PM (New York)* (February 16, 1944). [Clipping File on fiche, "U.S.-Army-Air Force-99th Pursuit Squadron," undated material, Schomburg Center for Research in Black Culture, NYPL. Copyright of the article is by the *Chicago Sun*]. First of two articles, "With the U. S. Air Forces in Italy." "... our men are being protected in part by Negro fighter pilots.

The famous 99th has leaped in a few days from comparative obscurity to leadership in pursuit and combat." They downed sixteen enemy planes since January 22, eight in one day. The author spoke to all the pilots involved and was inspired, and noted they had not lost any of their agreeable modesty. Both Charles B. Hall and Robert W. Diez describe battles, and there are photographs of Fred Hutchins, W.T. Foreman, C.P. Bailey, J.Y. Carter, and Paul Adams. Biographical information on Diez, who played bass violin in the Portland Symphony Orchestra and taught painting and sculpture.

790. Martin, Douglas. "35 Years Showing Warm Welcome at Carnegie Hall." *New York Times* (October 25, 1989): B1. To honor the 70th birthday of Thomas C. Martin, a maintenance worker for 35 years, the lobby will be named for him. Martin served in the Army Air Corps in World War II. A long sympathetic article.

791. "Mayor Greets Negro Pilot Home on Leave." *St. Louis Post-Dispatch* (November 28, 1944). Capt. Wendell O. Pruitt, first serviceman from St. Louis to return, completed 70 missions. He is credited with sinking an enemy destroyer, shooting down three planes, and destroying eight on the ground. He plans to marry Alice Charleton, of Detroit, who is also a pilot.

792. Mitchell, Mitch. "First Blood: The Saga of the 99th Fighter Squadron." *Air Classics* (February 1987): 14-20, 84, 86-88. An account of some of the air battles in World War II. Charles Hall is prominently featured, with biographical information. Others mentioned include Lemuel Custis, Spann Watson, Charles Dryden, and Robert Diez.

793. Murphy, Beatrice. *Ebony Rhythm: An Anthology of Contemporary Negro Verse*. New York: Exposition Press, 1948. Ritten Edward Lee III served in the Air Corps during World War II. He is now a college freshman in Indiana, pp.99-101.

794. "Negro Fighter Pilots Weather First Test Against Germans." *Call and Post (Cleveland)* (July 3, 1943): 1, 3. Article describes a June 18th battle over Italy in which two enemy aircraft were destroyed, while the Americans had no loss. The battle was led by Charles W. Dryden. The three flyers from Cleveland are: Sidney P. Brooks, Clarence C. Jamison, and Edwin B. Lawrence. Others were Lee Rayford, Willie Ashley, Spann

Watson, and Leon C. Roberts. Nearly twenty others are names with street addresses and home towns.

795. "Negroes Fill Vital Posts in Turning Out Wings for Army." *Chicago Sun* (October 1, 1942). [Fifth in a series on the Negro in America's war effort in factories and in the army]. "Of all industries devoted to the war effort aircraft production probably has been the most difficult for Negro workers to get into." Article focuses on the aircraft division of Pullman-Standard Car Manufacturing Co. Many Negroes are employed here, as they are in constructing railroad coaches and as porters in peacetime.

796. "Negroes' Flying Unit Scores First Victory." *New York Times* (July 4, 1943). First Lt. Charles Hall was congratulated by General Eisenhower when he returned from downing a Focke-Wolf 190. Hall describes the battle.

797. Ottley, Roi. "Dark Angels of Doom." *Liberty* (March 10, 1945): 13, 54. The story of the Red Tails, the all-Negro fighting group with the ace-high morale. They have run up an enviable record in sky battles from North Africa to Germany. More than 30 percent have attended college. Those mentioned or interviewed are: Bernie Jefferson, Jack Holsclaw, Vance H. Marchbanks, George S. Roberts, and Benjamin O. Davis.

798. Primack, Bret. "Bebop Above and Beyond the Fads." *Down Beat* (March 22, 1979): 16-17, 36-39. Interview with the Heath Brothers: Percy, Tootie, and Jimmy. Percy Heath is a bassist and a former fighter pilot in World War II.

799. "Segregation Banned as Air Corps Plans Bombing Unit." *Washington Afro-American* (September 11, 1943): 1, 2. The unit will be all colored, but the training will be in mixed classes - a first. The decision is believed to be based on the performance efficiency of the 99th Pursuit Squadron, now in Sicily.

800. Silvera, John D. *Negro in World War II.* [Baton Rouge, LA]: [Military Press, Inc.], [1946]. Consisting mainly of photographs, this book has unnumbered pages. There are nineteen pages on the Air Force, "Eagles at War," which also includes paratroopers.

801. Smith, Arnold Jay. "Jazzmobile: Magnetizing the Arts." *Down Beat* (December 1, 1979): 14-15, 41-43. Interview with Billy Taylor and S.

David Bailey, executive director of Jazzzmobile. Bailey flew P51s and P39s in World War II. He has FAA ratings for planes with a single propeller through multi-jet.

802. "St. Louis Negro Shoots Down Two Nazi Planes." *St. Louis Post-Dispatch* (April 2, 1945). Carl E. Casey is credited with shooting down two Nazi planes while escorting bombers over southern Austria.

803. Stewart, Ollie. "99th Squadron on Patrol From Base in Italy." *Afro-American (Baltimore)* (October 2, 1943): 1, 3. Reports of battles; John Rogers and Leon Roberts were promoted to First Lieutenants.

804. Stewart, Ollie. "One 'Lost' Flyer Returns to Base; Another Still Missing." *Call (Kansas City, MO)* (July 30, 1943). Lt. George R. Bolling parachuted from his burning plane into the sea near Sicily, was rescued by a ship, and returned to his base uninjured. Samuel L. Bruce guarded him from enemy planes. Second Lt. James L. McCullin is still missing.

805. Stewart, Ollie. "One Missing Pilot Safe; 3 Still Gone." *Call (Kansas City, MO)* (September 10,1943). Reporter is with the 99th Pursuit Squadron in Sicily. John Warren came back, but presumed dead are James L. McCullin, Sherman W. White, and Paul G. Mitchell.

806. Thompson, Vernon C. "Army to Honor First Black Pilot." *Washington Post* (February 7, 1980): 1, 5. As part of the Army's Black History Month celebration, they will honor Charles L. Brown at the Aviation Museum at Fort Rucker in Alabama. Biographical information about Brown, who fought both in World War II and Korea.

807. "World War II Air Force Hero Joseph Elsberry Dies." *Jet* 68:7 (April 29, 1985): 29. Major Joseph D. Elsberry was the first Air Force Squadron Leader to lead his men to sink a German destroyer with machine gun fire at Trieste, Italy. A month later he shot down three German planes in one day. He was buried at Arlington National Cemetery. Biographical information.

808. "Yesterday in Negro History." *Jet* (August 11, 1960): 9. On August 11, 1943 Sec. Lt. Paul G. Mitchell was shot down over Italy, and became the first Negro pilot to die in action in World War II.

Frank E. Petersen Jr.

809. Fleming, Robert. "Col. Frank Petersen: 'The Godfather' - in Line for Star Rank." *Encore* (April 2, 1979): 22. Biographical information on Petersen, the first black pilot in the Marines, and statistics on blacks in the Marine Corps.

810. Huntington, Tom. "An Eagle's Wings." *Air & Space/Smithsonian* (June/July 1988): 102-105. Lieutenant General Frank Petersen is a Silver Hawk, a Gray Eagle, and the Marine's [*sic*] first black aviator. Biographical information.

811. "It's Official; First Black Marine General is Installed." *Jet* (May 17, 1979): 13. The ceremony for Frank E. Petersen Jr. was held in Washington, D.C. Petersen was the first black Marine pilot 29 years ago.

812. Laluntas, N. "Col. Frank E. Petersen Becomes the First Black Marine Corps General." *Eagle & Swan* 2:2 (May 1979): 44. The Marine Corps' first black aviator has become the first black marine to attain star rank. Petersen gives his philosophical views, and there is biographical information.

813. "Marine Corps." *Tuesday* 8:4 (December 1972): 9. Frank E. Petersen is the first black Marine to enter the National War College. He has been recruiting blacks for three years and he comments,"The whole equality movement within the Corps is still in its embryonic stages." Although 12 percent of Marines are black, only 1.3 percent are officers.

814. "Marines Tab War Hero as First Black General." *Jet* (April 12, 1979): 8. [Col. Frank E. Petersen Jr., the first black Marine general, now serves as Chief of Staff of the 9th Marine Amphibian Brigade at Okinawa].

815. "Stars." *Washington Post* (April 28, 1979): C3. Photograph of Frank E. Petersen Jr. receiving his stars as brigadier general. This makes him the first black general in the Marine Corps.

816. "Top Man at Quantico." *Ebony* (December 1986): 140, 144, 146. Frank E. Petersen made history as the first black pilot in the Marine Corps in 1952. He is now commanding general of the Marines Development and Education Command in Quantico. Biographical information.

817. Toson, Jim. "Col. Frank Petersen, A Man of Many Firsts." *Eagle & Swan* 1:2 (March 1978): 27-29. [Cover story]. A candid interview with Frank E. Petersen, a Marine pilot for 28 years.

818. "Yesterday in Afro-American History." *Jet* (October 28, 1971): 10. On October 22, 1952 Frank E. Petersen Jr. was awarded his commission and wings at Pensacola, Florida, then the "Annapolis of the Air." He became the first black pilot in the Marine Corps. He is now a Lt. Colonel.

819. "Yesterday in Negro History." *Jet* (October 26, 1967): 11. On October 22, 1952 Frank E. Petersen Jr. of Topeka, Kansas became the first Negro flyer in the history of the Marine Corps, at Pensacola, FL, the then "Annapolis of the Air."

Other Individuals and Events

820. "Advertisement." *Ebony* (August 1979): 10. James White is now Project Manager of the ITT Avionics Division in Nutley, NJ. He served in Vietnam as an aircraft commander and squadron commanding officer, and he received a Distinguished Flying Cross.

821. "Aeronautics Board Executive." *Ebony* (January 1980): 6. Cressworth C. Lander is managing director of the Civil Aeronautics Board in Washington, D.C.

822. "AF is Ordered to Drop Loyalty Quiz of Officer." *Sunday News (New York)* (February 4, 1951): 16. Capt. Charles A. Hill was accused of reading the *Daily Worker*, and was ordered to resign his reserve commission or face an inquiry on his loyalty. His father was accused of being a Communist. Hill is a decorated pilot. The Air Force dropped the charges and expressed regret.

823. "African Mask Maker." *Ebony* (December 1952): 71-73. Now reproducing African masks, Perry J. Fuller has been a pilot and an aeronautical design consultant for Lockheed and Douglas. He has also been the technical advisor for such films as *Eagle Squadron* and *Victory through Air Power*. His mother was Meta Vaux Warrick, the sculptor, and his father was Dr. Solomon C. Fuller, a psychiatrist.

824. "Air Force Academy Names 1st Black Cadet Cmdr." *Jet* (September 8, 1977): 5. Edward A. Rice Jr. is the first black to be named Cadet Commander in the Air Force Academy's 23-year history. The selection is based on leadership abilty, academic achievement, and military development.

825. "Air Force Academy Sued over Sickle Cell Policy." *New York Times* (January 4, 1981). Stephen Pullens was forced to resign from the Air Force Academy in 1979 when he was found to have the trait for sickle cell anemia, but not the disease itself. He filed a class action suit in Minneapolis for reinstatement and damages.

826. "The Air Force Blows its Mind." *Ebony* (March 1972): 33-36, 38, 40, 42. Black cadets, less than two per cent of the student body, sponsored a five-day festival of black culture that included music, dance, fashion, poetry, art, film, religion, and food. Cadet Robert Gilbert originated the idea.

827. "Air Force Cadets." *Ebony* 15 (February 1960): 71-75. Three Negro youths are the first of the race to enter the five-year old U.S. Air Force Academy near Colorado Springs. They are Charles V. Bush, Isaac Payne IV, and Robert Sims.

828. "Air Force Contract Specialist." *Ebony* (June 1979): 5. Fred E. Obey is a supervisory contract specialist in the Electronics Systems Division, Air Force Systems Command, Hascom AFB, Massachusetts.

829. "Air Guard Appoints First Black General." *Jet* 63:19 (January 24, 1983): 53. Russell C. Davis became the first black general in the Air National Guard. He is commander of the 113th Tactical Fighter Wing, the major unit in the D.C. Air Guard.

830. "Air Official Gives Talk at A & T." *Daily News (Greensboro, NC)* (November 6, 1954). Major General Matthew K. Deichelmann is shown arriving at A & T College. Greeting him is Major Elmore M. Kennedy, professor of air science at the college, and head of the Air Force ROTC program.

831. "Air Traffic Controller." *Ebony* (May 1962): 6. Lewis Perry Jr. works at Baer Field Control Tower in Fort Wayne, Indiana.

832. "Airman of the Year." *Sepia* 30:8 (August 1981): 52, 78. Biographical information on John A. Norris. He was one of twelve airmen chosen annually to receive the award. He is stationed at Clark AFB in the Phillipines.

833. "Airport Concessions: New Opportunities for Black Business." *Ebony* (April 1987): 54-56, 58-59. Fourteen businessmen are mentioned, some history and a list of black-owned businesses at the 15 busiest U. S. airports.

834. "Airport Executive." *Ebony* (July 1982): 7. Melvin McCray is director of maintenance at Hartsfield Atlanta International Airport in Georgia. The airport is the world's largest and second busiest.

835. "Airport Executive." *Ebony* (April 1983): 6. Carroll H. Hyneson Jr. is director of information and trade development for the Maryland State Aviation Administration.

836. "Airport Superintendent." *Ebony* (April 1961): 6. Charles H. Rogers is superintendent at North Philadelphia Airport.

837. "Airport Superintendent." *Ebony* (December 1973): 7. Robert E. Quincey is Superintendent of Operations at Los Angeles International Airport.

838. "Alaska Crash Has its Hero." *Life* (December 2, 1957). S/Sgt. Calvin Campbell saved three men when their B-29 crashed in Alaskan snows. Six other men died.

839. Appelhof, Ruth Ann. *Jack White: The Flight Genesis.* Syracuse, New York: [Everson Museum of Art], 1977. Exhibition catalog. Jack White is a painter who served in the Air Force from 1950 to 1954 in North Africa. He has always been interested in flight, and this exhibition comprises two groups of abstract paintings: Horizontal Series and Glider Series. Information about the artist and his work.

840. "Arctic Test Board Member." *Ebony* (November 1957): 5. Capt. Charles L. Easley is the only Negro army officer assigned to the U.S. Army Arctic Test board at Ft. Greeley, Alaska. A pilot, he tests airplanes and helicopters for use in arctic regions.

841. "Army Helicopter Pilot." *Ebony* (April 1955): 5. Warrant Officer James Delaney is the only Negro helicopter pilot in the U.S. Army. He is a

member of the Eighth Transportation Battalion at Ft. Bragg, North Carolina.

842. "Army Pilot for VIPS." *Ebony* (January 1951): 5. William M. Bumpus flies VIPs and confidential cargo at Wright Patterson Field, Dayton, Ohio. Kentucky-born Bumpus had fighter training on P-51 Mustangs.

843. "Artist Sculptures JFK Doodles." *Ebony* (October 1969): 46-48, 51. Ralph M. Tate was asked to turn Pres. Kennedy's doodles into metal sculptures, which were then exhibited. Tate is also a pilot.

844. Baker, Martha. "Byronic Poses." *New York* 25:40 (October 12, 1992): 56-59. Discussion of prize-winning designer Byron Lars, whose latest collection is inspired by clothing worn by aviators.

845. Begeman, Jean. "The Air Force Tries Democracy." *New Republic* (May 15, 1950). E.W. Kenworthy toured Air Force bases and found the new integration policies working well everywhere except for Maxwell AFB at Montgomery, Alabama. Of the 25,891 Negroes in the Air Force, 18,489 are integrated, and the others will be soon.

846. Bergdall, Calvin. "A Day in the Life of a Jet Instructor." *Sepia* 8:8 (August 1960): 70-73. Lt. Al Daniels is one of the few members of his race to hold the position of instructor for jet planes in the Air Force. He is stationed at Vance AFB, near Enid, Oklahoma. The article describes an average day for Daniels, and gives biographical information.

847. Berry, Frank W. Jr. "The United States Air Force Aerospace Medicine Program." *Journal of the National Medical Association* 64 (January 1972): 48-51. [Berry, a flight surgeon, read this paper at the 76th annual convention of the National Medical Association in Philadelphia, August 1971]. Brief history of flight medicine, which became more specialized after World War I, and discussion of the achievements and goals of the U.S. program.

848. "Big Bomber Bears Name of Soldier." *Journal and Guide (Norfolk, VA)* (October 16, 1943). The black citizens of Birmingham raised $300, 000 to buy a bomber to be named after Julius Elsberry, killed at Pearl Harbor. The plane was named "The Spirit of Elsberry." The only other American bomber christened by Negroes was "The Spirit of the Memphis Belle."

849. "Black Aviators Part of Record Global Flight." *Jet* 58:23 (August 21, 1980): 24. Captains Thomas E. Clark and James A. McLauchlin are thought to be the first blacks to fly a non-stop operational mission around the world - 22,275 miles in 43 and a half hours. They were part of a 14-man crew, and they landed at Sawyer AFB, Michigan. Black aviators represent only about two per cent of the officer flying force.

850. "Black Pilot Gives Rare Personal Glimpse of Pope." *Jet* (October 25, 1979): 9. A brief article, with some biographical information, on Clarence Powell, the co-pilot of Shepherd I, Pope John Paul II's plane.

851. "Black Pilot to be Captive Until U.S. Leaves Lebanon." *Jet* 65: 16 (December 26, 1983): 31. Lt. Robert Goodman is a prisoner of war in Syria. He was captured after his plane was shot down and the pilot was killed. Goodman was the bombadier-navigator.

852. "Black Pilot's Portrait in Pentagon's Hall of Heroes." *Jet* 59: 26 (March 12, 1981): 5. The portrait is of Fred V. Cherry one of the nation's most decorated pilots.

853. "Black Rodeos." *Black Enterprise* 2:9 (April 1972): 42. Charles Evans, a radio announcer and calf roper, works five days a week as an aircraft repair shop machine operator in Oklahoma.

854. "Black Sergeant Selected as Outstanding Airman of '74." *Jet* 47: 5 (October 24, 1974): 19. Chief M/Sgt Isaiah N. White Jr. was selected as one of twelve outstanding Airmen of the Air Force for 1974. He was chosen for job knowledge and his leadership abilities. He is stationed at Offutt AFB in Nebraska.

855. "Black War Prisoners: Forgotten Men." *Encore* (October 1972): 10-11. Profile of Lt. Norris A. Charles, whose fighter plane was shot down over Vietnam.

856. "Blacks Make Great Pilots." *Chicago Daily Defender* (August 15-21, 1970): 5. Report on the Negro Airmen International, Inc., which was founded in 1967 by Edward A. Gibbs, who is still president. Other officers are Spann Watson, Perry Young, and Charles N. Smallwood. The address is P.O. Box 723, Westbury, New York, 11590. NAI was founded in response to the discrimination faced by blacks who want to enter

aviation. The organization attempts to educate young people and help them find employment.

857. Booker, Simeon. "Death of a Navy Pilot." *Ebony* (January 1967): 25-28, 31-32. Biographical information about Joseph Steven Henriquez, a Lt. Commander in the Navy, and his family. He died in Vietnam.

858. Booker, Simeon. "Washington Notebook." *Ebony* (July 1978): 68. At his death Col. Luther Joseph Brown was chief of the Air Force's social action division of the Pentagon. Holder of many medals, he is now memorialized annually with an award to the command which has made the most significant contribution to equal opportunity, human relations, education, and to drug and alcohol control. Biographical information.

859. "Boss of World's Biggest International Airport." *Ebony* (June 1985): 136-138, 140, 142. General Manager Richard L. Rowe thrives on the challenge of running Kennedy International Airport. Biographical information.

860. "Boston Pilot in Korea." *Boston Traveler* (September 25, 1951). Photo of First Lt. Vernon W. Burke in front of his F-51 Mustang fighter. Burke has completed 100 combat missions.

861. Boyne, Walter J., and Steven L. Thompson. *The Wild Blue*. New York: Crown Publishers, 1986. The novel follows six different men in the the U. S. Air Force, from 1948, when the armed services were ordered to integrate, to 1978. One of the fictional characters is an African American, Millard Washington, of East St. Louis.

862. "Brothers under the Skin." *Ebony* (September 1957): 82-86. Andrew M. Kea, 1st Lieutenant in the Alaskan Air Command's 64th Fighter Interceptor Squadron, lives and works with a white counterpart. Kea has been in the Air Force for seven years.

863. Brown, William Earl. *A Fighter Pilot's Story*. Washington, D.C.: Smithsonian Institution, 1992. [National Air and Space Museum Occasional Paper Series Number 4]. Lt. Gen. Brown, USAF (Ret.) gave the Charles A. Lindbergh Memorial Lecture on May 21, 1992. In this 40-page pamphlet, Brown tells of being inspired by the Tuskegee airmen, his mentor and friend, Woodrow Wilson Crockett, and of the many events of his career. Much of the article is technical, and describes the various fighter

planes he flew. Other black pilots briefly mentioned are: Beverly Dunjill, Fred Davis, and Dayton Ragland.

864. "Built Their Own Airport." *People's Voice* (February 21, 1943): 14. A & T College owns a hangar at Greenboro-Highpoint Airport (North Carolina). They built it themselves at a cost of $10,000 when they were refused the use of other hangars. Wladimir Terry of New York is in charge of training pilots in the CAA course. Over 200 men have been trained.

865. Burgen, Michelle. "Piloting the FAA Academy." *Ebony* (December 1976): 65-66, 68, 72, 74. Benjamin Demps Jr. is head of the school that trains personnel in air traffic control, flight safety standards, and airway facilities maintenance.

866. "Capt. Angelo Eiland is 1st Black to Pilot Lockheed F-117A Stealth Fighter." *Jet* 80:21 (September 9, 1991): 39. Biographical information on Eiland who is a veteran of the Persian Gulf War, and is now at Nellis AFB, Nevada. There are about 50 pilots who fly this plane.

867. Cash, C. "Morning Report." *Eagle & Swan* 2:6 (December 1979): 26. Profile of Navy Lt. John Douglas Jackson, who is the highest ranking black officer at the Naval Air Facility at Andrews AFB, Maryland. Jackson manages a warehouse with an inventory of $4 million.

868. "Ceramics by Tony Hill." *Ebony* (November 1946): 31-35. Now a successful maker of ceramic lamps, Tony Hill was a lathe operator at an aircraft plant in Los Angeles.

869. Cheers, D. Michael. "Bernard P. Randolph: The Armed Forces' Only Black Four-Star General." *Ebony* (November 1987): 154, 156, 159, 161. Biographical information about Randolph, who enlisted in the Air Force in 1955, and now is Commander of U.S. Air Force Systems at Andrews AFB, Maryland.

870. Cherry, Fred V. as told to Wallace Terry. "One Brave Man's Ordeal." *Parade Magazine* (July 29, 1984): 15-17. [Supplement to the Daily News (New York)]. Article is taken from *Bloods* by Wallace Terry. Cherry was a prisoner of war in Vietnam.

871. "Chief Engineer." *Ebony* (July 1981): 7. George Lee Frank Britton, at Aeronautical Systems Division at Wright Patterson AFB, Ohio, is

responsible for developing cost-effective solutions for Air Force weapons systems. He has been in the Air Force for 23 years.

872. "Chief Pilot at Municipal Airport." *Ebony* (May 1950): 5. Cecil Baker may be the only Negro chief pilot at a municipal airport in the United States today. Baker works in Decatur, Illinois. He instructs new pilots and has been flying since 1943.

873. Christmann, T. J. "'We All Shared a Common Bond'." *Navy Times* (December 16, 1985): 71. Pilots recall their rescue efforts for Jesse L. Brown, who was the first black pilot in the Navy in 1948. Brown died in Korea in 1950, despite the rescue attempt. A lengthy article with many details.

874. "Cigar-Smoking Kid Grows Up." *Ebony* (February 1970): 58-60, 62-63. ["Cigar-Smoking Kid." *Ebony* (October 1952) 94-98]. Charles R. Harris, who has been smoking and eating cigars since childhood, is now an airman who has served at Sheppard AFB near Wichita Falls and Luke AFB, Arizona.

875. "Civil Aeronautics Board to Get 1st Black - A Cuban Expatriate." *Jet* 56:23 (August 23, 1979): 5. George A. Dalley probably will become the first black member of the Civil Aeronautics Board in Washington, D. C. He has degrees from Columbia University in law and business.

876. Cleaver, James H. "Floyd Death Jolts Friends." *Los Angeles Sentinel* (February 15, 1979): A10. Obituary of Booker Floyd, a pilot who taught Ray Charles to fly an airplane. James T. Smith was also killed in the crash. Other black pilots in the Compton area after World War II are Rusty Burns, Paul Anderson, and Jim Woods, who comments on Floyd.

877. "Clevelander Graduates from Aviation School." *Call and Post (Cleveland)* (July 10, 1943): 2. [Second section]. Albert W. Herndon completed a course in airplane mechanics at the Army Air Base in Lincoln, Nebraska.

878. "Closing Ranks on Poverty." *Ebony* (August 1971): 86. Leroy Lewis, manager of the West Georgia Cooperative, was an aircraft assembly line worker.

879. "Col. Cherry Gets Partial Claim in USAF Pay Case, Vows to Continue Fight." *Jet* 63 (March 7, 1983): 32. Col. Fred V. Cherry began in 1974 to seek $122,000 from the Air Force. This money was paid to his wife, who was unfaithful to him while he was a prisoner of war in Vietnam for seven years. The Appeals Court ruled he was entitled to sixty percent.

880. Collier, Aldore. "The First Black Blue Angel." *Ebony* (June 1986): 27-30, 33-34. Lt. Cmdr. Donnie Cochran is the first black member of the U.S. Navy Flight Demonstration Squadron, the Blue Angels.

881. "Colonel Tests AF's Hottest Combat Jet." *Ebony* (May 1968): 44-46, 48, 50. James E.P. Randall, veteran of both wars in Korea and Vietnam, evaluates capability of 1,600 mph F-111 A fighter bomber. Biographical and scientific information.

882. "Combat on the Border." *Ebony* (April 1977): 104-106, 108, 110. Richard Biffle, retired Air Force pilot, flies as a U.S. Customs pilot in Tucson helping track down dope smugglers.

883. "Control Tower Boss at Kennedy." *Ebony* (March 1973): 72-74, 76, 78, 80. Arthur Varnado is one of three blacks in charge of air traffic control towers. The other two are: Marion Davis, Torrance, California and Larvano Grider, Ardmore, Oklahoma. There are 809 black controllers out of 23,635 nationwide.

884. "Convicted Airman Seeks Justice After Release from Prison." *Eagle & Swan* 2:2 (May 1979): 12-13. Frank E. Ross claims to be innocent of a crime for which he served time at RAF Lakenheth, England. He requests assistance in conducting an inquiry.

885. "Corporate Piloting: A New Trip for Blacks." *Ebony* (July 1972): 72-75, 77, 79. Joseph E. Armstead and Solomon H. Cates Jr. are pilots with the Xerox Corporation in Rochester, NY. Discusses the possibilities for blacks in corporate flying and such issues as seniority and racism.

886. "Councilman's Daughter Gets 5 Years for Mate's Death." *Jet* (October 2, 1975): 54. Mrs. Ninaking Calhoun Anderson was found guilty of manslaughter for stabbing her husband to death in Atlanta. The victim was Granville O. Anderson, a retired Air Force major.

887. Dabbs, Henry E. *Black Brass: Black Generals and Admirals in the Armed Forces of the United States*. Freehold, NJ: Afro-American Heritage House, 1984. Biographical information and photographs. The generals of the Air Force are: Benjamin O. Davis Jr., pp.48-53; Daniel James Jr., pp.58-62; William E. Brown, pp. 148-149; Rufus L. Billups, pp.150-151; Thomas E. Clifford, pp.152-153; Titus C. Hall, pp.154-155; Winston D. Powers, pp.156-157; Bernard P. Randolph, pp.158-159; Lucius Theus, pp.160-161; James T. Boddie, pp.162-163; Archer L. Durham, pp.164-165; Alonzo L. Ferguson, pp.166-167; David M. Hall, pp.168-169; Avon C. James, pp.170-171; Charles B. Jiggetts, pp.172-173; and Norris W. Overton, pp.174-175. Other generals included, without photographs, on the pages following are: Elmer T. Brooks, Horace L. Russell, John H. Voorhees, and William C. Banton.

888. Davis, George. *Coming Home*. New York: Random House, 1971. This is a first novel by a black veteran of the Air Force. It deals with the corrosive effect racism has on blacks, on whites, and on the United States' relations with the rest of the world. Its setting is the aerial war in Vietnam.

889. Davis, Lenwood G., and George Hill. *Blacks in the American Armed Forces, 1776-1983: A Bibliography*. Westport, CT: Greenwood, 1985. [Foreword by Benjamin O. Davis Jr.]. This bibliography of 2,386 citations is arranged by war, then alphabetically by author or title. Since there is no subject index, one must read through many citations to find the ones on aviation.

890. "Democracy at Mitchel Base." *New York Times* (March 9, 1953). [Editorial]. The editorial comments favorably that integration is working well at the base. Even so, "Civilian life on Long Island hasn't caught up with the high standards set by the Air Force." It notes that there are 27 officers and 448 other Negroes out of a population of 8,000.

891. "Denver's Swoop Club." *Our World* 4:4 (April 1949): 55-57. Four ex-aircorpsmen organized the Swoop Club in 1946 to keep pace with the ever-changing developments in aviation. They are Richard Biffle, Henry Jones, Harris Robnett, and John Moseley. Their purpose is to encourage youth, and there are now 55 young men and women members. Biographical information about the four organizers.

892. "Destination 'Moon' : Negro Navy Man Takes Tough 7-Day 'Flight'." *Ebony* 13:9 (July 1958): 120-122, 124. Charles Hayes is the first Negro to take a simulated space flight of 248,000 miles. Biographical information.

893. "Douglas Watson, First Black Aeronautical Engineer, Dies." *New York Amsterdam News* (June 12, 1993): 44. Watson died on May 30 in Queens, New York at the age of 73. He worked for Fairchild Republic Aviation Corporation for 27 years. Although he graduated with honors from New York University in 1941 he did not receive one job offer. A full obituary, this articles gives details of his long career and his family. His father and brother were judges, his sister an ambassador, his first cousins are Colin L. Powell and J. Bruce Llewellyn.

894. Duckett, Richard. "A Real Joker Must Have Been Author of Script for 'Aces'." *Telegram and Gazette (Providence, RI)* (June 13, 1992): 20. Review of *Aces: Iron Eagle III*, starring Louis Gossett Jr. as USAF Colonel Sinclair.

895. "Ebony Update: Lt. Robert O. Goodman." *Ebony* (May 1987): 124, 126. After being captured and freed in Lebanon three years ago, the Navy navigator and bombadier is studying for a post-graduate degree in space systems operations. Goodman was released through the negotiations of Jesse Jackson.

896. "[Eddie Hinton]." *Aviation International News [New Jersey]* (November 1, 1986): 115. Eddie Hinton, a former receiver for the Baltimore Colts, started a small unique service, Fly Clean, to clean aircraft. Now it is growing, publically held, and franchised.

897. Eff, David. "Chief Master Sgt." *Eagle & Swan* 3:5 (November 1980): 19-21. [Cover story]. Robert L. Ellis is the Chief of Social Actions at Laughlin AFB, Texas. He is the first enlisted man to serve in that post at any wing in the Air Force. His job deals with human relations, alcohol and drug problems, and equal opportunity. He also develops training programs to head these problems off. There is a thoughtful discussion about blacks in the Air Force, also personal and family information about Ellis.

898. "Engineering Supervisor." *Ebony* (April 1973): 6. Jack F. Charlton is a licensed pilot in Ohio.

899. "Ens. Brown, Navy Pilot, Dies a Hero." *Journal and Guide (Norfolk, VA)* (December 12, 1950): 1, 2. Jesse L. Brown was the first colored naval aviator in the history of the Navy, and the first colored officer in the Navy to lose his life in any war. He drowned in his plane when it was forced down behind enemy lines.

900. "Ensign Carter To Become First Negro Carrier Pilot." *New York Amsterdam News* (September 30, 1950): 4. [The date is not clear on the photocopy examined; it could be September 20]. Earl L. Carter of Harlem is the first Negro USN pilot to complete advanced flight training for carriers. He is at Cabaniss Field, Corpus Christi, Texas. While this article is largely composed of photos, the public information office of Cabaniss Field issued a three-page press release on Carter about two weeks later.

901. "FAA Aircraft Manager." *Ebony* (July 1979): 6. John M. Howard is the senior aircraft manager for the Federal Aviation Administration in Washington, D.C. He was formerly chief of branches in Alaska and Japan.

902. Fabre, Michel. *From Harlem to Paris: Black American Writers in France 1840-1980*. Urbana: University of Illinois Press, 1991. Melvin Van Peebles was a navigator on an Air Force bomber, p.261.

903. "Faithful Navigator for K. of C." *Ebony* (December 1960): 7. Senior Master Sgt. Calvin Hobbs, maintenance supervisor for long-range bombers at Mather AFB, California, is the first Negro to be elected Faithful Navigator in the Knights of Columbus.

904. "Favorite Hobbies of Famous Faces." *Ebony* (March 1989): 54. Ray Parker Jr., singer-composer, took up flying so he'd have a quick getaway to the California mountains.

905. "Federal Airways Flight Inspector." *Ebony* 17 (August 1962): 66-70. Elliott H. Blue is the first Negro flight inspector for the Federal Aviation Administration. He was a captain in the Air Force, and is based in Minnesota.

906. "Fighting Weathermen from the Sky." *Buffalo* 1:2 (December 1980): 18-20. The "jumping weathermen" who forecast conditions for parachuting are Kenneth J. Bradley and Donny Weaver, stationed at Ft. Bragg, North Carolina.

907. File, Nigel, and Chris Power. *Black Settlers in Britain*. London: Heine-mann Educational Books, 1981. Alfred Moore, born in Guyana, was a volunteer for the RAF in 1943. He did not fly, but spent the war in Wales. Biographical information,.

908. "First Navy Jet Pilot." *Ebony* (May 1951): 4. Earl L. Carter of New York City is the first Negro jet pilot to win his wings in the U.S. Navy. He has been in the Navy since 1945.

909. "First Negro Flight Instructor." *Sepia* 11 (January 1962): 43-44. Lt. Louis Alvin Williams became the Navy's first Negro flight instructor on October 20, 1958. Biographical information.

910. "Flight Unlimited." *Ebony* (October 1971): 123-124, 126, 128, 130. A native of Jamaica, Rev. Linton Scott, set up Flight Unlimited Inc. in 1968 in Minneapolis. The purpose is to assist young people (17-23) who want training but can't afford it. Students are mostly black, but it is open to all. Article states there are 51 blacks among the nation's 35,000 commercial pilots.

911. "The Flying Preacher." *Ebony* (February 1961): 52-54, 56. Julius Carroll, pastor of the Randall Memorial Methodist Church in Washington, D.C., finds flying a pleasant adjunct to ministerial duties. Licensed in 1951, he is an organist and chaplain for the local Civil Air Patrol. Some of his sermons are entitled, "Flying from Dusk to Darkness" and "Takeoff at Sunset."

912. Foresman, Bob. "Negro Makes Airport Pay at Muskogee." *Tulsa Tribune* (July 6, 1956). Pilot Nathan Sams, a former flight instructor at Tuskegee, now operates a municipal air field, the largest operated by a Negro. Hatbox Field was in a decline until Sams took over in January. He has reversed that trend. He also owns the Sams Flying School. He credits his success to "long hours."

913. Fowler, Elizabeth A. "Careers: Air Force Recruiting Mission." *New York Times* (November 30, 1977). Profiles Lieut. Michael A. Cross, a recent graduate. Cross has been assigned to increase enrollmentin the Air Force Academy in Colorado, especially among minority men and women. There is information about the Academy's requirements and programs.

914. Fowler, Glenn. "Dr. Jasper F. Williams Killed." *New York Times* (April 17, 1985): D27. Williams was piloting a light plane when it crashed near Terre Haute, Indiana. Williams had been flying for twelve years. He was a physician, banker, and television station co-owner.

915. Franklin, Ben A. "Ex-P.O.W. Seeks Money Paid to Wife." *New York Times* (June 30, 1981). Col. Fred V. Cherry, veteran of over seven years of captivity which included surgery without anesthesia and 702 days in solitary confinement, gives details of his battle to win his pay and savings. A painting of Cherry, "Portrait of a Fighter Pilot, " recently installed at the Pentagon, is shown.

916. Franklin, Ben A. "Former P.O.W., Money Taken by Wife, to Reject Court Award." *New York Times* (April 25, 1982). Col. Fred V. Cherry, a decorated fighter pilot and P.O.W. for seven years, came home in 1973 to find his wife had deserted him and vanished with $121,998 the Air Force had paid her. The article gives details of the case, including testimony by relatives.

917. Friedman, Robert. "Dare a Civil Servant Speak His Mind?" *Newsday* (July 18, 1983). Harold Brown, an air traffic control supervisor, was fired for expressing support for the strike of air traffic controllers. After his attempt to be reinstated failed, he decided to take his case to the Supreme Court.

918. Garvin, Roy. "Negro Aviator First to Land Aircraft on Turks Island in Bahama Group." *Negro History Bulletin* 16:1 (October 1952): 19. James O. Plinton, flying his own plane, had to make a forced landing on Grand Turks Island March 12, 1947. It was the first time an airplane had landed on the island. Biographical information on Plinton.

919. "General Clifford Picked for Pentagon Post." *Eagle & Swan* 1:4 (1978): 8. Major General Thomas E. Clifford became the Deputy Secretary of Defense for Public Affairs in September. Clifford had been a fighter pilot.

920. "Ghana's Leader Wins Election as President." *New York Times* (November 6, 1992): A5. Jerry J. Rawlings, a former air force pilot, received 58.7 percent of the vote.

921. "GI Risks Death 65 Times for Science." *Ebony* (May 1959): 68-70, 72. Airman Alton W. Yates risks life on the bopper sled, a machine that simulates space flight. He is at Holloman AFB, New Mexico.

922. Gite, Lloyd. "On the Wings of Suds." *Black Enterprise* 15:11 (June 1985): 52. Eddie Hinton owns Fly Clean, a company that's been scrubbing airplanes since 1977. Hinton, a former football player, got the idea while at the car wash he owned. Six banks refused to lend him money because they said it wouldn't work.

923. "Gives Pupils Lofty Hopes." *Sunday News (New York)* (November 22, 1970). Joseph Haynes, a mechanical engineer and a pilot, began an aviation workshop at Muse, the children's museum which opened a few years ago. Haynes teaches aerodynamics, navigation, meteorology, regulations, and the instrument board. The students have hands-on practice when he rents a plane and takes them up about once a month. More information about the workshop and Haynes, who also started a workshop in Harlem.

924. Greene, Robert E. *Black Defenders of America: A Reference and Pictorial History.* Chicago: Johnson Publishing Company, 1974. This work provides one or two pages of biographical information on twenty-four men in the Air Force. Citations accompanying the medals many of the men won are included, and provide useful information. Joseph D. Elsberry, p.194; Charles Hall, p.196 (photo only); Jack D. Holsclaw, p.198; Clarence D. Lester, p.200; Andrew D. Marshall, p.201; Wendell O. Pruitt, pp.204-205; Jesse L. Brown, p.214; Ernest Craigwell Jr., p.215; Vance H. Marchbanks, p.216; Dayton Ragland, p.216; Eugene Ashley Jr., pp.222-223; Thomas E. Clifford, p.239; Woodrow W. Crockett, p.241; Benjamin O. Davis Jr., pp.242-243; Clarence L. Davis, p.244; Edward J. Dwight Jr., p.249 (photo only); James F. Hamlet, p. 264; Daniel James Jr., p. 267; Milton Olive III, p.279; Frank E. Petersen, pp.280-281; John E. Peterson, p.281; Roscoe Robinson Jr., p.286; Chester C. Sims, pp.292-293; Lucius Theus, p.296; Robert H. Lawrence, p.328 (photo only).

925. "Guardians Under Guard." *Life* (March 17, 1958). Picture of Airman Lemuel Riddlespreger with the guard dog Bonzo at a German air base.

926. "Guided Missiles." *Ebony* (May 1956): 132-134. Negro airmen play big roles in the Air Force's first Pilotless Bomber Squadron at Bitburg, Germany.

927. Haden-Guest, Anthony. "Just Plane Folks." *New York Magazine* (January 23, 1978): 32-27. An article about people who build planes in basements, garages, living rooms, barns and in a rectory in Brooklyn. Al Doyle, p. 37, is building a jet plane in a loft on lower Broadway. The Doylejet I will have two seats and a 500 mile range. Doyle is a New Yorker, studied art at Pratt, and made his career in advertising. He also writes a newsletter that goes to about 100 people.

928. Harris, Lorenzo D. "Britton's Bright Idea." *Airman* (January 1985): 34-36. George Britton is chief engineer in the Air Force's Productivity, Reliability, Availability and Maintainability Office (PRAM), at Wright-Patterson AFB in Ohio. Biographical information about him and his work.

929. Haynes, Joseph H. "Letter to the Editor." *Flight Instructor's Forum* 9:1 (January 1983): 8. [Supplement to *Flight Instructor's Safety Report*]. The letter is in answer to the question posed in the October issue, "When teaching instrument rating applicants to fly on partial panel, what procedures/techniques do you use?" Because of the many responses received only a few selected responses were printed.

930. "He Flies the Largest Airplane in the World." *Ebony* (April 1979): 98-100, 102, 104. Major Willie L. Farrow flies a C-5 Galaxy, whose cargoes include missiles, tanks, trucks, and complete hospitals. Biographical and technical information.

931. "He Needed a Lift to Town." *Daily News (New York)* (March 16, 1972): 77. Pilot George Bailey, who was uninjured, watches police prepare stricken chopper for the airlift. Bailey's Bell 206-A helicopter went down in the East River.

932. "Helicopter Systems Engineer." *Ebony* (October 1983): 6. Otha L. Stubblefield is the assistant department manager for Helicopter Systems Engineering at Hughes Aircraft Company in California.

933. Hevesi, Dennis. "Douglas C. Watson, Design Engineer, 73, in Military Aviation." *New York Times* (June 3, 1993): D23. Watson, an

aeronautical engineer, died on May 29, at his home in Jamaica, Queens. He worked for 27 years with the Fairchild Republic Aviation Corporation. He was proudest of his role in the design of the P-47N, a bomber escort, and considered that his major contribution to aviation. Biographical information.

934. Hillinger, Charles. "A Boost in Black Air Force Cadets." *New York Post* (May 20, 1970): 36. John W. Blanton, a former Harlem Globetrotter, is such a successful recruiter for minority cadets for the Air Force, that West Point and Annapolis have adopted similar programs.

935. Hillinger, Charles. "Inner-City Youths Soar to Excellence." *Los Angeles Times* (November 30, 1986): 10. [Part 6]. For eleven years Rev. Russell White of East Orange, New Jersey, has operated Eagle Flight, a flying academy. There have been 239 graduates. The current enrollment is fifty: forty-four men and six women.

936. Hincher, Lee. "Boxer with Talent." *Encore* (February 16, 1976): 44. Sgt. John Vaughn, George AFB, California, is a boxer. Biographical information.

937. "Hot Pilots." *Our World* 5 (December 1950): 58-59. "The tan flyboys have arrived. At home and in the Far East they're doing their bit to keep the world's greatest flying powerhouse in the blue." They are important in the new, integrated Air Force. Mentioned are: John Whitehead, Russell Stewart, Frank Lee, Vance Marchbanks, W. Haywood, Lewis Lynch, and Eugene Briggs.

938. Howe, John L. "Home-Front Vets." *The Black Vet [Brooklyn]* 1:4 (June/September 1990). Paratrooper John L. Howe recounts his experiences in Vietnam, and the toll it took on his family and himself.

939. Hudson, Neff. "At Andrews: 'The Folks on the Floor' One Source of Problem-solving Ideas." *Air Force Times* (August 31, 1992): 12-13. [Cover story]. The two problem solvers are MSgt. Carl Buckmon, who with his team, successfully solved the 10-year problem of maintaining oxygen carts used to service aircraft; and SSgt. Kevin Hewitt (on cover), an electrical technician with 1st Helicopter Squadron.

940. Hunter, Charlayne. "Stabbing of Boy Led to Career Training Plan for Slum Youths." *New York Times* (February 1, 1971): 23. Sidney

Augstein's son was stabbed in the back by a band of boys. When he recovered, Augstein wanted to offer a release to the anger and idleness of youth. He bought Flight Products, Inc. and set up a 33-week aviation training course in Harlem. Joseph Haynes, who soloed when he was sixteen years old, is the instructor. The outlook for employment as a pilot is not good, "One in a million," says Augstein. According to a 1969 survey of fourteen major airlines taken by the *Christian Science Monitor*, there were only 51 employees at the "cockpit level," out of 35,000 employees.

941. "I Spied on Castro's Cuba." *Ebony* (April 1963): 114-116, 118, 120, 122-123. In October 1962 Thomas LeRoy Hennagan flew unarmed over Cuba to take aerial photos which revealed a missile buildup. Much of the story is told in Hennagan's own words.

942. "Images of Pride." *Jet* (March 9, 1978): 21. Air Force Major Amos Roscoe Otis displays his art. He is at Wright-Patterson AFB in Ohio.

943. "Ind. Univ. Alumnus Pays a Visit." *Eagle & Swan* 3:3 (July 1980): 9. Brig. Gen. Norris Overton visits his alma mater. He is now deputy commander of the Army and Air Force Exchange Service at Dallas, Texas.

944. Innis, Doris Funnye, and Juliana Wu. *Profiles in Black: Biographical Sketches of 100 Living Black Unsung Heroes.* New York: CORE Publications, 1976. [There is a page of text and a photograph for each entry]. Lawrence W. Carroll, pilot, pp.94-95; Alonza Cummings, Air Force mechanic and air traffic controller, pp.60-61; Katy Harper, first black, first woman air traffic controller in east Texas, pp.194-195; Ruth Bates Harris, space program administrator, pp. 88-89; L. B. Jackson, aircraft supplier, pp. 132-133; Johnny L. Jones, school superintendent who served in the Air Force, pp. 180-181; William R. Norwood, pilot, pp. 12-13; Ida Van Smith, pilot, pp.138-139; William T. Syphax, construction company owner, was an officer in the Air Force, pp.170-171; James A. Tilmon, pilot, pp. 30-31; O. S. Williams, aeronautical engineer, pp.84-85.

945. "Integration in the Armed Forces." *Ebony* 13:9 (July 1958): 17-20, 22-24. The Air Force is discussed on p. 18. In one decade, America's military services have virtually eradicated their color lines. Armed service integration is still not without flaws.

946. "Jet Ferry Pilot." *Our World* 10 (October 1955): 64-67. Captain Charles Cooper is commander of a group which delivers fighter planes to U.S. airbases.

947. "A Jet Pilot's Dream Comes True." *Ebony* (May 1975): 82-84, 86, 88, 90. Captain Lloyd Newton wins a position with the Air Force Thunderbirds. He is the first black pilot to fly with the prestigious U.S. Air Force's Air Demonstration Squadron.

948. Johnson, Ralph F. "Ravens Rise to New Heights..." *New Jersey Connection* (December 1-15, 1983): 8-9. The Ravens Flight Club held a salute to black aviation on November 26. Many photographs and the officers of the club are listed: Ed Haddon, Steve McPherson, James Randolph, Orville O'Brien, John Harley, Russell White, Augustus Jenkins, Joe Clark, Bravelle Nesbitt Jr. Among those pictured are: Willis Brown, Rosco [sic] Brown, Leslie Morris, E. Raymond Hadden.

949. Kamen, Al. "Route to NTSB Runs Through Tennessee." *Washington Post* (May 28, 1993): A-21. The article deals with the replacement of Christopher A. Hart, a private pilot and aviation lawyer, by Jim Hall on the National Transportation Safety Board. Hall's nomination is said to be totally political, and Kamen details his connections.

950. "Karate: The Gentle Art of Killing." *Ebony* (April 1960): 104-106. Air Force dental technician Nathan B. Young teaches karate in his off-duty hours to paratroopers at nearby Ft. Bragg. Young is stationed at Pope AFB in North Carolina.

951. Keating, Susan Katz. "The Outstanding Airmen of the Year." *Air Force Magazine* 74:9 (September 1991): 61. SM Sgt. Arthur L. Haney was one of the twelve enlisted men honored by the Air Force Association. He executed an urgent action order, completing 363 engine safety modifications to a bomber's GE F101 engine in fewer than ninety days. Haney is at Tinker AFB, Oklahoma.

952. "Kennedy Airport Police Chief." *Ebony* (February 1964): 7. Capt. Ross L. Morgan Jr. is commander of the 101-man police department at Kennedy Airport. He is the first Negro assigned to the post.

953. "The Last Days of a Navy Pilot." *Ebony* (April 1951): 15-24. Jesse LeRoy Brown's last days in Korea are recollected by colleagues. His last letter to his wife is published.

954. Lee, George L. *Inspiring African Americans: Black History Makers in the United States, 1750-1984.* Jefferson, NC: McFarland and Co., 1991. A collection of Lee's newspaper illustrations and brief facts. The history makers in aviation are: Benjamin O. Davis Jr., p.73; Otis M. Smith, p.95; Isaac T. Gillam IV, p.110; Jim Tilmon, p.112; and Mary E. Tiller, p.129.

955. Lee, George L. *Interesting People: Black History Makers.* Jefferson, NC: McFarland and Co., 1989. A collection of Lee's newspaper illustrations and brief facts. The history makers in aviation are: William H. Hastie, p.74; Willa B. Brown, p.104; Daniel James, p.121; Jesse L. Brown, p.122; Frank E. Petersen, p.149; Guion S. Bluford, p.189; Jill Brown, p.202; Otis B. Young, p.202; and Milton L. Olive III, p.203.

956. "Leo C. Maitland, 64, Harlem Surgeon, Dies." *New York Times* (February 7, 1992): A19. Dr. Maitland served two years in the Air Force.

957. Livingston, Jane, and John Beardsley. *Black Folk Art in America 1930-1980.* Jackson: University of Mississippi, 1982. [Pp. 110-115]. Leslie Payne (1907-1981) was a black folk artist who created flight vehicles. "The absence of literal flight did not discourage Payne... took a series of imaginary journeys... entering the flights in a log book."

958. "Lloyd 'Fig' Newton: Play-by-Play Narrator for Air Force Thunderbirds." *Black Sports* 5:3 (September 1975): 46-48. Newton is the first black officer and pilot to join the Thunderbirds, a crack flying team. Other blacks, however, have served in other capacities on the team. Newton will narrate the first season, and then he will become one of the five flyers who perform the stunts. The stringent requirements, experiences, and activities are described. Biographical information.

959. "Looking and Listening." *Crisis* 68 (December 1961): 620-622. Biographical information on Flight Captain Charly Eboue, "probably the first African flight captain," employed by UAT (Aeromarine Transport Union).

960. "Maj. Gen. Clifford Receives Award." *Eagle & Swan* 2:6 (December 1979): 10. Thomas E. Clifford was awarded the Defense Distinguished Service Medal on September 26, 1979.

961. "Major 'Fig' Newton a Thunderbird in the Sky." *Eagle & Swan* 1:3 (June 1978): 28-29. Lloyd Newton is the first black pilot to join the prestigious team, the Thunderbirds, the Air Forces' crack demonstration team. He has been a member since 1974, and is the first airman who was asked to extend his three-year assignment. Three years is the usual term. He has fought in Vietnam, and he wants more blacks to join the Air Force. There are 70,000 blacks among 473,000 enlisted men, and 3,500 officers of 100,000.

962. "Man whose 'Brain' Steers the X-15." *Ebony* (December 1960): 73-74, 76, 78. Luther Prince is supervisor of the project that developed the adaptive autopilot for the X-15, America's first rocket ship. An engineer and mathematician, Prince works for Honeywell in Minneapolis.

963. "Many Problems Delay Graduation of Air Force Cadet." *New York Times* (May 27, 1980). Vaughn Benjamin, who was to graduate from the Air Force Academy with his sister Gail, was denied graduation and commissioning because of debts run up on credit cards. The Air Force will develop a plan with Benjamin to clear the debts. He will probably be able to graduate in late summer or fall.

964. Marriott, Michel. "Mincing No Words, Ex-Pilot Drops a Bomb on Would-Be Dropouts." *New York Times* (May 23, 1992): 26. [Drew (Bundini) Brown Jr., his father, was Muhammad Ali's trainer]. Drew Timothy Brown 3d is a lieutenant in the United States Naval Reserve and a former jet pilot. He now works for Federal Express, and in his free time, travels to schools to motivate young people to go to college. He has written an autobiography, *You Gotta Believe!* published by Morrow last year. Biographical information.

965. Maslin, Janet. "She's the Wrong Woman to Mess With." *New York Times* (June 13, 1992): 16. Review of *Aces: Iron Eagle III* starring Louis Gossett Jr. as Chappy Sinclair, aviator.

966. Massaquoi, Hans J. "The 'New' Navy: Trying to Put the Past Behind." *Ebony* (September 1989): 30-32, 34. Once notoriously racist service

branch offers wide range of career opportunities to blacks interested in becoming officers.

967. "Master of Air Defense." *Ebony* (October 1969): 124-126, 128, 130. Major James J. Kelly leads a 150-man team, the 924th Aircraft Control and Warning Squadron in Northern Labrador. Biographical information.

968. Mazza, Frank. "This Air Force Vet Wins in Bias Battle." *Daily News (Queens edition)* (October 28, 1979): 3. Air Force veteran George Gaynor had to support himself with temporary jobs from 1975 to 1979 because of employers' bias against veterans of the Vietnam war. They believe them to be drug users. Gaynor is now being assisted by a federally-funded program, Hire-Two.

969. McAlpin, Harry. "Race Bombers to Fly B-26's Army Reveals." *Chicago Defender* (September 11, 1943): 1, 18. According to Asst. Secretary of War John T. McCloy, Negro and white students will go to school together to train as navigators and bombadiers. There are many quotations from William H. Hastie, as this new setup upholds his argument against separation.

970. McDaniel, Jean. "A POW Wife Writes." *Encore* (October 1972): 14. Mrs. McDaniel writes to her husband, Air Force Major Norman McDaniel, a POW since July 29, 1966.

971. McPeak, William. "Genealogy and Grace: A Parable." *Interracial Review* 35 (December 1962): 270-272. Avery C. Mann Jr., born December 25, 1956, is an orphan at the New York Foundling Hospital. The article traces his genealogy. His father was Avery C. Mann, who died a hero's death in the Gulf of Mexico, and was awarded a Congressional Medal of Honor posthumously.

972. "The Men of the USS Saratoga." *Ebony* (March 1980): 44-46, 48, 50. There are 350 black crewmen on the USS Saratoga, one of 13 aircraft carriers now on duty. There is mention of pilot Paul D. Thompson and others.

973. "Military Brothers Assist in Promotion Ceremony." *Eagle & Swan* 3:2 (May 1980): 8. William Murphy, 2nd Lt. in the Air Force, assisted in the promotion of his brother Thomas, to Captain in the Army. Another brother, Tyrone, is in the Marines.

974. Miller, Jack. "Black Youths Get Pilot Training." *Minneapolis Tribune* (November 2, 1970). Rev. Linton Scott, a part-time minister, pilot and auto repairman, started an aviation training program for black youths two years ago. Biographical information. Some students are pictured and named.

975. Morris, Rachel. "Essencemen." *Essence* 9:4 (August 1978): 11. Edward A. Rice Jr. was named Air Force Academy Wing Commander last fall. He is the first black cadet to hold this post. His father is a retired Air Force major.

976. Morris, Steven. "Alaska: Bonanza for Blacks?" *Ebony* (November 1969): 123-126, 128, 130, 132, 134. Profiles a number of blacks who live in Alaska, where there are more planes per person than anywhere else in the world because roads are scarce. The three air traffic controllers are: Frank Austin, Freeman L. Lathan Jr., and Harold Richardson.

977. "Musician Solves a Problem." *Ebony* (December 1958): 115-118. Marvin Chandler, formerly of the gospel group, the Chandler Trio, and a former Baptist minister, was licensed as a pilot in 1953. He is a partner in the Musical Commercials Service in Nashville, Tennessee, and he pilots the company plane.

978. "NAACP to Defend Negro Suspended by Air Force for 'Association'." *Daily Worker* (August 18, 1954). Theodore Griffin, an Air Force worker and president of the Asbury Park-Neptune branch of the NAACP, was suspended for associating with communists. He worked with the 2847 Patrol Wing of the Air Force in Newark, New Jersey.

979. Nash, Colleen A. "All-Stars on Call." *Air Force* 74:9 (September 1991): 71. The Earl T. Ricks Award was given to 2nd Lt. Leonard W. Isabelle of the 107th Tactical Fighter Squadron at Selfridge, MI. "Lt. Isabelle displayed excellent airmanship under a highly stressful situation with only thirty-five hours in the F-16."

980. "Navy 'A Family Affair' for Ali's Ex-Aide Bundini Brown and Jet Pilot Son." *Jet* 65:16 (December 26, 1983): 30-31. Drew T. Brown III earned his jet pilot wings, one of few blacks in the Navy to be certified to fly jet fighters.

981. "Negro Air Command Pilot Earns Outstanding Award for Part in Cuban Reconnaissance." *Sepia* (February 1963): 82. Capt. Thomas L. Hennagan is awarded the Distinguished Flying Cross for his role in the photo reconnaissance of Cuba.

982. "Negro Airman Gets Top Award for Valor." *St. Louis Post-Dispatch* (March 31, 1951). Cpl. Burnett J. Hale, of St. Louis, will get the Army's highest peacetime decoration for rescuing a motorist from his burning car in California. Hale was severely burned. Biographical information.

983. "Negro Airman in England Granted Execution Stay." *Daily Worker* (August 16, 1956). James C. Jordan will have a new trial in the death of a civilian in Leeds, England. The trial will begin on August 21, with new evidence that the man died of dysentery, and not of a stab wound.

984. "Negro Helped by Nixon Plans to Quit Air Force." *New York Times* (October 9, 1968). Major Lewis Olive applied for resignation because "Air Force conditions do not allow me in good conscience to speak out on racial unrest." Olive has been in the Air Force for fourteen years.

985. "Negro Plane Builders." *Ebony* 8 (October 1953): 19-22. The Lockheed jet bomber plant in Marietta, Georgia, decided to train 1,000 Negroes because of their manpower shortage in 1951. White instructors request more Negro classes because the students are alert and eager. Segregation reigns - there are separate dining rooms, restrooms, and drinking fountains. The union local is segregated, too.

986. "Night People." *Ebony* (December 1983): 44, 46, 48. Carroll M. Waters has been a pilot for Federal Express for ten years. He flies at night, and is a board member of the Organization of Black Airline Pilots.

987. "163 Nigerians Dead As a Military Plane Crashes Near Lagos." *New York Times* (September 28, 1992): 6. The crash of the Hercules C-130 occurred on September 26. Many of the dead were middle-level personnel of the Nigerian Air Force, and were on their way to attend a course at a staff college.

988. "Our Man in Saigon." *Ebony* (June 1963): 121-122, 124, 126. Joseph S. Grant Jr. is a member of "The Dirty Thirty," a group of U.S. Air Force pilots serving as combat support for the South Vietnamese Air Force. Grant has been an airman since 1954.

989. "Outstanding Airmen of 1984." *Airman* (January 1985): 12. Sgt. Kevin M. Brown was selected as one of the twelve outstanding airmen of 1984. He saved the Air Force $100,000 by helping to design and build a test set for troubleshooting an antenna control assembly. He is at Wright-Patterson AFB in Ohio.

990. Perry, Jean. "Engineer Builds Second Career as Company President." *Black Enterprise* 4:3 (October 1973): 49-50, 52. Luther Prince Jr., former supervisor of 14-man team working on the experimental Air Force plane X-15, is now the president of Ault Inc., which manufactures electronic components in Minneapolis.

991. Peters, Art. "High-Flying Soldier of Fortune." *Ebony* (June 1964): 37-38, 40, 42, 44, 46. Wendell W. Levister is the personal pilot to the vice-president of Honduras. He left the U.S. in 1957 because he was unable to obtain employment with a commercial airline. Biographical information about Levister's life and dashing adventures.

992. "Pilot Reaction Specialist." *Ebony* (February 1971): 7. Preston L. Dent is a human-factors specialist at Bunker-Ramo, an aeronautics corporation in Canoga Park, California. He was in the Air Force.

993. "Pipeline Patrol Pilot." *Ebony* (November 1981): 7. Cornell Alexander Mauney is a pipeline patrol pilot for McCord's Aerial Patrol Systems at Gastonia Airport, North Carolina.

994. Ploski, Harry A., and James Williams. *The Negro Almanac: A Reference Work on the African American*. Detroit: Gale Research, Inc., 1989. [Fifth edition]. "Black Graduates of the United States Air Force Academy (1963-1988)," pp. 887-891. The list is chronological. There is biographical information on more than twenty high-ranking members of the Air Force.

995. Ploski, Harry A., and Warren Marr II. *Negro Almanac: A Reference Work on the Afro-American*. New York: Bellwether, 1976. Biographical information on: Thomas E. Clifford, p. 653; James Frank Hamlet, p.655; Daniel James Jr.,p.656; Roscoe Robinson Jr.,p. 656; Lucius Theus, p. 656; Jesse Leroy Brown, p.658; and Benjamin O. Davis, pp. 658-659.

996. "Pope Talks of Hope During Visit to Harlem." *Jet* (October 18, 1979): 7. Clarence Powell is the co-pilot who flies Pope John Paul II on his trips around the world.

997. Porterfield, Byron. "4 Bias-Free Years Hailed at Air Base." *New York Times* (March 8, 1953). The men at Mitchel AFB on Long Island can scarcely recall the segregation era they get along so well. The only thing they can't agree on is the type of dance music to play at socials. Both Negroes and whites praise the Air Force's non-segregation policy.

998. Precopio-Mann, Lee S. "The Airman is a Unicyclist." *Eagle & Swan* 1:3 (June 1978): 36. New Yorker Derrick Foster, a Senior Airman, has been riding a unicycle since 1973, and does so on the base at Misawa [Japan?]. One advantage is that his hand is free to salute on-coming staff cars. Biographical information.

999. Price, Yvonne. "Navy Honors Black Hero." *Crisis* 80:8 (October 1973): 277-278. The destroyer escort, USS Jesse L. Brown, the first Naval vessel named to honor a black man, was launched in Boston on February 17, 1973. Biographical information and report on the ceremony.

1000. "Private Plane Owners." *Ebony* 6:2 (December 1950): 76, 78, 80-81. Although Negro pleasure flyers triple in boom since war's end, private flying is still considered in the hobby stage. There are hair-raising stories of close calls. Gratuitous acts of racism are described, but there is the perception that discrimination is lessening. Aviators, with their home town, occupation, type of plane and cost, are: A. Porter Davis, Janet Harmon, Lewis R. Williams, Raymond L. Jackson, Robert T. Chestnut, Alfred H. Bulkley, Herman L. Waterford, Clark Waterford, James E. Levy, Grover C. Nash, William Paris, William P. Foreman, James O. Plinton, and James Long.

1001. "Radar Program Director." *Ebony* (June 1978): 7. Lt. Col. Raymond V. McMillan directs "Seek Igloo," a multi-million dollar program to upgrade 13 Alaskan Air Command radar installations. McMillan has been in the Air Force for 27 years.

1002. Rayner, Bob. "Air Force Salute: Woman's Seven Sons Served in the Military." *Richmond-Times Dispatch [Virginia]* (July 28, 1991): C 4. At a ceremony at Mt. Olivet Baptist Church in Petersburg Erma Riley was honored as the mother of seven sons who served in the Air Force. They are: James, Rudolph (killed in a car crash), Edward, Theodore, Kenneth, Norman, who was a photographer, and Raymond.

1003. "The Real Iron Eagles." *EM (Ebony Man)* 6:2 (December 1990): 46-47. Blacks are on the teams that keep America's best precision flying squads soaring: the Thunderbirds of the Air Force and the Blue Angels of the Navy. Thunderbirds include James Daniels, Louis Edwards, and Dale Sullivan. The Blue Angels are: Bruce Dillard, Cravon Ford, Mark Hopkins, Michael Riley, Darrin Williams, Claude Numa, and Kathleen Pettaway. Dillard is the only pilot in the group; the others are on the ground as draftsmen, mechanics, etc.

1004. "Retired Air Force Officer is Airport Manager." *Jet* (December 7, 1967): 10. Charles E. Walker, retired Lt. Col., is the first Negro manager of a major airport, Ventura County Airport, California.

1005. Reuter, Henry. "A Modern Masai." *Ebony* (April 1971): 87-91. Shadrack ole [*sic*] Sainepu is the only African commercial pilot in East Africa. He is the chief pilot for Wings for Progress air service. Biographical information.

1006. "A Ridiculous Case." (February 7, 1951): [Source unknown]. The Air Force was ordered to drop disloyalty charges against Capt. Charles A. Hill Jr. Hill was accused of having read the *Daily Worker*, and his father and sister were interested in communist activities. This appears to be an editorial, and it quotes from an editorial in the *New York Times*.

1007. Robinson, Louie. "Soaring Sailplane Pilot." *Ebony* (October 1976): 64-66, 68, 70. Dan Pierson is one of the nation's top-ranked glider pilots, and the only black glider pilot. He was in the Air Force for eight years, other biographical information.

1008. "Room 222 Star Reveals Mixed Marriage on TV Panel." *Jet* (October 28, 1971): 16-18. Lloyd Haynes' single-engine plane is at the Santa Monica airport. Haynes has been flying since March 1970. He has always wanted to fly, but hasn't had the money or time until recently.

1009. "SAC." *Ebony* (August 1968): 50-54. The Strategic Air Command (SAC) is an elite branch which controls bombers and nuclear forces. Several black men are part of that force. They are: Edgar V. Lewis, Fred Sabbs, Charles James, David L. Smith, Fitzroy Newsum, Dean B. Mohr,

Oliver W. Ellington, David Grudger, Charles O. Carter, and Aldred Ennett. Others are mentioned.

1010. Schiro, Anne-Marie. "The Sweet Smile of Success." *New York Times* (June 7, 1992): Section 9 - 1, 9. Profile of Byron Lars, a standout among young fashion designers. Lars' latest collection is inspired by aviation, and includes jackets, caps, goggles, leggings, and shorts with airplanes printed on them.

1011. Scott, Roland B. "US Air Force Revises Policy for Flying Personnel with Sickle Cell Trait." *Journal of the National Medical Association* 74:9 (September 1982): 835-836. [Guest editorial]. The new policy took effect May 26, 1981. All restrictions on personnel with sickle cell trait have been removed. The Air Force, however, will monitor symptoms or complications that may develop. Author applauds the fact that now policy will be based on carefully gathered data instead of anecdotal incidents. Mentions the case of Stephen Pullens who filed a class action suit in 1979, and Col. Vance H. Marchbanks, a flight surgeon who has done research in sickle cell anemia.

1012. "Sect Figure Denies Ordering Killings." *New York Times* (April 26, 1992): 27. Yahweh ben Yahweh was born Hulon Mitchell Jr. in Oklahoma 56 years ago and served honorably in the Air Force.

1013. Severo, Richard. "Air Academy to Drop its Ban on Applicants with Sickle-Cell Gene." *New York Times* (February 4, 1981): A-1, D-22. The Air Force Academy, since 1973 the only service academy to exclude applicants with a single gene for sickle cell anemia, dropped its ban yesterday. It did so, not because of the class action suit brought by Stephen Pullens, but because of new medical evidence.

1014. Sewall, George Alexander, and Margaret L. Dwight. *Mississippi Black History Makers.* Jackson, MS: University of Mississippi, 1984. "Jesse Leroy Brown: First Black Naval Aviator," pp.395-398. Further bibliography is included.

1015. "Sickle Cell Trait Turns Academy Off." *Jet* 44 (August 16, 1973): 42. Rodney Vessels enrolled at the Air Force Academy, but was then ousted because he has the trait for sickle cell anemia. Arrangements allowed him to enter the U.S. Naval Academy. This policy is said to be discriminatory because it is based on little medical fact.

1016. "'Sitting Ducks' of Aerial War." *Ebony* (November 1966): 58-60, 62-63. Members of the Forward Air Control (FAC) fly low at under 120 miles to locate enemy targets, then drop smoke bombs as markers for bombers.

1017. "Sloane Honored with Aviation Industry Top Award." *New York Amsterdam News* (April 14, 1990): 11. Morris Sloane, director of Aviation Operations and Redevelopment at the Port Authority, received the agency's highest award, the Howard S. Cullman Distinguished Service Medal.

1018. "State Aviation Director." *Ebony* (March 1986): 6. George M. Boyd is director of aviation for the Kansas Department of Transportation. He was a major in the U.S. Air Force and is the author of articles in *Flying Magazine* and *Air Force & Space Digest*.

1019. "'Suicide' Jones Out to Beat 'Bombshell'." (May 16, 1947): [I was not able to locate the periodical, the date or the page]. Willie "Suicide" Jones is flying his plane around the world to beat the record established by Milton Reynolds last month, 78 hours and 55 1/2 minutes. Jones gave a press conference at the Harlem YMCA yesterday. The flight is sponsored by the National Negro Day Committee to highlight National Negro Day on June 27. Biographical information on Jones.

1020. Sutherland, Don. "Lee Owens: You Can Do Anything You Want to Do." *Eagle & Swan* 3:6 (December 1980): 6-7. S/Sgt.in the Air Force, Owens is also a football star and photographer. Biographical information about Owens, who was born in Mississippi and is now in Germany.

1021. "Taking Off." *Black Enterprise* 20:7 (February 1990): 92. Since 1969 Greg Holloway has been a design engineer and manager of General Electric's Aircraft Engine Division. Some biographical information, but the emphasis is on his designs, patents, and awards.

1022. Taylor, Harold W. *One Tenth of a Nation*. Corona, NY: Progressive Book Shop, 1946. Blacks involved in aviation are briefly mentioned on p.27. Among them are Bessie Coleman, Willa Brown, John C. Robinson, Albert Forsythe, Alfred Anderson and Willie "Suicide" Jones who was a champion parachute jumper in 1938. The Pacific Parachute Company of California was owned and operated by Eddie (Rochester) Anderson and Howard Smith. "The plant hired mixed help."

1023. "Television News Cameraman." *Ebony* (April 1962): 7. An amateur aviator, Bill Baker is the only full-time television news cameraman for station KOA in Denver, Colorado. He is the only Negro so employed in the city.

1024. Terry, Wallace. *Bloods: An Oral History of the Vietnam War by Black Veterans*. New York: Random House, 1984. The Air Force veterans are: Norman A. McDaniel, 135-147; Don F. Browne, 160-175; William S. Norman, 191-205; Robert E. Holcomb, 206-224; Arthur E. Woodley, 243-265; and Fred V. Cherry, 274-300.

1025. "They Monitor Safety in the Skyways." *Ebony* (June 1979): 146-147, 150. The mission of the inspector pilots of the Federal Aviation Administration is to check on airspace navigation facilities. The only black pilots are William Owens and Theos McKinney Jr. Roger Smith is an electronics technician.

1026. Thompson, Era Bell. "Black Leaders of the West Indies." *Ebony* (October 1967): 77. Errol Walton Barrow, Prime Minister of Barbados, was a pilot for the RAF.

1027. Tisdal, Derrick. "Sassafras Lady." *Sepia* 27:10 (October 1978): 34. Judy Ann Lee accompanied her husband Airman First Class Wyman Lee to Okinawa, even though wives were not sponsored, i.e., no housing on the base or transportation to and from the U.S. The title is not explained.

1028. "Top Black in Air Force Quits as Inquiry Begins." *New York Times* (May 15, 1982). Maj. Gen. Titus Hall elected to retire yesterday. His subordinates complained of his authoritarian manner and his preference for blacks over whites. Hall's last service was at Lowry AFB in Colorado.

1029. "Top Blacks in Armed Forces." *Crisis* (March 1983): 24-26. Those in the Air Force are shown on p.25. There are sixteen photographs with name and rank.

1030. "Tracking Station Chief." *Ebony* (June 1959): 77-80. Anderson G. McPhaul is in charge of a U.S. Army satellite tracking station near Lima, Peru.

1031. Turner, Estelle Beasley. "The Great Call." *Pittsburgh Courier* (July 7, 1945). Poem dedicated to Lt. Othel Dickson, of the 332nd Fighter Group, who died over Italy in June 1944, and to the 87 fliers killed in action in the Mediteranean theatre of war. Photograph of Dickson.

1032. Twombly, Mark R. "Pilots: William Campbell." *Pilot (Aircraft Owners & Pilots Association, AOPA)* (October 1992): 168. Campbell has taught instrument flying to 2,500 pilots, and now operates his school, Air Experts, Inc. at Islip, New York. Some biographical information as well as information about instrument flying.

1033. "U. S. Administrator for Aeronautics." *Ebony* (December 1985): 7. Robert F. Smith Is U.S. administrator for aeronautics, a part of the U.S. Mission in Berlin.

1034. "Up, Up and Away." *Encore* 5 (February 16, 1976): 42-43. Survey of different jobs available in the airline industry: flight attendants and crew, mechanics, clerical, sales, etc.

1035. "Up, Up, and Away: Black Aeronauts Discover Thrills of Hot-Air Ballooning." *Ebony* (July 1977): 88-90, 92, 94, 96. Bill Costen, an insurance underwriter in Hartford,Ct, and Paul Roberson, a photographer in Atlanta, Georgia are the only known black balloonists.

1036. "U.S. Air Force Comptroller." *Ebony* (April 1981): 7. Brig. Gen. David M. Hall is deputy chief of staff and comptroller at Air Force Logistics Command at Wright-Patterson AFB in Ohio. He has been in the Air Force 29 years.

1037. "USAF Cadets Awarded Rhodes Scholarships." *Jet* 80:11 (July 1, 1991): 29. Micul Thompson Jr. and Christopher Howard, cadets at the U.S. Air Force Academy, have won Rhodes Scholarships for two years of study at Oxford. These scholarships were awarded to only 32 Americans. Both cadets plan to make their careers in the Air Force.

1038. Volz, Joseph. "Top Black AF General Has His Wings Clipped." *Daily News* (May 15, 1982). Maj. Gen. Titus Hall, the highest ranking black in the Air Force, has been forced into early retirement because of allegations that he showed favoritism toward blacks in his command, Lowry AFB, Colorado.

1039. "VW Tool Design Chief." *Ebony* (September 1972): 7. Gerard Georges, born in Haiti, is a designer in a Volkswagen plant in Wolfsburg, Germany. He invented and flies a unique one-man turbine helicopter.

1040. "Wanted: Black Air Traffic Controllers." *Ebony* (April 1970): 54-56, 58, 60. The Federal Aviation Administration is increasing recruiting among blacks because of a dangerous manpower shortage. Mentioned, among others, are: Eugene Stewart Jr., Lloyd H. Johnson Jr., Rodney L. Butler, and Richard Huff.

1041. "What Was Bill Thinking?" *Congressional Record* (May 27, 1993). Mr. Inhofe addressed the House for one minute on the subject of the new member of the National Transportation Safety Board. The member who was replaced is Chris Hart [Christopher A. Hart], "the most qualified member of the NTSB...and an African American." Hart is an instrument-rated pilot with degrees from Princeton and Harvard Law School. His replacement is a real estate developer and a lawyer, Jim Hall. Hall worked for Albert Gore and managed Clinton's Tennessee campaign.

1042. "Where Are They Now ?" *Black Stars* 7:8 (March 1978): 50. Lloyd Haynes was unable to get work for two years after his television program, *Room 222*, was cancelled. He became the West Coast representative for Air Center, Inc., a company which maintains corporate jets; directed Education Through Aviation, a school program to motivate under achievers; and continued to serve as Lt. Commander in the Air Force Reserves.

1043. "Whirlybird Whiz of the Coast Guard." *Ebony* (May 1965): 26-28, 30, 33. The only Negro pilot in the Coast Guard, Lt. Robert C. Wilks is a rescue flight officer at the Brooklyn station.

1044. White, Hugh J. "Mr. Death." *Ebony* [Letter to the Editor]. Capt. White worked with John L. Whitehead and writes to comment on the article in the January 1951 issue: The U.S. Air Force and the nation as a whole might well be proud of the great "John L."

1045. *Who's Who in Colored America: An Illustrated Biographical Dictionary of Notable Living Persons of African Descent in the United States.* Yonkers-on-Hudson, New York: Christian E. Burckel & Associates, 1950. [Seventh edition]. A. Porter Davis, b. November 13, 1890,

physician, Kansas City, KS. Davis received his license in 1928, the
Dwight H. Green Trophy in 1939 from the National Airmen's Association, p. 137. He is listed in earlier editions. Elliott Henry Gray, b. January 28, 1920, university professor, Nashville, TN. He was supervisor of
maintenance at Tuskegee airport, 1940-1943, a fighter pilot from
1943-1946, a commercial pilot and parachutist, p.223. Harold Carl
Hayes, b. November 25, 1916, Air Force meteorologist, pilot, instructor,
pp.250-251. Eugene R. Henderson, b. June 16, 1917, housing manager,
bomber pilot 1943-45, civilian commercial pilot, p. S-13 (Supplement).
Robert L. Maxwell, b. April 5, 1922, engineer, pilot in the Army Air
Corps 1944-1946, p. 612.

1046. "World Champ of the Mini-Plane." *Ebony* (May 1968): 64, 66, 68, 70.
Herb Stockton is a champion in international competition in motorized
model plane races.

1047. "World Record Flight." *Ebony* (August 1963): 85-86. Capt. Luther Joseph Brown and his co-pilot broke the altitude and gross weight records
for the HU-16 Albatross, previously held by the Russians. The new record of 19,500 ft. eclipsed the old by 2,337 ft. Brown began as an aircraft
mechanic after enlisting in the Air Force in 1948.

1048. "World Tour." *Ebony* (June 1950): 46-49. Charles J. Dorkins, a former
B-25 pilot with the 477th Bomber Group, is now a photographer. He was
the official photographer with a Youth Argosy tour around the world.

1049. Writers' Program, Work Projects Administration, Illinois. *Who's Who in
Aviation 1942-43: A Directory of Living Men and Women Who Have
Contributed to the Growth of Aviation in the United States.* Chicago:
Ziff-Davis Publishing Company, 1943. Entries on Charles Alfred Ander-
son, p.11; Willa Beatrice Brown, p.61; Cornelius R. Coffey, p.87; and
A. Porter Davis, p.104.

1050. Wynn, Commodore. *Negro Who's Who in California.* [Los Angeles]:
[Negro Who's Who Publishing Co.], 1948. Charles Williams, an aerial
photographer, photographed parachute jumps by Skippy Smith, owner of
the Pacific Coast Parachute Company, p.64; Claude C. Davis, an ardent
flyer in private life, flies at Hamilton Field in Marin County, was a
bomber pilot in the 474th Bomb Group, p.71; Maceo B. Sheffield, photographer, stuntman, actor, and policeman, was the first Negro aviator on

the West Coast. He trained at the Roger School of Aeronautics in 1927, and received his license in 1929, p.80.

1051. "Yesterday in Negro History." *Jet* (June 9, 1960): 9. Lawrence C. Chambers became the second Negro to graduate from the U.S. Naval Academy on June 6, 1952.

Eugene J. Bullard, author's collection.

Bessie Coleman, courtesy of the Security Pacific Collection/Los Angeles Public Library.

J. Herman Banning, courtesy of the Security Pacific Collection/Los Angeles Public Library.

Hubert F. Julian, author's collection.

SPORTING huge wings of spun gold and the emblem of the (ex) Conquering Lion of Judah, Colonel John C. Robinson. "The Brown Condor," late of the Ethiopian air corps, returns to this country on the liner Europa.—AP Wirephoto from New York.

Newsclipping of John C. Robinson from the Omaha, NE *World Herald* dated May 20, 1936. (Chicago Historical Society, Claude A. Barnett collection, Box 171-5).

Willa B. Brown in padded flight suit, courtesy of the National Air and Space Museum, Smithsonian Institution, photo no. 90-13119. © Smithsonian Institution.

Cornelius R. Coffey, courtesy of Smithsonian Institution, photo no. 91-6606. © Smithsonian Institution.

Chauncey E. Spencer, Dale L. White, Ben Hall, and Cornelius R. Coffey prepare to resume flight to Washington, D.C. in the repaired *Lincoln-Paige*, May 11, 1939, author's collection.

Eight Tuskegee Airmen, U.S. Air Force Pre-1954 Photo Collection (USAF No. 33440 AC), courtesy of the National Air and Space Museum, Smithsonian Institution. © Smithsonian Institution.

Benjamin O. Davis, Jr., courtesy of the National Air and Space Museum (photo no. 90-379), Smithsonian Institution. © Smithsonian Institution.

Daniel James, Jr. with Black Panther helmet, U.S. Air Force (USAF photo no. 102092 USAF), courtesy of the National Air and Space Museum, Smithsonian Institution. © Smithsonian Institution.

Robert H. Lawrence, Jr., courtesy of the National Air and Space Museum (photo no. 86-3662), Smithsonian Institution. © Smithsonian Institution.

Ronald E. McNair, National Aeronautics and Space Administration (NASA photo no. 78-H-642), courtesy of the National Air and Space Museum, Smithsonian Institution. © Smithsonian Institution.

Charles F. Bolden, Jr.

Frederick D. Gregory

Guion S. Bluford, Jr.

Mae C. Jemison

Photo courtesy of the National Aeronautics and Space Administration.

Janet Waterford Bragg with relatives, courtesy of the National Air and Space Museum (photo no. 91-6610), Smithsonian Institution. © Smithsonian Institution.

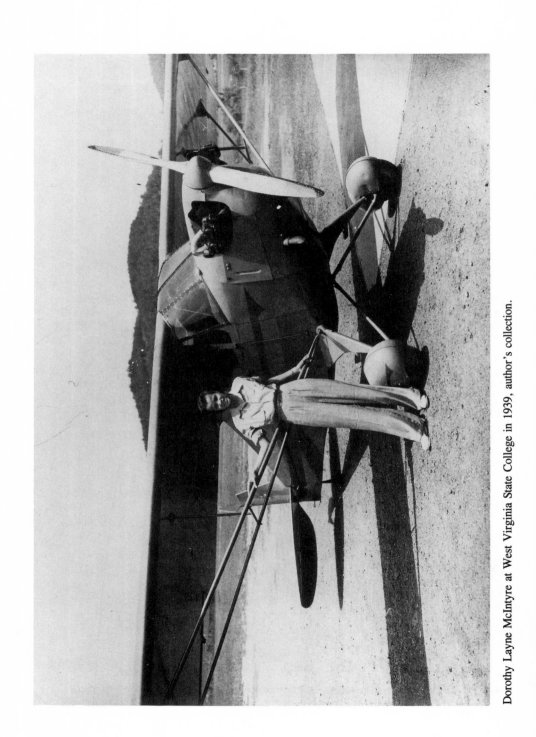

Dorothy Layne McIntyre at West Virginia State College in 1939, author's collection.

Astronauts and
Space Scientists

Edward J. Dwight

1052. Anderson, Susan Heller. "Chronicle." *New York Times* (September 22, 1990): 27. Edward Dwight is to be the sculptor for a memorial to the black soldiers of the American Revolution, to be erected on a two-acre site on the Mall in Washington, D.C. Dwight, who in 1962 was named as the first black astronaut, has retired from the Air Force and is now a full-time sculptor.

1053. Cohen, Jean Lawlor. "Ed Dwight the Realistic Dreamer." *American Visions* 7:2 (April/May 1992): 26-31. Dwight was to have been the first black astronaut. The emphasis is on Edward Dwight's sculptures in bronze. There are lists of galleries and museums which hold his work.

1054. Minerbrook, Scott. "No Room in Space for Earlier Black." *Newsday* (September 4, 1983). Edward Dwight's account of the discrimination he faced as the the first black selected for astronaut training in 1962. Some experiences of Robert H. Lawrence, selected the following year, are included. Dwight resigned in 1966 and Lawrence died in an accident in 1967. The next astronaut was Guion S. Bluford Jr. in 1978.

1055. Sanders, Charles L. "The Troubles of 'Astronaut' Edward Dwight: Official Excuses Cloud Routine Assignment of Nation's Only Negro Trained for Role in Space." *Ebony* (June 1965): 29-32, 34-36. Two years ago Edward Dwight was headlined internationally as the first Negro astronaut. Today he has apparently been dropped from consideration for space flight. Answers to questions are evasive and rumors abound. This article attempts to sort them out and provides biographical information. It concludes the nation deserves a full accounting of what really happened in Ed Dwight's case.

1056. Seymour, Gene. "The Black Pilot Who Almost Made it into Space." *S.F. Sunday Examiner & Chronicle* (August 28, 1983): A17. An interview with Edward Dwight, in which he describes his treatment as an astronaut trainee starting in 1962, and ending with his resignation from the Air Force in 1966.

1057. "Symbol of Excellence." *Jet* 65:12 (November 28, 1983): 47. Ed Dwight, the astronaut who left the space program, is shown with one of his sculptures. It will be presented to the winner of the contest, "Black Athlete of the Year," sponsored by Gordon's Gin early next year.

1058. White, Frank III. "The Sculptor who Would Have Gone into Space." *Ebony* (February 1984): 54, 56, 58. Twenty-one years ago, Capt. Edward Dwight Jr. reportedly had Pres. Kennedy's personal backing to become the first black astronaut. With Kennedy's death, Dwight's space hopes fizzled. He is now a sculptor in Denver. Biographical information and discussion of racism.

1059. Wolfe, Tom. *The Right Stuff.* New York: Farrar, Straus and Giroux, 1979. [This book has no index]. Wolfe writes of Edward Dwight on pp.419-420.

1060. Yeager, Chuck, and Leo Janos. *Yeager: An Autobiography.* Toronto: Bantam Books, 1985. Discusses the selection of Edward Dwight as the first black astronaut candidate, pp.269-272.

Robert H. Lawrence Jr.

1061. Brown, Charles E., and Reginald McCafferty. "Polar Orbiting Spacemen Will Observe Every Point on Earth." *Jet* (July 20, 1967): 14-19. Biographical information on Robert H. Lawrence, the first Negro astronaut. There is also discussion of Edward Dwight and the current racial situation in the U.S.

1062. "First Negro Astronaut Killed in Crash Landing." *Jet* (December 21, 1967): 6. Less than five months after he became the first Negro astronaut to begin training for the 30-day long Manned Orbiting Laboratory (MOL) space flight, 31-yr-old Robert Henry Lawrence was killed while making a landing at Edwards AFB, California.

1063. Llorens, David. "A Farewell to an Astronaut." *Ebony* (February 1968): 90-94. Description of the last rites for Major Robert H. Lawrence Jr. in Chicago. Major Lawrence was the first black astronaut; he died in an accident in California in December 1967. Biographical information.

1064. "Our First Negro Astronaut." *Sepia* (September 1967): 76-79. Biographical information about Major Robert H. Lawrence, the first Negro to become an astronaut. Information is also included about Edward J. Dwight, who failed to become an astronaut.

1065. "Pres. Johnson Wires Widow, Chicago Passes Resolution." *Jet* (December 28, 1967): 10. A description of the funeral services for Robert H. Lawrence, and of events in Chicago relating to the memorial services.

Ronald E. McNair

1066. Buchanan, Jay. "Is There a Future for Blacks in Space?" *Black Collegian* (December 1980/January 1981): 131, 134-138. Biographical information on Ronald E. McNair, and a long interview with him.

1067. Cheers, D. Michael. "'Touching the Face of God'." *Ebony* (May 1986): 82-84, 88, 90, 92, 94. Biographical article on the life and death of Ronald E. McNair, the astronaut who was killed in January in the Challenger explosion. A poem by John G. Magee Jr. is included; it was read by President Reagan at the funeral rites.

1068. "Cheryl McNair: Surviving the Shuttle Disaster." *Ebony* (May 1987): 162, 166. Ron McNair's widow has been sustained by her faith and the steady support of her family, friends, and strangers. She works in many programs to enhance the futurist thinking of her husband.

1069. Clendinen, Dudley. "Two Paths to the Stars: Turnings and Triumphs." *New York Times* (February 9, 1986): 1, 28. Feature articles on Ronald E. McNair and Judith Resnick begin a three-part series on the crew of the Challenger.

1070. Haskins, Jim. *One More River to Cross: The Stories of Twelve Black Americans.* New York: Scholastic, 1992. Chapter 12, pp.182-200, gives biographical information on Ronald E. McNair.

1071. Knox, Margaret L. "Ron McNair was Always a Dreamer." *Atlanta Journal and Constitution* (February 1, 1986): A1+.

1072. McConnell, Malcolm. *Challenger: A Major Malfunction*. Garden City, NY: Doubleday & Co., 1987. Ronald E. McNair and family members are briefly mentioned on a dozen scattered pages.

1073. Naden, Corinne. *Ronald McNair*. New York: Chelsea House Publishers, 1991. A biography for young adults.

Charles E. Bolden Jr.

1074. "Charles Bolden Jr.: He Gives Stargazing a Different Meaning." *EM (Ebony Man)* 5:10 (August 1990): 20, 22-23. In August of 1981 Bolden became the fourth black astronaut. Bolden gives his impressions of being in space, and tells of the value of space exploration. Some biographical information.

1075. "Congressman Set to Go Up in Space Shuttle Today." *New York Times* (December 19, 1985): n.p. Rep. Bill Nelson, Florida Democrat, who heads House subcommittee that oversees the budget of NASA will be on board the Columbia. Lieut. Col. Charles F. Bolden, Jr. of the Marine Corps is the pilot.

1076. "The Crew of the Atlantis: 7 in the 46th Shuttle Flight." *New York Times* (March 25, 1992): A 20. Brief biographical information on Charles F. Bolden Jr., Mission Commander.

1077. Harris, Greg. "Marine Col. Bolden Pilots Hubble Telescope Shuttle." *New York Amsterdam News* (April 14, 1990): 4, 53. Bolden is scheduled to pilot the "Discovery" space shuttle mission that will launch the Hubble Space Telescope. Biographical information.

1078. Johnson, Thomas L., and Phillip C. Dunn. *A True Likeness: The Black South of Richard Samuel Roberts 1920-1936*. Columbia, SC: Bruccoli Clark, 1986. [I am indebted to Wilhelmina Wynn, the daughter of the photographer, for this information]. On pp. 70-71 there is a photograph of Martha P. Grier and her daughters. Malinda, on the right, is the grandmother of Charles F. Bolden. Thomas S. Martin, the maternal uncle of Bolden, is shown on p. 71.

1079. "Maj. Bolden Joins NASA Space Shuttle Project." *Eagle & Swan* 3:4 (September 1980): 42. A frank interview with Charles F. Bolden. He shows his elation at being selected as an astronaut on May 29. He describes the events and tests that led to his selection, including the fact that he applied for Test Pilot School five times before he was accepted.

1080. "NASA Extends Shuttle's Flight by One Day." *New York Times* (March 30, 1992): A8. A day was added to the mission of the space shuttle Atlantis so that its crew could conduct more research on the atmosphere. Col Charles F. Bolden Jr. is the mission commander.

1081. Wilford, John Noble. "Shuttle Lifts Off to Study Atmosphere." *New York Times* (March 25, 1992): A 20. The space shuttle Atlantis thundered into orbit today (Mar. 24), carrying an array of scientific instruments to conduct atmospheric studies that could influence major policy decisions for protecting the global environment. Commanding the crew is Charles F. Bolden Jr., making his third trip into space.

1082. Young, Gwen. "Astronaut Tells Blacks Aim for Sky." *Newsday* (February 18, 1984): 11. Charles F. Bolden was the featured speaker at a luncheon to celebrate Black History Month at the Grumman plant. The luncheon, jointly sponsored by the Navy, is for workers at Grumman. Celebrations in the last two years featured black aviators and Tuskegee Airmen. Bolden told the group to ask for what you want, and never place limitations on yourself.

Guion S. Bluford Jr.

1083. "Astronaut Guion Bluford Jr. Resigns From NASA to Join Engineering and Computer Firm." *Jet* 84:10 (July 5, 1993): 32. Bluford will join NYMA in Greenbelt, Maryland, as vice president and general manager of the Engineering Services Division.

1084. "Astronauts' stuff right for success, Bluford says." *Chicago Sun Times* (June 25, 1985): n.p. In Chicago to receive an honorary doctorate from Chicago State University, Bluford comments on colleagues, is learning German for second flight in October, which will have German and Dutch specialists aboard.

1085. Benedict, Howard. "Shuttle Breaks the Racial Barrier." *Chicago Tribune* (August 29, 1983): n.p. On the occasion of Guion S. Bluford's flight, a capsule history of blacks in aviation.

1086. "Bluford, Guion S." *Current Biography* 45:9 (September 1984): 3-6. Cover story.

1087. Broad, William J. "First U.S. Black in Space: Guion Stewart Bluford, Jr." *New York Times* (August 31, 1983): B6. Man in the News article provides scientific, as well as biographical information.

1088. Broad, William J. "Shuttle is Off at Last, on 8-Day Military Mission Without Secrecy." *New York Times* (April 29, 1991): B6. Guion S. Bluford Jr. is a mission specialist on this flight. There is a brief profile of him.

1089. Dunlap, David. "Astronauts are Honored at City Hall." *New York Times* (October 25, 1983): [n.p.]. Welcome for the five astronauts from the eighth space shuttle flight. Guion S.Bluford, the first black American to fly into space, was for many the hero of the day. Music was provided by Lionel Hampton's band and the Emerald Society bagpipers of the Police Department.

1090. "50 Pathfinders." *Ebony* 48:1 (November 1992): 146, 150. Brief notes on Guion S. Bluford Jr., Benjamin O. Davis Jr.

1091. "First Black American to Probe Space Keeps a Low-Orbit Profile." *Washington Post* (August 21, 1983): A8-9. An in-depth profile of Guion S. Bluford, with much information provided by his younger brother, Kenneth. Scientific information about the flight on August 30th is included.

1092. Harris, Lorenzo D. "The 'Blue' in Bluford." *Airman* (February 1984): 8-11, 13-14. Biographical and scientific information, with many comments by Bluford.

1093. Haskins, James, and Kathleen Benson. *Space Challenger: The Story of Guion Bluford*. Minneapolis: Carolrhoda Books, Inc., 1984. An authorized biography for seven to ten year olds, but because of the subject matter (space science and America's first black astronaut) the book would be suitable for older children as well.

1094. Hoffman, Werner. "Black Astronaut Urges Kids to Follow Suit." *New York Tribune* (October 26, 1983): n.p. Guion S. Bluford appeared before over 500 sixth graders and adults at Frederick Douglass Intermediate School in Harlem.

1095. "JPC Babies." *Ebony* 48:1 (November 1992): 86. [Johnson Publishing Company's (JPC) 50th anniversary]. Guion S. Bluford is one of those born in 1942, who was asked to comment on the influence of *Ebony* and *Jet* in his life.

1096. Kalette, Denise. "Bluford seen as a milestone, role model." *USA TODAY* (August 29, 1983): 1A-2A. Biographical information on Guion S. Bluford. Statistics: Blacks at Johnson Space Center - 6.4% of 3,300; at NASA - 7% of 22,000. Louis Purnell, former fighter pilot and now curator at the National Air and Space Museum, comments on racism then and now. Gen. B.O. Davis, Jr. recalls some of his experiences and states "In the flying business, there is no question we have come a long way — from a zero start."

1097. Leavy, Walter. "A Historic Step into Outer Space." *Ebony* (November 1983): 162-164, 166, 168, 170. Guion S. Bluford Jr., America's first black astronaut breaks the aerospace color barrier 22 years after the United States' first orbital flight. Biographical and technical information. Other astronauts and NASA personnel mentioned.

1098. McKee, Clarence V. "Guy Bluford, King's Dream, and Last Month's March." *Washington Times* (September 20, 1983). Discusses the irony of the Rainbow Coalition's condemnation of military spending, which made possible the space launch by Bluford, America's first black astronaut.

1099. Minerbrook, Scott. "Devotion to a Dream in Flight." *Newsday* (August 29, 1983): Part II, 4-5. Biographical article includes interviews with teachers, relatives, friends and colleagues of Guion S. Bluford.

1100. Prochnau, Bill. "Guy Bluford: NASA's Reluctant Hero." *Washington Post* A1+. [Date unavailable, but before August 30, 1983]. Biographical information, but little comes from Bluford himself. He prefers to protect his privacy, "a trait ingrained in him by an extraordinary and insular family that fits no stereotype, black or white."

1101. *Washington Post* (December 7, 1983): n.p. Guion S. Bluford received an award from the NAACP on December 4, 1983 at the Hollywood Palladium.

1102. *Washington Times* (November 18, 1983): n.p. Guion S. Bluford receives Ebony's Trailblazer Award for being the first black astronaut to fly into space.

Frederick D. Gregory

1103. "Astronaut Says Soul No Excuse for Lousy Grades." *Jet* (June 21, 1979): 19. In a talk to school children in Baltimore, Frederick D. Gregory told them that watching too much television is depriving them of education. "We are not behind because of our genes, but because of our agenda. We do best what we do most." He also stated that excellence is achieved with effort, not with soul.

1104. Baillou, Charles. "Boys and Girls High Warmly Welcomes Black Astronaut." *New York Amsterdam News* (May 11, 1991): 6, 37. Fredrick D. Gregory addressed eleventh-graders at their Career Day assembly program. He told them that without the Tuskegee Airmen he would not have become an astronaut, and that without him, his son would not now be in the Air Force. He encouraged the students to consider a flying career.

1105. "Black Leads Spaceship." *New York Amsterdam News* (December 10, 1988): 13. Frederick D. Gregory will command Discovery on its August 10, 1989 flight. This will make him the first black to commmand a shuttle mission.

1106. Broad, William J. "Shuttle Atlantis is Launched With Military Satellite." *New York Times* (November 25, 1991): A7. Scientific information, and sketches of crew members and the mission commander, Col. Frederick D. Gregory.

1107. "Careers Behind the Launchpad." *Black Enterprise* (February 1983): 59-60, 64. [Guion S. Bluford is on the cover]. Description of the black professionals behind the scenes in space exploration. Of NASA's 22,000 employees, more than seven percent are black. Some of these are: Isaac T. Gillam, Curtis Graves, Robert Shurney, Christine V. Mann Darden, Willy Wright, and Patricia S. Cowings. Interview with Guion S. Bluford, who on July 4, 1983, will become America's first black astronaut to fly into space. Information on other black astronauts: McNair, Gregory, and Bolden. Mention is made of Arnaldo Tamayo Mendez, a black Cuban, who was the first black astronaut in the world. He went into space three years ago on the Soviet Soyez 38.

1108. "Gregory Remembered." *Washington Post* (April 30, 1986). The Fort Davis regional branch library is to be renamed to honor Francis Anderson Gregory. Gregory, who died in 1977, was chairman of the library board, and assistant superintendent in the D.C. schools. His son is Col. Frederick Gregory, an astronaut.

1109. Gregory, Frederick. "D.C. Astronaut Locks onto a View of Unity from Space." *Washington Times* (January 12, 1990). Gregory describes the beauty of the earth from space, and how each astronaut could see his own home town. Gradually each member of the space team began to see the world as his home, and to focus on their common desire to explore the unknown: space.

1110. Hunt, Rufus A. "Profile of an Astronaut Candidate." *Chicago Defender* (March 22, 1982): 6. Biographical information on Frederick D. Gregory. When the space shuttle Columbia is launched, Gregory will be at Edwards AFB as Director of Contingency Operations.

1111. Marriot, Michel. "Astonaut's Dream Comes True." *Washington Post* (April 28, 1985): A1, 18. Black D.C. youth defied odds to become shuttle pilot. Lengthy biographical article about Frederick Drew Gregory.

1112. Marriott, Michel. "District Celebrates Local Astronaut's Homecoming." *Washington Post* (June 4, 1985): C1, 5. Report of a day-long celebration in honor of Frederick Drew Gregory. Strangers, politicians, relatives, and friends honored him. He gave the Disrict a city flag he had carried into space.

1113. Milloy, Courtland. "An Inspiring Alumnus." *Washington Post* (June 6, 1985). Col. Frederick D. Gregory returns to Anacostia High School, his alma mater.

1114. Narine, Dalton. "First Black Space Commander." *Ebony* (May 1990): 78, 80, 82. Col. Frederick Drew Gregory made history as the first black to command a space ship, but hardly anyone knew as the Discovery was a top secret mission. Biographical information.

1115. Runco, Mario Jr. "An Alumnus in Orbit." *Alumnus (City College of New York)* 87:2 (Spring 1992): 11-13. In November 1991 Mario Runco Jr. '74 became the first CCNY graduate to be launched into space as one of six crew members aboard the space shuttle Atlantis. Frederick Gregory was the mission commander; there are photographs of him on the cover and on p.11.

Mae C. Jemison

1116. Abdullah, Khalil, and Grady Wells. "A Galaxy of Expectations." *Sisters* 2:4 (Spring 1989): 31-33. [Cover story]. Biographical information on astronaut Mae Carol Jemison.

1117. "Another Giant Leap..." *Emerge* 4:3 (December 1992): 18. Brief note about the space flight of Dr. Mae C. Jemison on September 11 [*sic*]. Accompanying the article is a handsome, not often seen, photograph of the astronaut.

1118. "Astronauts Study Motion Sickness on Second Day of Shuttle Mission." *New York Times* (September 14, 1992): 12. Dr. Mae C. Jemison is the only one among Endeavor's seven-member crew who is trained in biofeedback, and she used it to control her pulse and sweating. There is also a brief biographical sketch about her.

1119. "'Be Your Own Role Model': 1st Black Woman Astronaut." *Jet* (August 17, 1987): 22. "If I am a role model, I hope it will be for those who want to do something different." As a child Mae Jemison did not look to models, but committed herself to her studies and her own career objectives.

1120. Blount, Carolyne S. "Our Place Among the Stars." *about...time* (March 1993): 22-23, 25. [Cover story]. This interview with Mae C. Jemison stresses her deeply-felt view that everyone should inform themselves about scientific and mathematical concepts because of their impact on our rapidly changing world. This is especially true for the people who have been left out, i.e., developing nations and African Americans. Jemison describes the experiments she helped design and conduct on the Space Shuttle Endeavor in September 1992. She took into space more than a dozen items, and their significance is explained. There is an editor's note that at press time Dr. Jemison announced that she would leave NASA to follow her interests in "teaching, mentoring, health care issues and increasing participation in science and technology for those who have been traditionally left out."

1121. Brozan, Nadine. "Chronicle." *New York Times* (September 16, 1992): B4. Dr. Mae C. Jemison, the first black woman astronaut, is also an aficionado of modern dance. She asked Judith Jamison of the Alvin Ailey American Dance Theater if she could take a costume of hers into space. As it was unavailable, Jamison sent a signed poster, which Dr. Jemison took into space with her. In her request, Dr. Jemison wrote, " Many people do not see a connection between science and dance, but I consider them both to be expressions of the boundless creativity that people have to share with one another."

1122. "Dr. Mae Jemison Quits NASA; Has New Mission." *Jet* (March 29, 1993): 6. Mae C. Jemison, at NASA since 1987, has left to teach a course at Dartmouth College. She will also develop a project to improve health care in West Africa. There are four other black astronauts, all men, out of 88.

1123. "For a Black Woman, Space Isn't the Final Frontier." *New York Times* (March 3, 1993): B13. Dr. Mae C. Jemison is teaching a course on space-age technology and developing countries this term at the Thayer School of Engineering at Dartmouth College.

1124. Green, Constance M. "To Boldly Go..." *Ms.* 3:1 (July/August 1992): 78-79. Mae Jemison prepares to become the first black woman in space, aboard the STS-47 Spacelab J for seven days in August. She will be the science mission specialist, studying the effects of space on the human organism, i.e., the rapid loss of calcium. Biographical information, and Jemison's opinions on feminism and abortion rights.

1125. Haynes, Karima A. "Mae Jemison: Coming In From Outer Space." *Ebony* (December 1992): 118, 120, 124. Dr. Jemison describes her excitement at the launching of the Endeavor space shuttle last September, as it was what she had wanted to do for a long time. The article quotes her on a number of subjects and shows her in a personal light. Chicago, where Jemison was raised, gave her a six-day tribute.

1126. Kimbro, Dennis, and Napoleon Hill. *Think and Grow Rich: A Black Choice*. New York: Fawcett Columbine, 1991. Biographical information on Mae C. Jemison on pp.58-60, which stresses the role imagination plays in success.

1127. Leary, Warren E. "A Determined Breaker of Boundaries: Mae Carol Jemison." *New York Times* (September 13, 1992): 42. Woman in the News feature gives biographical information. Jemison downplays her role as model for little black girls. Rather, the people who should know are "older white males who sometimes make decisions on the careers of those little black girls." About the future of space exploration she says, "We need to get every group of people [small, less-industrialized countries] involved because it is something that eventually we in the world community are going to have to share."

1128. Leary, Warren E. "U.S.-Japan Mission is a Shuttle First." *New York Times* (September 13, 1992): 42. [Mae C. Jemison is pictured on p. 1]. The 50th flight in the space program, on the shuttle Endeavor, is marked by innovations. These include cooperation with another country, the first married couple in space, and the first black woman astronaut, Dr. Mae C. Jemison. She will conduct fertilization studies on South African clawed frogs, and use biofeedback techniques to test their ability to reduce space motion sickness.

1129. "Mae Jemison to Appear on TV's 'Star Trek'." *Jet* (May 3, 1993): 34. Mae C. Jemison will make a guest appearance on the television program during the week of May 31. She will play a transporter operator. Jemison says her inspiration to become an astronaut was Lt. Uhura, as played by Nichelle Nichols on the original program.

1130. Marshall, Marilyn. "Child of the '60s Set to Become the First Black Woman in Space." *Ebony* (August 1989): 50, 52, 54-55. Biographical information on Mae Carol Jemison, who is both a doctor and an engineer, and who will serve as mission specialist.

1131. Marshall, Marilyn. "Close-Up: A New Star in the Galaxy." *Ebony* (December 1992): 122. A profile of Dr. Mae C. Jemison in her new role as "star." She speaks to many groups, urging them to become involved in space exploration now by mastering science and mathematics. She wants people to know she is "not the first or the only African-American woman who had the skills and the talent to become an astronaut."

1132. Scott, Gilbert L. "Space Exploration." *Class* (February 1993): 38, 40. [Cover Story]. Information on Mae C. Jemison.

1133. "She's Out of this World." *New York Amsterdam News* (May 25, 1990): 1. Mae C. Jemison was Grand Marshall of the 369th Annual Martin Luther King Jr. Day Parade.

1134. "Space is Her Destination." *Ebony* (October 1987): 93-95, 98. Mae C. Jemison, low-key physician is propelled to fame as NASA's first black woman astronaut candidate. Biographical information.

1135. "Trailblazers." *Jet* (November 30, 1992): 44. Photograph of Mae Jemison, congratulated by Nichelle Nichols, for winning the Trailblazer Award at the American Black Achievement Award ceremony in Hollywood.

1136. Whigham, Marjorie. "The Right Stuff." *Essence* (December 1987): 15. Dr. Mae Carol Jemison has been accepted into NASA's astronaut program. Her special interest is in the health of black people, and of black women in particular. Biographical information.

1137. "The Year of the Black Woman." *Ebony* (October 1992): 112, 118. [Cover]. Mae C. Jemison is one of the black women of the year. There is not much information, but there is a new photograph.

NASA

1138. "Aerodynamics Staff Chief." *Ebony* (June 1969): 6. Linwood C. Wright is chief in the preliminary design department of AiResearch Mfg. Co. in Los Angeles. An aeronautical engineer and a pilot, he plans designs for NASA's projects.

1139. "Ants in Space." *Ebony* (September 1983): 83-84, 86, 88. Report of NASA's efforts to increase students' awareness of the opportunites in space science. Three hundred students from Camden, New Jersey participated in experiments, field trips, and meeting astronauts.

1140. "Astronauts Conduct Life Science Studies on 2nd Day of Flight." *New York Times* (April 27, 1993). This flight, on the space shuttle Columbia, was financed and directed by Germany. Dr. Bernard A. Harris Jr., a civilian medical doctor and mission specialist, performed experiments in a wall-mounted biology laboratory, with his German counterpart. [Harris was selected as an astronaut candidate in 1990].

1141. Atkinson, John, and Jay M. Shafritz. *The Real Stuff: A History of NASA's Astronaut Recruitment Program.* New York: Praeger, 1985. [Foreword by Alan Shepard and Guion S. Bluford]. This book traces the thirty-year development (late 1950s to the mid 1980s) from all-white male veteran test pilots to men and women, whites and minorities. Ch. 5, "The First Efforts of Women and Minorities to Become Astronauts," pp.87-109, includes the difficulties experienced by Edward Dwight, pp.100-105, and mentions Robert H. Lawrence, pp.36, 104-105.

1142. *Black Americans in Aerospace.* Washington, D.C.: Association for the Study of Afro-American Life and History, 1981. This nineteen-page pamphlet is part of the Association's 1982 Afro-American History Kit. There are photographs and brief biographical information about 35 black Americans working for NASA, arranged by location.

1143. Burns, Emmett C. "NASA and Blacks: Triumph in Tokenism." *Crisis* 89 (December 1982): 12-16. Article briefly covers these topics: 1) history of American space program, 2) relates NASA's own statistics to show limited progress, 3) reviews NASA's affirmative action programs, 4) role (or non-role) in critical analysis, 5) what individual blacks or civil rights organizations can do to redress problems.

1144. Burt, Yumeka. "Up and Away." *Class* (February 1993): 37. How one becomes an astronaut: description of the different categories and the address to obtain an application package.

1145. "50 Leaders of Tomorrow." *Ebony* 48:1 (November 1992): 220, 224. Brief notes on Luther Neal Jenkins, aerospace engineer at NASA Langley Research Center; and Chaka L. Wade, a military intelligence officer at Ft. Huachuca, Arizona and an aeronautical engineer.

1146. "The Future-Makers." *Ebony* (August 1985): 62-63. Astronauts Bluford, Bolden, Gregory and McNair are profiled. Also noted is William Harwell, who designs the hardware astronauts use in space.

1147. "Gillam Elected Fellow to American Astronautical Society." *Eagle & Swan* 2:2 (May 1979): 9. Isaac T. Gillam IV, Director of NASA's Dryden Flight Research Center, was elected to the American Astronautical Society. Gillam was honored for his contributions to aeronautics.

1148. Graves, Curtis M., and Ivan Van Sertima. "Space Science: The African-American Contribution." *Journal of African Civilizations* 5 (April/November 1983): 238-257. [Also published as *Blacks in Science*, edited by Ivan Van Sertima, New Brunswick, NJ: Transaction, 1983]. Information about prominent men and women employed by NASA. They are Frederick D. Gregory, Isaac Gillam IV, Robert E. Shurney, Patricia Cowings, and Christine Darden. Curtis M. Graves is also employed by NASA.

1149. Johnson, Terry E. "First Visit With New Astronauts." *Jet* (March 9, 1978): 22-26. Interviews with Bluford, Gregory and McNair. Other black employees of NASA are Curtis Graves, Hattie Terry and Joseph Atkinson.

1150. Jones, Wilkins O. "Careers in Aerospace: Flying High, Flying Low?" *Black Collegian* 21:1 (September/October 1990): 88, 173-174, 176. Jones says the aerospace industry is an excellent source of career opportunities for African-American engineers and scientists. The companies making recruitment efforts are Boeing and Jet Propulsion Laboratory. The personnel mentioned are: Gregory Frazier, an engineer for NASA; Cecil McQuilken at American Airlines; Betty S. Goldsberry, Lockheed; John Beavers, Trans World Airlines; Janice Buckner and Carrington Stewart of NASA.

1151. Morris, Steven. "How Blacks View Mankind's 'Giant Step'." *Ebony* (September 1970). Various viewpoints are voiced. Sixteen black men are named as behind-the-scenes participants, besides Carl Echols and Kenneth Lowry. Echols is the project engineer for the lunar lander vehicle. Lowry designed the lunar module's fuel loading controller.

1152. Murray, James B. *Black Visions '90: African Americans in Space Science*. New York: Mayor's Office of Minority Affairs, 1990. Catalogue of exhibition at the Tweed Gallery February 1-28, 1990. Murray, the curator, interviewed Guion S. Bluford and Patricia S. Cowings. Information and photographs are included on the astronauts and on many other historical and support figures.

1153. "NASA Auditor." *Ebony* (October 1976): 7. Carroll Samuel Little is an associate auditor at Langley Research Center in Hampton, Virginia.

1154. "NASA Computer Whiz." *Ebony* (March 1986): 62, 64, 66. Mathematician David R. Hedgley Jr. at Edwards AFB solved, in 1982, a decades-old computer problem. He devised a method to show 3-dimensional objects despite their complexity, and has won many awards for this. Biographical information.

1155. "NASA External Affairs Deputy." *Ebony* (December 1984): 7. Harrison Allen Jr. is deputy director of external affairs at NASA's station in Cleveland, Ohio. He was an aerospace research scientist and holds a patent on rocket motors.

1156. "NASA Space Flight Information Chief." *Ebony* (August 1965): 6. Peter L. Robinson Jr., as chief of visual information in the office of Manned Space Flight Headquarters in Washington, is responsible for all artwork and photography used in NASA presentations.

1157. "Obituary." *Alumnus (City College of New York)* 87:2 (Spring 1992): 22. Dudley George McConnell, director of NASA's Earth Science and Application Division died of a heart attack on October 28. He was to have assumed a new post in Space Nuclear Affairs, but died before he could begin.

1158. Odum, Karen. "The Race in Outer Space." *Black Enterprise* 12 (July 1982): 17. The selection of Guion S. Bluford to become the first American black in space raises doubts about the non-military benefits of NASA's programs, especially for black civilians. There are statistics on NASA's employment of blacks.

1159. Robinson, Rosetta. "Space is the Place." *Essence* 15:7 (November 1984): 38. The article profiles Anngienetta R. Johnson, at NASA 16 years, who is now a manager of a space-lab operations implementation. The article describes selected space-related jobs in an industry that employs more than a million people. Dr. Christine M. Darden, an engineer at NASA, says, "Persevere. The opportunities are there."

1160. Sawyer, Kathy. "Reviving Aeronautics: Space Agency Focuses on Global Contest." *Washington Post* (May 27, 1993): A-23. Wesley L. Harris, a former professor at the Massachusetts Institute of Technology, was appointed head of NASA's aeronautics office. Nasa is asking for 1.02 billion for aeronautics research, which has as one of its goals, the development of a supersonic jet liner that would be environmentally friendly. Harris was interviewed for the article.

1161. Seabon, Pamela. "Preparing for Liftoff." *about...time* (March 1993): 24. Profile of Henry Eckhardt Greene Jr., a Field Engineer III for twelve years at NASA in Houston. He is responsible for the upkeep of four different types of stimulators used to train astronauts for their space missions.

1162. Sehlstedt, Jr Albert. "Being the 1st Black off the Launchpad is Secondary for NASA's Guy Bluford." *The Sun* (August 10, 1983): A1+. [First of two articles]. Besides biographical information, there is also a description of the Johnson Space Center in Texas, and comments about its racial climate by Guion S. Bluford, Charles F. Bolden, Jr. and Frederick D. Gregory.

1163. "Space Center Opens its Doors to Student Aides from Ghetto." *Product Engineering* 38 (October 23, 1967): 137. NASA opened Goddard Space Flight Center to 25 Washington teenagers for a summer of challenging tasks. They were selected from teachers' recommendations, and the hope is that the experiment will spread to the business sector.

1164. "Space Trio: New Faces Among Shuttle Crew." *Ebony* (March 1979): 54, 56, 58, 60, 62. Biographical information on Guion S. Bluford, Frederick D. Gregory, and Ronald E. McNair.

1165. Spady, James G. "Blackspace." *Journal of African Civilizations* 5 (April/November 1983): 258-265. [Also published as *Blacks in Science Ancient and Modern*, edited by Ivan Van Sertima, New Brunswick, NJ: Transaction Books, 1983]. Information about Dr. George Carruthers, an astrophysicist at NASA, in the emerging discipline of the space sciences. Information is also included on Dr. Elmer Imes, an early black physicist.

1166. Still, Larry. "Many Negroes Helped in Glenn's Epic 'Team Effort'." *Jet* (March 8, 1962): 20-23. On his return from space Lt. Col. John Glenn stressed the team effort in Project Mercury. More than a dozen Negro experts worked on every phase from the planning to the completion of the successful flight. They are: Katherine Johnson, Ted Scopinsky, James Langston, Leonard Beale, Harold Thames, Joseph Swafford, Nathaniel Crump, Clinton Rayford, Tom Gentry, William Pynter, and Vance Marchbanks.

1167. Sye, Robert J. "Blacks in Space." *Sepia* 30:3 (March 1981): 39-41, 68-71. [Cover story]. Biographical information on astronauts Ronald McNair, Frederick Gregory and Guion Bluford. Charles Bolden is an astronaut candidate. Brenda Robinson is mentioned as a pilot with the credentials to become an astronaut.

1168. Tryman, Mfanya Donald. *A Study of the Minority College Programs at the NASA Johnson Space Center*. Houston, TX: NASA, Johnson Space Center, NASA/American Society for Engineering Education, 1987. [20 pages]. This report examines the Minority Graduate Researcher's Program and the Historically Black College and University Program, as they train and further the capabilities of minorities in space science. Topics covered include organization, management, differences between the two, and suggestions for improvement.

1169. "Weightless Flight Test Engineer." *Ebony* (February 1971): 7. Robert E. Shurney is a space flight test engineer at NASA's Marshall Space Flight Center at Huntsville, Alabama. He leads a 15-man team in experiments to simulate weightlessness.

1170. "Wind Tunnel Supervisor." *Ebony* (July 1986). Lonnie Reid is head of the Aerodynamic Section at NASA Lewis Research Center in Cleveland. He is working toward his Ph.D. in mechanical engineering at the University of Toledo.

Other Individuals and Events

1171. "Aeorospace Engineer." *Ebony* (August 1965): 7. Silas G. Garrett is an aerospace engineer in the Directorate of Research, Development and Engineering Dept., U.S. Aviation Material Command in St. Louis, Missouri.

1172. "Aerospace Dept. Manager." *Ebony* (November 1983): 6. George W. Jordan Jr. manages day-to-day flight simulations, is responsible for budget, personnel, and technical aspects for Lockheed in Marietta, Georgia.

1173. "Aerospace Firm Analyst." *Ebony* (July 1984): 7. Ernie Thompkins is a quality assurance analyst with United Space Boosters, at Kennedy Space Center, Florida.

1174. "Aerospace Firm Program Head." *Ebony* (February 1989): 9. Shelly W. Riley II is director of mission simulation and support systems programs for LTV Missiles and Electronics in Dallas.

1175. "Aerospace Test Engineer." *Ebony* (June 1978): 7. Erwin S. McCalla is a director at the Grumman Aerospace Corp. in Bethpage, New York. He developed a facility to test vehicle components.

1176. "Air Force Picks Black to Head Space Division." *Jet* 63 (March 7, 1983): 32. Maj. Gen. Winston D. Powers is Deputy Chief of Staff for communications, electronics, and computer resources for North American Aerospace Defense Command in Colorado Springs.

1177. "Air Surveillance Scientist." *Ebony* (November 1970): 7. James Thomas is research psychologist for Goodyear Aerospace Corporation in Akron, Ohio. Formerly with the Air Force, he studies ways to increase the amount of intelligence available from visual reconnaissance systems.

1178. Black, Austin. "The Rocket Fuels Expert." *Sepia* 10:10 (October 1961): 22-24. Joseph H. Johnson Jr. started as a mechanic in the Air Force, became a chemical engineer, and now is in charge of administering $5,000,000 of U.S. Air Force liquid fuels contracts. Biographical and scientific information.

1179. "Black Pilot Appointed Dean at D.C. Med School." *Jet* 63 (March 7, 1983): 32. Leonard W. Johnson has been appointed Dean at the School of Medicine of the Uniformed Services University of the Health Sciences in Washington D.C. In 1968 Dr. Johnson became the first black physician to become certified in the specialty of aerospace medicine. Biographical information.

1180. "Earth's Eye on the Moon." *Ebony* (October 1973): 61-63. Dr. George R. Carruthers developed the first moon-based observatory. Biographical and scientific information.

1181. Gregory, William H. "Aerospace and Social Challenge." *Aviation Week and Space Technology* 88:24 (June 10, 1968): 39, 42-44, 47, 49, 51-52, 57. [Part 1 of a three-part article: "Industry Probes Socio-Economic Markets"]. Dicusses job programs for minorities. "We have a modest amount of altruism and a lot of interest in profits." Information on financing business in ghettoes, and emphasis on Watts, California.

1182. Gregory, William H. "Aerospace and Social Challenge." *Aviation Week and Space Technology* 88:25 (June 17, 1968): 43, 45-46, 48-49, 50-51, 53, 55. [Part 2 of a three-part article: "Job Training Programs Expanding"]. Discusses on-the-job training for the hard-core unemployed.

1183. Gregory, William H. "Aerospace and Social Challenge." *Aviation Week and Space Technology* 89:1 (July 1, 1968): 38-40, 45-46, 51. Part 3 of a three-part article: "Several Firms Planning Urban Programs, but Sales Prospects are Vague."

1184. Haskins, James. *Against All Opposition: Black Explorers in America.* New York: Walker and Co., 1992. Chapter 8, "The Stars, My Goal: Guion Stewart Bluford, Jr.," pp. 62-71. Chapter 9, "Ronald E. McNair and the *Challenger* Disaster.," pp. 72-80. For grades 5 to 8.

1185. "Industrial, Aerospace Engineer." *Ebony* (November 1986): 7. Christopher L. Dawkins manages the support program at Eaton Corporation, New York.

1186. Marchbanks, Vance H. "Effects of Flying Stress on Urinary 17-Hydroxycorticosteroids Levels Observations during a 22 1/2 Hour Mission." *Aero-Medical Journal* (September 1957). [Author is a doctor in the space program].

1187. Marchbanks, Vance H. "Noise Levels in the KC-135." *Noise Control* (May 1957). [Author is a doctor in the space program].

1188. Marchbanks, Vance H. Jr. "Sickle Trait and the Black Airman." *Journal of the National Medical Association* 73 (1981): 1117. [Reprinted from *Aviation Space Environment Medicine* (March 1980) 290]. This article was not seen.

1189. Mathes, Bernard. "Marchbanks: Man of Space." *Sepia* 10:12 (December 1961): 32-34. Col. Vance Hunter Marchbanks is one of 23 physicians trained in aviation medicine to take part in Project Mercury. Biographical information. Marchbanks has written numerous scientific articles.

1190. "Member of California Space Team." *Ebony* (January 1965): 7. L. Warren Morrison is in the advanced systems engineering department at Northrup Space Laboratories in Hawthorne.

1191. "Missile Evaluation Chief." *Ebony* (May 1985): 7. Captain Dalton C. Nicholson is chief of an evaluation team for the Titan II (ICBM) at McDonald AFB, Wichita, Kansas and Little Rock AFB, Arkansas.

1192. "Moon Project Physician." *Ebony* (Octber 1964): 6. Dr. Vance Hunter Marchbanks Jr., a retired Air Force flight surgeon, is developing a space suit and life support system for the Apollo moon project.

1193. "Moon Shot Technician." *Ebony* (December 1964): 45-46, 48, 50, 52. James E. Martin is part of the team that developed Ranger VII's intricate television system which sent 4,316 photographs of the moon's surface to earth.

1194. "Rocket Team Boss." *Ebony* (May 1964): 46-48, 50, 52. Employed by Aerojet-General at Sacramento, California, Willis Sprattling Jr. is an expert on rocket testing, and has been involved with rocketry since 1949. He served in the Army Air Force in the Far East. Biographical information.

1195. "Senior Astrophysicist." *Ebony* (September 1985): 7. George R. Carruthers is a senior astrophysicist at the Hulbert Space Center in Washington D.C. He has been involved in rocket experiments since 1966.

1196. "Soviets Launch World's First Black Cosmonaut." *Jet* 59:4 (October 9, 1980): 8. Arnaldo Tamayo Mendez, a Cuban from Guantanamo, joined Yuri Romanenko in a planned link up of the Soyez-38 space capsule with the manned Salyut-6 space laboratory.

1197. "Space Corp. Administrator." *Ebony* (April 1975): 6. Charles A. Brown works for McDonnell Douglas Corporation at Edwards, California.

1198. "Space Flight Engineer." *Ebony* (July 1967): 6. R.T. Mackey is a senior tool engineer for North American Aviation.

1199. "Space Stars." *Ebony* (August 1985): 150, 152, 154, 156. Article discusses two stars in futurist dramas: Nichelle Nichols and Billy Dee Williams. Nichols played Lieut. Uhura on *Star Trek* (1966-1969), the first time that race was irrelevant on television. She went on to work with NASA as a consultant, and this year she received an award for her work in humanizing science. Williams played Lando Calrissian in *The Empire Strikes Back* and *Return of the Jedi.* Discussion of the future.

1200. Stinson, Sonya. "African Americans in Aerospace and Defense." *National Technical Association Journal* (Fall 1989): 50-58. [Article not seen].

1201. "TV: Black Stars in Orbit." *People's Daily World* (February 8, 1990): 18. This one-hour documentary, to be shown on PBS stations on February 12, details the achievements of black scientists and astronauts in the space program.

Airlines

1202. "Advertisement." *Ebony* (May 1958): 89. Advertisement shows James O. Plinton Jr, Assistant to the President, TWA. He now flies his own two-engine plane for pleasure.

1203. "Advertisement." *Harper's* (June 1961). A history of Ethiopian Air Lines, "Fifteen Years Ago He Created an Airline." Haile Selassie is "He."

1204. "Advertisement." *Ebony* (October 1961): 118. Perry H. Young, a helicopter pilot for New York Airways, advertises Viceroy cigarettes. Some biographical information.

1205. "Advertisement." *Ebony* (November 1965): 57. Hayes Jones is a sales representative in Detroit for American Airlines. Jones is the winner of a bronze medal in the 1960 Olympics in Rome and a gold medal in the 1964 Olympics in Tokyo.

1206. "Advertisement." *Ebony* (July 1981): 1. Advertisement for Eastern Airlines, featuring Captain Leslie A. Morris.

1207. "Advertisement." *Black Enterprise* (June 1983): 66. Charles Wright, manager of market development for Eastern Airlines, is featured. Aspects of his job are described.

1208. "Aeronautical Engineer." *Ebony* (April 1987): 7. Michael C. Hardware is a structural engineer at American Airlines in Tulsa, Oklahoma.

1209. "Air Afrique Gets $6.6 Million Export-Import Bank Credit." *Wall Street Journal* (January 6, 1971).

1210. "Air Engineering Section Head." *Ebony* (October 1962): 6. Maurice Jones heads the design engineering section at Hughes Aircraft Company's Aerospace Group at Culver City, California. With the company 13 years, Jones formerly taught at Prairie View University, Texas.

1211. "Aircraft Line Inspector." *Ebony* (January 1962): 7. Frank L. Lewis is an aircraft inspector with Northeast Airlines at New York's International Airport. He is the first Negro to hold this position at Northeast.

1212. "Airline Captain." *Ebony* (May 1981): 6. Leslie A. Morris is the captain of a Boeing 727 for Eastern Airlines. Morris is the only black captain among Eastern's 4,400 pilots, which include 2,000 captains.

1213. "Airline Cargo Training Manager." *Ebony* (April 1980): 6. William Leroy Murphy trains Pan American employees in international tariffs, rules, and regulations in New York.

1214. "Airline Executive." *Ebony* (September 1974): 6. William J. Allen is reservations and ticketing sales manager for United Airlines in Detroit.

1215. "Airline Industry Insider." *Emerge* 3:9 (August 1992): 22. Jack E. Robinson, President of Florida Air, has written *Freefall*, which describes the failure of Eastern Airlines. Robinson worked for Eastern Express, and is now a consultant to the industry, and a bankruptcy lawyer in New York.

1216. "Airline Manager." *Ebony* (October 1973): 6. Jean-Claude Holly, Haitian, is the American Airlines manager at Alexander Hamilton Airport in St. Croix.

1217. "Airline Operation General Manager." *Ebony* (May 1987): 7. James A. Watkins Jr. is the general manager for American Airlines, Grannis Field Airport in Fayetteville, North Carolina.

1218. "Airline Sales Assistant." *Ebony* (May 1955): 5. Walter Brandford, an engineer, assists the sales controller in scheduling and planning flights for Pan American Airways in New York.

1219. "Airline Services Manager." *Ebony* (April 1985): 6. Ronald W. Williams is the customer service manager for United Airlines in Cleveland.

1220. "Airline Vice President." *Ebony* (July 1976): 6. Charles J. Patterson is senior vice president of World Airways, a charter airline.

1221. "Airline Vice President." *Ebony* (February 1985): 6. Stephen E. Daniels is staff vice president for reservations for Trans World Airlines in New York.

1222. "Airlines: Flying High Out of Africa." *Time* (April 19, 1968). Description of East African Airways, a 22-year old company with an estimable safety record. The countries which own it are Kenya, Uganda, and Tanzania. Heading EAA is Chief Abdulla Said Fundi-Kira. Only six of the pilots are African, and they are all co-pilots.

1223. "Airlines Sales Representative." *Ebony* (December 1978): 6. Bette G. Saunders works for KLM Royal Dutch Airlines in New York. She specializes in market development of emerging African nations who have never used KLM.

1224. "Airlines: Wheeler Flying Service." *Black Enterprise* 6 (April 1976): 35. Warren Wheeler's airline has grown from one airplane and one employee to eleven planes and 31 employees. It is based at Raleigh/Durham airport.

1225. "The Airport That Maynard Built." *Ebony* (December 1980): 52-54, 56, 58, 60, 62. Blacks reap bonanza at world's biggest airport in Atlanta, Georgia. Mayor Maynard H. Jackson insisted that blacks get at least 25 percent of the action, in all areas, or there would be no airport.

1226. "Airways Sales Manager." *Ebony* (October 1969): 6. W. Alvin Hunter, born in the Netherlands Antilles, manages district sales for Trans Caribbean Airways in New York and five New England states.

1227. Alexander, James Jr. "Air Atlanta's in a Holding Pattern." *Black Enterprise* 15:11 (June 1985): 228-230. "Despite a rocky takeoff, officials of this black-owned airline believe that marketing to the business traveler is the key to weathering the industry's competitive storm." Michael Hollis discusses the business he founded.

1228. "All-Black Crew Makes Transcontinental Flight for Flying Tigers." *News from Flying Tigers* (October 16, 1979). [This is a nine-page press release. Address is 7401 World Way West, Los Angeles, CA 90009]. On

October 16, three black pilots were at the controls of a four-engined heavy jet aircraft on a three-day scheduled transcontinental flight. They are George M. Raynor, Franklyn D. Campbell, and Fred E. McClurkin. Raynor was the first black pilot for the airline (1966), Campbell (1972), and McClurkin (1978). There are ten black pilots at Flying Tigers, reportedly the highest percentage in the airline industry. Of more than 40,000 pilots in the country, only 143 are black. The other pilots are: James Bailey, Dennis Cropp, Michael Flemons, Joey Johnson, Wayne Norris, Harold Thomas, and Thomas Witts. Campbell is listed in *Who's Who Among Black Americans.*

1229. Anderson, Monroe. "Jim Tilmon: Jet Age Renaissance Man." *Ebony* (April 1973): 56-58, 60-62. Tilmon, a commercial pilot, TV personality, businessman, and concert clarinetist, devotes 18 hours a day to his careers. He has been flying for 15 years, in the Army and for American Airlines.

1230. "Aviation's Only Black 747 Pilot." *Sepia* 20 (June 1971): 19-25. Biographical information on Otis B. Young.

1231. "Black Airline Pilots." *Black Enterprise* 4 (April 1974): 15-17, 19, 22-23, 61-62. Piloting is an attractive career, but for blacks the "last hired, first fired" looms large. Five pilots participated in a round table discussion. Their names and airlines are: Alexander Lambert, United; Clarence Powell, TWA; Joseph Bryant, Eastern; Otis Young and Edward Moon, Pan Am. There are also photographs of 69 other pilots from these airlines and from Delta Airlines, American Airlines, Allegheny Airlines, Flying Tiger Line, New York Airways, North Central Airlines, Piedmont Airlines, and Southern Airways.

1232. "Black Pilots." *Ebony* (January 1978): 58-60, 62, 64, 66. Report of the second annual convention of the Organization of Black Airline Pilots. Ben Thomas of Atlanta is the president. Their membership consists of seventy of the 100-110 black pilots flying for major airlines. "Currently black pilots represent less than one-half of one per cent of the total number of pilots in the industry." There are photographs of ninety-eight pilots, arranged by company.

1233. "Blacks Behind the Scenes." *Black Enterprise* 4 (April 1974): 31-34. Airline employment is opening up for black managers in senior positions.

Those profiled are: Donald B. Young, Eastern; James A. Watkins Jr., American; Thawn T. Johnson, Seaboard World; and Maurice Wardlaw, Pan American.

1234. "Breakthrough on the Airlines." *Ebony* (November 1965): 112-114, 116, 118-119. Four Negro airmen join the 15,750-man cockpit crew (.0002 per cent). Marlon Green, Continental; David E. Harris; American; Jack A. Noel, American; William R. Norwood; United. William R. Norwood is featured, with biographical information. Marlon Green's litigation with United is noted: the suit continued from June 1957 until February 1965, when he was hired.

1235. "Cargo Services Manager." *Ebony* (December 1981): 6. William E. Holden is manager of cargo services for Eastern Airlines at Miami International Airport.

1236. Chandler, Jerome Greer. "How Color-Blind Are The Skies?" *Frequent Flyer* (May 1987): 87-96. An in-depth article about the struggle minority pilots undergo for acceptance by the airlines and by frequent flyers. Chandler reports on a House of Representatives panel which met last fall. Statistics show fewer than one percent of 46,000 commercial airline pilots are black, despite the hiring of 8, 000 new pilots in 1985. That makes them rarer than black brain surgeons or nuclear physicists, percentagewise. The article abounds with historical information, personal anecdotes, other statistical information, and analysis. It also mentions organizations of African-American pilots and airlines in Africa. Pilots interviewed are: Eddie Hadden, Organization of Black Airline Pilots (OBAP); Don Barton, American Airlines; and William F. Broadwater. There is also a full-page box on Harry Brown, now at Air Atlanta. Brown was a helicopter pilot in Vietnam and worked for Continental Airlines. Federal Express has the highest percentage of black pilots in the U. S. - four percent. Organizations active in recruiting blacks into aviation are, besides OBAP, are Negro Airmen International and Afro-American Aviation Foundation, P.O. Box 86, LaGuardia Airport, NY 11371.

1237. "Charter Airline Executive." *Ebony* (March 1969): 6. Charles J. Patterson is vice president of World Airways in Oakland, California.

1238. "Chicago Weatherman Has Resolve for Job Madness." *Jet* (July 24, 1975): 20-22. Jim Tilmon has been a pilot for American Airlines for ten years, is a television weatherman, hosts a television show, runs a television production company, and plays clarinet with the Lake Forest Symphony. He would like to own his own plane and helicopter. Tilmon on his many activities: "Man is like a computer... you don't want to have any down time."

1239. "Colin Moore, Others Protest B.W.I.A. All-White Management." *New York Amsterdam News* (June 6, 1992): 9, 35. Attorney Moore held a press conference on March 19 to declare a disturbing trend in personnel changes at BWIA, owned by Trinidad and Tobago. Moore also cited Guyana Airlines for replacing black pilots with white pilots.

1240. "Control Systems Designer." *Ebony* (July 1962): 6. Leonard W. Massey designs all-weather interceptors for the U. S. Air Force at Hughes Aircraft Company in Culver City, California.

1241. Cronin, Lisa. "Negro Pilots are Sought by Airlines." *St. Paul Sunday Pioneer Press* (May 18, 1969): 9. [Third section. The same article is in the *Chicago Tribune*, May 18, 1969]. Airlines are eager to hire qualified Negroes for flight and management jobs but can't find them. Numerous statistics for both commercial airlines and the Navy and Air Force. The Army does not keep personnel records by race. Among those quoted are Carol Johnson, a stewardess at United and Jim Tilmon, a pilot for American.

1242. "Dalton James." *Jet* (February 24, 1977): 22. Dalton James, a technical writer for Eastern Airlines, has been promoted to public relations representative for Eastern Airlines in Miami, Florida.

1243. DeKnight, Frieda. "Food in Flight." *Ebony* (June 1956): 128, 131-132. Highlights black chefs and cooks for United Airlines: Willie Flowers, Edward Gerber, Jerry Roland, Walter Pryor, and Frank Payne.

1244. "Democracy Flies the Airways." *Ebony* 12 (August 1957): 47-50. British West Indian Airways, seventeen years old, has a non-bias hiring policy.The black staff pictured are Lysle Bailey, an engineer; Clair Benjamin, a clerk; and two hostesses Koala Cockburn and Pearl Marshall.

1245. DeWitt, Karen. "When Social Services Have a Bottom Line." *New York Times* (June 7, 1992): 20. [Section 4]. Cessna Aircraft built a training factory in a depressed area of Wichita, Kansas.

1246. "Doctor, Inventor." *Ebony* (August 1963): 6. Dr. Clarence Larry has invented an instrument to take still and moving pictures of astronauts' eyes during simulated space flight. He works in the bioastronautics section of Boeing Aircraft in Seattle, Washington.

1247. "Employing the Unemployable." *Aerospace* 6:2 (Fall 1968): 2-7. Companies in the aerospace industry have been acutely aware of the plight of the hard-core unemployed, for many of their plants are in or near the major cities of the nation. Programs of numerous companies are described.

1248. "Employment Director." *Ebony* (June 1966): 7. Norman Lincoln is Director of the Employment and Manpower section at Hughes Aircraft Co. in Los Angeles.

1249. Feaver, Douglas B. "TWA Jet's Accidental Aerobatics Under Exhaustive Study." *Washington Post* (May 13, 1979): A3. A 727 airplane dropped five miles in 30 seconds, but the pilot was able to recover control. It is not known what caused the incident. The captain was Harvey Gibson. The lengthy article is mainly about the mechanical aspects if the incident, with very little about Gibson. There is, however, a photograph of him.

1250. "50 Top Black Executives in Corporate America." *Ebony* (January 1992): 112, 116. John W. Cox is the vice president of community affairs for Delta Air Lines at the company's headquarters in Atlanta, Georgia. Gary S. Jefferson is the vice president for the Northeast Region of United Airlines in Chicago. Roger A. Gibson is the vice president for the mountain region of United Airlines at Denver, Colorado.

1251. "First Black Airline Gets off the Ground." *Ebony* (April 1976): 44-46, 48, 50, 52. Warren Wheeler's airline is the only black-owned regularly scheduled airline in the country.

1252. "First Black Man Flies Pan Am's Jumbo 747 Jet." *Jet* (July 2, 1970): 28. Otis B. Young Jr. flew the "Midnight Sun," a 747 Jumbo Jet on its inaugural voyage from London to Los Angeles. Young has worked for Pan American Airlines since 1966; the article includes biographical information and his comments on piloting the 747.

1253. "First Negro Airline Captain Will Spend Ground Time on Long Island." *Long Island Sunday Press* (April 21, 1957). Perry Young will move to Nassau County soon. Biographical information.

1254. "Flying High as Texas International VP." *Ebony* (March 1978): 64-66, 68, 70, 72. Evans Joseph McKay, as vice president, helps develop his company's greatest asset - its people, including those in management.

1255. "Gary S. Jefferson." *Jet* (June 8, 1978): 20. Gary S. Jefferson was appointed Manager of Station Operations for United Airlines in Detroit. His former position was assistant to the president and chief executive officer of United Airlines.

1256. Gregory, William H. "Airlines Focus on Special Interest Groups." *Aviation Week and Space Technology* 95:5 (August 2, 1971): 32-34. Among the hottest areas of interest at this time is the ethnic market, primarily the black market in the case of U.S. domestic carriers. Describes the programs of a number of airlines, and Jim Plinton is interviewed.

1257. Gunther, John. "The Emperor's Airline." *Coronet* (May 1954): 137-140. Information about Ethiopian Air Lines, and its chief pilot, Waldo G. Golien, who is Swedish. The Emperor sits in the cockpit with him when he flies.

1258. Harmon, George. "Restless Black Pilot Eyes Better Skies for 'Brothers'." *Cincinnati Enquirer* (April 13, 1969). Profile of Jim Tilmon, one of ten blacks among 3,000 pilots for American Airlines. Biographical information, and Tilmon's philosophy of reaching out to others so that they can succeed too. "The fact is you're not free as long as there is one person in the country who isn't free."

1259. "Hayes Jones." *Jet* (December 28, 1967): 44. Hayes Jones is taking a two-year leave of absence from his post as American Airlines sales representative to become New York City Commissioner of Recreation, a position newly created by Mayor John Lindsay.

1260. "He Helps Jockey the 'Jumbo'." *Ebony* (September 1970): 54-56, 58. Otis B. Young was the co-pilot on Pan American's recent inaugural flight from London to Los Angeles of the Boeing 747, the largest and most complicated passenger aircraft now in the air. Biographical information.

1261. Heintz, Paul C. "Aviation Makes Move for Black Education." *Philadelphia Bulletin* (April 12, 1970). The Philadelphia Urban Coalition spurred the creation of the Academy of Aerospace and Aviation at a high school here in an effort to inspire black students to stay in school. They are learning mechanics, electronics, reservations, and pilot training. The pilot training has not gotten past classroom work because they have no access to an airplane. Trans World Air Lines and United Airlines are assisting. Photograph shows Capt. David Harris, one of the few black pilots, talking to students. Harris flies for American Airlines.

1262. Holahan, Sharon. "Black Pilots Breaching Corporate Cockpit Barriers." *Aviation Convention News (Midland Park, NJ)* (September 1, 1980): 74, 76-77. Article discusses the scarcity of black pilots flying for corporations. There are between twenty and thirty black pilots, which is about one-tenth of one percent. The reasons given are color discrimination, lack of money for training, lack of contacts in the industry, and lack of role models. Seven pilots are interviewed and they relate their experiences. They are: Bob Dodd of Burlington National; Orville O'Brien of Becton Dickinson; Coleman Radar of Northwestern Bell; Bill Henderson and Tony Mixon of General Motors; Glenn Noonan and Walt Branch of Mobil Oil; and George Raynor of Flying Tigers Airlines. Also mentioned are Wheeler Airlines and Wheeler Flying Service, which runs a CETA program, Frank Campbell, Fred McClurkin, and Charles F. Bolden Jr.

1263. James, Dalton. "James O. Plinton Jr. Eastern Airlines." *Black Collegian* 8:4 (March/April 1978): 47. Plinton, vice president for marketing development for Eastern Airlines, and in aviation for 35 years, offers his philosophy of life.

1264. "Jet Aircraft Test Engineer." *Ebony* (November 1969): 6. Thomas H. Gray is a flight test instrumentation engineer for the Boeing Co. in Seattle. He tested Air Force One before its delivery to President Kennedy, and he now tests 747 jets.

1265. "Jim Tilmon: The Tempo is Multivocational." *Chicago Tribune* (September 15, 1974): 14. [Magazine section]. Jim Tilmon flies 727s out of Chicago for American Airlines; he hosts a weekly television show; he's first clarinetist for the Lake Forest Symphony; he is president of a company that makes commercials for radio and television, industrial films and slide shows.

1266. Johnson, Darlene. "Wings Over Cleveland." *Black Enterprise* 10 (November 1979): 19. Arthur Fantroy, a former combat pilot, is the founder and owner of Cleveland Air Transport, an airplane and helicopter charter service. He also covers late-breaking news stories for television.

1267. Johnson, Herschel. "Airline Pioneer: Vice-Presidency at Eastern crowns Jim Plinton's 34 Years in Aviation." *Ebony* (November 1976): 103-104, 106, 108-109. Only black vice president of a major airline. Biographical information.

1268. Johnson, Herschel. "Ed Green: On the Wings of Success." *Black Enterprise* 15:11 (June 1985): 251-253. Ed Green is the vice president of sales and services for Eastern Air Lines. A marine lieutenant colonel for 21 years, he now battles to keep Eastern's most profitable division in the black. He is the highest-ranking black executive working for a major carrier in the industry.

1269. Knoch, Joanne. "Asks Training Negroes for Better Jobs." *Chicago Tribune* (February 15, 1964). George A. Spater, executive vice president and general counsel of United Airlines, said companies should do a little more than the law requires to break a vicious circle. That circle is one where young Negroes aren't motivated to train for better jobs because the potential is unreal to them.

1270. Lane, Bill. "Sepia Hollywood." *Sepia* (January 1980): 14, 16. Imara R. Yokely, manager of convention sales for United Airlines in San Francisco, has received movie offers because of his good looks.

1271. Lara, Edna B. "Paving a Way for Other Black Pilots." *Kansas City Star* (October 5, 1972). Profile of U.L. (Rip) Gooch, pilot/owner of Aero Services, Inc., founded in 1959 in Wichita, Kansas. The company owns thirteen planes and one helicopter, and employs 42 people. Biographical information.

1272. Leary, William M. *Encyclopedia of American Business History and Biography: The Airline Industry*. New York: Facts on File, 1992. Theodore W. Robinson, a pilot and a historian, has written "African Americans in the Airline Industry, " pp. 9-11.

1273. Lucas, Caryl R. "Group of Black Pilots Targets Recruitment." *Newark Star Ledger* (August 16, 1992). M. Perry Jones, president of the Organization of Black Airline Pilots, says fewer than 500 of the 52,000 pilots flying are black. The group held their annual convention last week in Boston. OBAP was formed in 1976 to advance career opportunities in commercial aviation for blacks and other minorities. Interviewed are Jones, now at Delta, having been the black pilot hired by Pan American Airlines; Eddie Hadden, formerly at Eastern Airlines; and Jim Harrison who flies for USAir.

1274. "Making it: A Business Grows in Boulder." *Black Enterprise* 7: 10 (May 1977): 14. Bob and Marietta Stevens converted their dry-cleaning business into an industrial cleaning plant. Their customers include Lowery AFB near Denver and United Airlines.

1275. "The Man Who Won't Give Up." *Ebony* (April 1957): 17-24. ["Wheel Chair Wedding" *Ebony* (July 1959) 134-138. Pan Am Jets attend the wedding of Junius Kellogg]. Junius Kellogg, the basketball star who was paralyzed after an automobile accident in 1954, coaches a team of paraplegic basketball players. Kellogg is employed by Pan American World Airways, and the team is called the Pan Am Jets.

1276. "Market Expert for TWA." *Ebony* (November 1964): 7. James O. Plinton Jr. is director of special market affairs for Trans World Airlines, which he joined in 1957.

1277. Miller, Charles. "Amazing Record of the 'World's Wackiest' Airline." *Reader's Digest* (August 1960): 115-119. In September of 1945 Haile Selassie negotiated a contract with Trans World Airlines to bring air service to Ethiopia. The changes include the ability to reach remote isolated areas, and communication is now much improved. The training is the most rigorous for any airline because of Ethiopia's difficult terrain. There has not been a single fatality in its fifteen years of existence, and fifteen Ethiopian pilots are employed.

1278. Moses, Knolly. "BWIA Grounded by Strike and Strife." *Black Enterprise* 8 (May 1978): 12. A strike was called last February in the midst of Carnival, the major tourist attraction. It was called by the Trinidad Airlines Pilots Association over the grounding of Malcolm Hernandez.

Another point of contention is BWIA's hiring policy: currently 80 per cent of pilots are not nationals.

1279. Nash, Malcolm. "A Dare Led to Negro Pilot's Career as 'Copter Captain." *New York Amsterdam News* (April 20, 1957): 20. Biographical information on Perry Young Jr., a helicopter pilot for New York Airways. His brother William is a mechanic for Pan American Airways.

1280. "Nation's Only Black Scheduled Airline." *Sepia* 25 (April 1976): 18-23. Warren Wheeler is the owner of the first and only black-owned airline, which makes a dozen daily flights between North Carolina and Virginia.

1281. "Navajo Airlines: A Dream Takes Wing." *Black Enterprise* 1 (June 1971): 23-24. Ken York has just started a cargo business in Miami with one plane.

1282. "Nigerian Airways Plans Expansion." *New York Times* (March 16, 1962). Article details amounts and programs.

1283. Olesky, Walter. "The Blue Yonder's Really Wild For Charlie." *Black Sports* (December 1974): 40, 46. Charlie Chambers, a pilot for Ozark Airlines, has built his own Formula One Cassette. It took him four years and $5,500. He is interested in racing; other biographical information.

1284. "Passenger Helicopter Pilot." *Ebony* (June 1957): 128-130. Perry H. Young Jr. celebrated 20 years as a pilot by becoming a captain for New York Airways, the world's first regularly scheduled helicopter line. Young's appointment made him the first Negro to crack aviation's long-time color barrier.

1285. Pearson, Trevor. "Local Caribbean Group Calls for Reversal of BWIA Appointments." *New York Amsterdam News* (June 20, 1992): 9, 26. The Caribbean-American Action Committee met at Medgar Evers College in Brooklyn to protest the all-white management team running British West Indian Airways.

1286. "People." *Jet* (January 31, 1980): 20. Fred Pitcher has been elected chairman of the Organization of Black Airline Pilots at their convention in Washington, D.C. Pitcher was the first black engineer and co-pilot hired by Western Airlines.

1287. "Production Control Coordinator." *Ebony* (June 1962): 6. Ronald E. Hyman works at New York's Idlewild Airport for Pan American Airways. He was in the Air Force from 1952-1956.

1288. Robinson, Jack E. *Freefall: The Needless Destruction of Eastern Air Lines and the Valiant Struggle to Save It.* New York: HarperCollins Publishers, 1992. Robinson, as vice president of corporate development at Eastern Air Lines and president of Eastern Express, was one of the key players. He describes the negotiations and the participants, concluding that the fall was not inevitable. He is now president of Florida Air.

1289. "Room at the Top." *Black Enterprise* 2:2 (September 1971): 15-18. 'Showcase' jobs persist, but fight continues for more meaningful positions. Interviews and discussions with James O. Plinton, Lee Archer, Paul Gibson, and Earl Estwick.

1290. Salpukas, Agis. "Air Atlanta's Buoyant Founder." *New York Times* (June 9, 1985): 7. [Business section]. Profile of Air Atlanta, the first airline largely owned by blacks, and its founder, chairman, and chief executive, Michael R. Hollis. There is considerable financial information about the company and its chances for success, as well as biographical information on Hollis.

1291. Schwartz, Jerry. "After Three Years of High Hopes, Air Atlanta is Out of Cash." *New York Times* (April 12, 1987): 8. [Business section]. Almost a full-page story of the economic trials and failure of Air Atlanta, and an analysis of the reasons for it.

1292. "Sierra Leone to Have Airline." *Christian Science Monitor* (March 11, 1961). Sierra Leone, to become independent next month, has signed a contract with British United Airways to form a new airline.

1293. Simmons, Judy D. "Airlines of the Caribbean." *Black Enterprise* 7 (April 1977): 61-62, 64-66. Simmons discusses four airlines, giving their history, atmosphere, safety record, and the general problems of tourism. The airlines are: Air Jamaica, British West Indian Airways (BWIA), Leeward Islands Air Transport (LIAT), and Caribbean Airways.

1294. Simon, Francesca. "Air Atlanta Takes Off." *Essence* 15 (September 1984): 66. Profile of Michael Hollis, founder and president of Air Atlanta, which started in February.

1295. Stephenson, Olivier. "Caribbean Activists Press their Fight Against BWIA's White Management." *New York Amsterdam News* (August 15, 1992): 9-8 [*sic*]. The Caribbean-American Action Committee just returned from a meeting in Trinidad with BWIA officials. This committee is opposed to the government's decision to privatize BWIA. They see white foreigners being brought in to top management positions while local Trinidadian employees are dismissed.

1296. "Study Analyzes Negro Hiring in Industry." *Aviation Week and Space Technology* 89:21 (November 18, 1968): 118-120. Comments on Ford Foundation-funded study by Herbert R. Northrup. Northrup concludes the hostile attitude toward Negro labor in the aeronautics industry at the beginning of World War II has shifted over the years to an active effort to recruit and upgrade Negro workers. Statistics.

1297. Suehsdorf, Adie. "Wings for the Lion." *Saga: True Adventures for Men* (September 1952): 22-29, 94. A profile of Ethiopian Air Lines, whose pilots are mostly American. There are three Ethiopian pilots, but the only one named is Bedane Girma. Ethiopia's terrain is a challenge to the highly-skilled pilots. The cargoes too are sometimes unusual: lions, gold, frankincense and myrrh.

1298. "Teaching Airline Pilots Their ABCs." *Ebony* (July 1964): 33-34, 36, 38, 40. Retired Air Force Major George H. O. Martin is an instructor at United Airlines Flight Training Center in Denver, Colorado. Twenty years in the Air Force, Martin has a Distinguished Flying Cross and other medals.

1299. Thompson, Era Bell. "African Safari." *Ebony* (February 1969): 114-118, 120, 122. James O. Plinton Jr., TWA Special Market Affairs Director, joins four others in "probably the world's first all-Afro big game hunt."

1300. "Trinidad Is Planning to Operate British West Indian Airways." *New York Times* (October 8, 1961).

1301. "TV Weatherman in the Skies." *Sepia* 24 (December 1975): 56-61. A television weatherman in Chicago, Jim Tilmon is also a pilot for American Airlines.

1302. "Welcome Aboard." *Sepia* 15 (December 1966): 26-30. The article discusses the five Negro pilots employed by American Airlines to fly "the giants of the sky," the 707 Astrojets. It recounts the training, education, pay, and gives biographical information for: Jim Brame, A. J. Price, Jack A. Noel, James A. Tilmon, and D. E. Harris.

1303. Whitaker, Charles. "The $90 Million Dream: The Rise and Fall of Michael Hollis." *Ebony* (November 1987): 188-190, 192, 194. Hollis founded Air Atlanta, the nation's first major airline controlled predominantly by blacks. Hollis raised, almost alone, the $90 million. Biographical information and discussion of reasons for failure.

1304. White, Frank III. "Spreading Their Wings." *Ebony* (February 1986): 75-76, 78, 82. Black pilots, numbering 175, want to increase their numbers because retirement age for pilots is 60, and the military is cutting back. This will continue the shortage of black pilots. Eastern and American Airlines are cited as employing the largest number. There are statistics on the other airlines. Mentioned are: Dave Harris, Herman Samuels, William Norwood (president of the Organization of Black Airline Pilots), Theresa Newsome (first black woman commercial pilot), Marlon Green, Fred Pitcher, Warren Wheeler and others.

1305. White, George. "Detroit Wings." *Black Enterprise* 10 (October 1979): 28, 31. Michigan Peninsula Airways, the first black-owned air cargo company started this summer. The partners, George Reasonover and Larry Mathews, had to borrow money from friends because banks would not lend to them.

1306. Williams, Brenda. "He's Up on Flying, Down-to-Earth on Trying." *Encore* 5 (March 8, 1976): 44-45. Biographical sketch of Otis B. Young, the first black pilot to fly the 747. He works for Pan Am, where he says his treatment is professional, not preferential. He discusses race relations and tells of his work with youth groups.

1307. "Wings of Progress." *EM (Ebony Man)* 5:6 (April 1990): 54-55. According to Eddie R. Hadden, general counsel of the Organization of Black Airline Pilots (OBAP), blacks make up less than one-half of one percent of the roughly 45,000 persons in the profession. There are more black brain surgeons and nuclear physicists than airline pilots. Other pilots included in the discussion are: David E. Harris, of American Airlines and president of OBAP; Leslie Morris, head of Negro Airmen International; and Larry Parker, chief pilot recruiter for United Parcel Service. Jim

Tilmon fears "that aviation will be yet another one of those careers where you just don't see us."

1308. Witherspoon, Roger. "The Crash Of Air Atlanta." *Black Enterprise* 17:11 (June 1987): 59-60. Relates the story of the three-year old airline that had been a "shining example of black capitalism." Michael Hollis, the owner discusses the financial aspects.

1309. Witherspoon, Roger, and S. Lee Hilliard. "Navigating a Steady Course." *Black Enterprise* 14 (May 1984): 61-63, 99. British West Indian Airlines, Trinidad's national airline has gone through years of major deficits. They now have a new management team and are trying new marketing methods.

1310. Xanthakos, Harry. "The Man Junius Kellogg: Former Cage Whiz Content as Antipoverty Executive." *Black Sports* 5:4 (October 1975): 53, 59-60. Kellogg was a senior accountant for Pan American Airlines from 1959-1965. He also coached a wheelchair basketball team for the airline. Medical aspects of his accident and rehabilitation are detailed; other biographical information.

Chicago

1311. "Airline Convention Sales Manager." *Ebony* (November 1978): 7. Imara R. Yokely is United Airlines' national sales manager in Chicago.

1312. "American Airlines Representative." *Ebony* (February 1964): 6. Harry L. Parson is a sales representative for American Airlines in Chicago.

1313. "Aviation." *Opportunity* 7:11 (November 1929): 353. The first national aviation meet of Negro flyers under the auspices of the Universal Aviation Association was held at Yackey Checkerboard airfield in Maywood, Illinois. Photograph of Louis Melgoza, Ira V. Evans, Eugene White, Robert Miller, Charles Watkins, and W.C. Mareno, all of Chicago; and Dr. A.P. Davis of Kansas City, Missouri, who flew his own plane to Chicago.

1314. "Black Pilot Finds Reward in Operating His Own School." *Chicago Defender* (April 2, [1969]). Emmett Stovall runs a pilot training school out of the Butler Aviation hangar out of Midway Airport. He opened the school in 1965, and has 100 students, 90 of whom are black. He has twenty years of flying experience and has flown the late Dr. Martin Luther King Jr., the late Robert Kennedy and other dignitaries. Biographical information.

1315. Brown, Roxanne. "Blacks with Unusual Businesses." *Ebony* (December 1988): 116. Clancy Wright, Allen Dandridge, and Ronald Leveston launched a national air courier service called All-Night Air (ANA) seven years ago in Chicago.

1316. Campbell, Clifford J. "They're Learning to Fly in Chicago." *Opportunity* 19:5 (May 1941): 132-134. Describes the courses in flying and aviation mechanics at the Wendell Philips Evening School. Willa B. Brown is Federal Coordinator. Cornelius R. Coffey, President of the National

Airmen's Association, trains student pilots. Other pilots mentioned are :
Lewis Jackson, Larry Green, Dale White and Chauncey Spencer.

1317. "Chicagoans Attend Preview of 'Black Wings' Exhibit." *Chicago Defender* (September 28, 1982): 10. Description of the role played by Rufus
Hunt, aviation historian, in the preparation of the Smithsonian's exhibition, "Black Wings." Photograph of Hunt with Janet Harmon Waterford
Bragg, an early aviator in Chicago.

1318. "Chief Pilot." *Ebony* (April 1993): 6. Capt. Louis L. Freeman is the first
black to be named chief pilot for any major U. S. airline. He oversees all
operations of the 150-pilot base of Southwest Airlines' Chicago base.

1319. Chilton, John. *Who's Who of Jazz: Storyville to Swing Street*. New York:
Da Capo Press, 1985. Charles Cyril Creath, a famous player of the saxo-
phone, trumpet and accordion, worked as an inspector in an aircraft factory (1944) in Chicago, p. 82.

1320. "Chopper Coppers." *Ebony* (July 1971): 78-80. Chicago crime fighters
take to air for improved law enforcement. August Sylvain and Lovell
Swanigan are the only black helicopter pilots of the nine-man aerial police force.

1321. Dombrowski, Louis. "Air Line to Train 500 Jobless." *Chicago Tribune*
(August 27, 1969): 2. United Air Lines will hire and train 500 hard-core
unemployed at eleven major airports with the assistance of a federal
grant. The Chicago area will have 129 jobs of the 500. Training will be
as food assemblers, clerks, airport service men, and ramp service men.

1322. Fax, Elton C. *Seventeen Black Artists*. New York: Dodd, Mead and Co.,
1971. John Cortor, the father of the artist, Eldzier Cortor, flew a small
plane in Chicago during the twenties. He was influenced by Bessie Coleman and Hubert Julian.

1323. "Jim Tilmon." *Jet* (May 7, 1970): 56. Jim Tilmon, host of Chicago's
Television program, "Our People," has formed Tilmon Productions to
make video and audio tapes, sound/slide presentations, and motion pictures. He is currently making two films for the Federal Aviation
Administration.

1324. "Model Airplanes." *Ebony* (November 1948): 39-43. Frank L. Cummings of Los Angeles has won 49 trophies, 14 medals, and 65 ribbons for his model airplanes. Henry Dumminie is president of Chicago's 25-member Skyscrapers, a Negro club in the American Model Association.

1325. "Negro Flyers Take Part in Amateur Show." *Louisiana Weekly* (October 29, 1938). [ANP release, Claude A. Barnett Papers, Chicago Historical Society]. Chicago's colored flyers made history at Harlem airport in Chicago. It was the first time that Negroes had participated in a white air show in America. Of 30,000 spectators, 5, 000 were black. Chauncey Spencer was the first prize winner in parachuting, and Charles Johnson took second prize in the precision flying event. Other pilots participating or present were: Lola Jones, Albert Cosby, Herman Ray, Cornelius Coffey, Fred Hutchison, Dale White, and Willa Brown.

1326. "Orthodontist." *Ebony* (March 1955): 38-42. Earl Wiley Renfroe, in Chicago, was the first Negro orthodontist. Article is mainly about his practice, but notes Renfroe was a pilot, and his son, Earl Jr., is an Air Force jet pilot.

1327. Rather, Ernest R. *Chicago Negro Almanac and Reference Book.* Chicago: Chicago Negro Almanac Publishing Co., 1972. Biographical information on Willa B. Brown on pp.52-53; school named for Robert H. Lawrence at 1 No. Kildare Avenue, p.129 and biographical information on p.12; Dr. Earl W. Renfro at 127 No. Dearborn, p.150; James A. Tilmon on p.78.

1328. "Retired Air Force Officer Named O'Hare's New Chief." *Jet* 66:3 (March 26, 1984): 13. Col. Edward Levell Jr. is deputy commissioner for operations at Chicago's O'Hare International Airport.

1329. "The Sky's No Limit for Black Airplane Whiz Emmit [*sic*] Stovall." *Chicago Defender* (October 20, 1969). Stovall's name is spelled Emmit, Emmitt, and Emitt in this article. It appears as Emmett in another article. Stovall's flying school is called National Air, Inc., and it does charter flights, rentals, and freight flights, as well as give flying lessons.

1330. "'Suicide' Jones." *Ebony* (February 1950): 35-36. Biographical information on Willie "Suicide" Jones. For more than twenty-two years Jones, of

Chicago, has been doing trick parachute jumps, specializing in the
delayed opening of the parachute. He has made 375 leaps.

1331. Waters, Enoch P. *American Diary: A Personal History of the Black
Press*. Chicago: Path Press, 1987. [Waters worked at the *Chicago Defender* for twenty-five years, and was part of the aviation activities there].
Chapter XIII, "Little Air Show Becomes A National Crusade,"
pp.195-210, tells how Waters and the newspaper became involved when
Willa Brown came to the office to request publicity for an air show the
black aviators were planning. It was 1936. Six years later the first pilots
were commissioned at Tuskegee. Waters relates personal anecdotes about
Willa Brown and Cornelius Coffey and others.

1332. Young, A. S. (Doc). "From Plane Janitor to Boss of Air Taxis." *[Chicago
Defender]:* (n.d.). [Young was a syndicated columnist whose work often
appeared in the *Chicago Defender*,] Article on William Barnett who is
president of Lake Air Services in Chicago. The company is interracial,
has four planes, and employs seven pilots. Biographical information on
Barnett.

Discrimination

1333. "Again: Caught Between." *Interracial Review* 36:1 (January 1963): 5.
Editorial on Marlon Green, a pilot who can't find employment with airlines that cross state borders.

1334. "Air Force Jim Crow." *Crisis* 77:6 (June/July 1970): 227-229. Account
of the incident at Goose Bay, Labrador air force base. On March 20-22
there were near riots over the kind of music to be played, a stabbing, and
a beating. The intensive probe of the NAACP resulted in the dropping of
court martial proceedings against five men, and the transfer of the commanding officer. Other racist conditions emerged during the probe.

1335. "Air Force Negroes Fight North Dakota Curbs." *New York Times*
(December 3, 1961). Negroes stationed at Grand Forks AFB and their
families are forcing compliance with a new law that forbids discrimination in public places. The first case was brought by Joseph McClendon
who was charged $5.00 for a Coca-Cola.

1336. "Airline Bias Case Will Get Hearing." *New York Times* (June 10, 1957).
The first public hearing in an airline bias case is set for July 9. Dorothy
Franklin, an employee of the New York Public Library, has accused
TWA of refusing to hire her as a stewardess because of her race. Articles
appeared the same day in the *New York Post*, the *Daily Worker*, and oth-
er papers.

1337. "Airline Creates Affirmative Action Program to Settle Job Bias Suit."
New York Times (May 12, 1991): 20. Northwest Airlines has agreed to
create a multimillion-dollar affirmative action program to settle a job-
discrimination suit brought on behalf of thousands of its black employees,
former employees, and job applicants.

1338. "Airline is Accused." *New York Times* (July 15, 1959). The State Commission Against Discrimination accused Capital Airlines of discrimination for its refusal to hire Patricia Banks.

1339. "Airline Ordered to Hire a Negro." *New York Times* (March 10, 1960). The State Commission Against Discrimination ordered Capital Airlines to abandon its policy of barring Negroes from flying jobs, and ordered them to hire Patricia Banks.

1340. "Airlines Agree to Hire Negro Pilots, Hostesses." *Daily News (New York)* (October 13, 1956). The eighteen major airlines in New York State have agreed to hire Negro personnel. The decision was the result of a five-month study by the State Commission Against Discrimination, headed by Charles Abrams.

1341. "Airport Files Reply in Integration Suit." *New York Times* (August 30, 1961): 21. Officials of Moisant International Airport, New Orleans, contend no law is being broken in the exclusion of Negroes from an airport dining facility.

1342. "Airport is Scene of Negro Protest." *New York Times* (January 2, 1960): 4. [See also the *New York Post*, January 3, 1960]. The municipal airport at Greenville, South Carolina, was the scene of a demonstration to protest the treatment of Jackie Robinson last March. He had been asked to leave the waiting room for whites.

1343. "Airport Race Ban Upset in Memphis." *New York Times* (March 27, 1962). The Supreme Court ordered an end to racial segregation in a restaurant at the municipal airport, and at all publicly-owned airports in the U.S.

1344. "The Airport Test." *Newsweek* (January 10, 1949): 23. Despite the Civil Aeronautics Administration's ban (last week) on discrimination or segregation based on race, color, or creed at the National Airport, race bias remains. Article offers two instances, including an eight-hour sit in at a coffee shop's lunch counter.

1345. "Alabama Airport Target of U.S. Suit." *New York Times* (July 22, 1961). The Justice Department filed suit against Montgomery's municipal airport. Segregated restaurants, waiting and rest rooms, and water fountains violate the Federal Aviation Act of 1958.

1346. Bedwell, Don. "Blacks Excluded from Aviation Board." *Miami Herald* (September 7, 1972). A list of nominees for a proposed Greater Miami Citizens Aviation Board excludes blacks and Latin Americans.

1347. "Bias Fight Won in Court, Negro Pilot Waits a Job." *Detroit News* (April 23, 1963): 1, 8. Marlon D. Green won a unanimous decision from the U. S. Supreme Court in his discrimination suit against Continental Air Lines. Green began his battle in 1957, and during that time sent out 600 applications.

1348. "Bias Protest Received." *New York Times* (September 2, 1953). Gov. G. Mennon Williams of Michigan has received no direct complaint of racially discriminatory practices by Sault Ste. Marie businesses towards the Negro airmen guarding the Soo locks. He has only received a telegram from Roy Wilkins of the NAACP, and he can't act on that, as the aggrieved party must file suit. The men can't find housing, eat in restaurants, or use barbershops.

1349. "Blacks End Protest at N.D. Base." *New York Post* (January 16, 1975). Twenty-five black enlisted men and women ended a protest today. They had locked themselves in the dining hall of the Minot AFB for six hours to protest the difficulty of blacks in Minot, North Dakota.

1350. Bombadier. "The Story of the 477th Bombardment Group." (June 1944): 141-142. [No source, but the article is reprinted from the *Pittsburgh Courier*, March 11, 1944]. This group began training early in the year at Mather Field, California, with no segregation, and all went well. When Maj. Gen. Ralph P. Cousins came on an inspection trip he ordered separation in the mess hall. The Negroes no longer use the mess hall. After this the group was shifted to Selfridge Field, Michigan, and then to Godman Field, Kentucky, where conditions were separate and definitely unequal.

1351. Brown, Drew T. III. *You Gotta Believe!: Education + Hard Work - Drugs = The American Dream.* New York: William Morrow, 1991. A former Navy jet pilot, Drew Brown now flies for Federal Express and has established a foundation to help youngsters continue their education and aim high in their career goals. It is an engaging autobiography, with his aviation experiences and the types of planes he flew chronicled in an epilogue, pp.271-285. Brown thinks that story could be another book.

1352. Carter, Elmer A. "Wanted: Jobs in Aviation." *Opportunity* 18 (November 1940): 323. Editorial cites inexcusable racial discrimination and prejudice in American industry. Aviation plants have inaugurated huge training programs for mechanics, but will not hire graduates of the High School of Aviation because they are black.

1353. Christmas, Faith. "Skycap." *Black Enterprise* 11 (January 1981): 15. Losing their jobs, or fighting to keep them, are 2,500 skycaps across the country. Continental has been charged with racial discrimination because it has not discharged in other job categories with so heavy a racial impact.

1354. Cockerham, William. "Black Soldiers Battled Against Racism, Prejudice During War." *Hartford Courant* (September 28, 1992). This article is about all branches of the armed services during World War II, but two former members of the Air Force describe their experiences of discrimination. They are Ralph Cloud and Ambrose Andrews, who both live at the Rocky Hill Veterans' Home and Hospital.

1355. Connes, Keith. "Can a Black Man Fly?" *Flying* (July 1969): 53-57. The answer is "yes." The pilots interviewed are: David E. Harris, American Airlines; Edward A. Gibbs, founder of Negro Airmen International; S. David Bailey, International Aviation; and Pat Connell, pilot and CBS announcer. Each man relates the discrimination he has encountered in the field of aviation, and Gibbs, whose flying experience goes back to the 1940s, gives a historical perspective.

1356. "Court Refuses Job Bias Review." *New York Times* (May 8, 1957). The Appelate Division refused to review the case of Wendell Jeanpierre, who charged that Pan American World Airways denied him a job as a flight steward because of race. His case was dismissed by the State Commission Against Discrimination because his work record consists of eighteen jobs in sixteen years.

1357. "Curbs on Negroes Eased by Airport." *New York Times* (June 28, 1961). Moisant International Airport, New Orleans, has a new policy. It will serve Negroes in the coffee shop. This is the result of a suit brought by the Justice Department because the airport failed to abide by a non-discrimination clause in the agreement, under which Federal funds were used for half the construction costs.

1358. Drew-Holland, Carol. "People & Places." *New York Voice* (October 15, 1983): 10. Biographical information on George Gay Daniel, a pilot and retired NYC Transit Police officer. Recounts incidents of discrimination. Appended to the article is an excerpt from a Department of Commerce report on Negro Aviators, September 1940.

1359. Drew-Holland, Carol. "People & Places." *New York Voice* (October 22, 1983): 10. Biographical information about Theodore W. Robinson, the black pilot who did research for and provided contacts with early black aviators for the exhibition, "Black Wings: The American Black in Aviation." Robinson learned to fly at Tuskegee, and eventually became the first black General Aviation Inspector for the FAA. His attempts to have a career in commercial aviation were thwarted by discrimination.

1360. "Federal Judge Orders USAir to Recruit Blacks." *Jet* 80:11 (July 1, 1991): 38. Judge Donald Zeigler ordered USAir to use standard hiring practices instead of nepotism or backdoor policies. This was the settlement of lawsuits filed by two pilots, Larry Curtis Taylor and Philip Garland in 1986.

1361. "Full Air Unit is Assembled." (April 17, 1943): 1, 2. [No source, but clipping was found on "United States-Army-Air Force-99th Pursuit Squadron" microfiche at the Schomburg Center for Research in Black Culture, New York Public Library]. The 332nd Fighting Group was transferred from Alabama to Selfridge Field in Michigan. This is the first time Negro pilots have been trained in the North. It is believed to be a result of Judge Hastie's resignation because of discrimination. There is a list of names of about 100 commissioned officers.

1362. Greenaway, John. *American Folksongs of Protest*. Philadelphia: University of Pennsylvania, 1953. [The song has been reprinted in *Hammer and Hoe: Alabama Communists During the Great Depression* by Robin D. G. Kelley on p. 209, Chapel Hill: University of North Carolina Press, 1990. The original poem appeared in *Cavalcade* 1:4 (October 1941)]. A song, "Uncle Sam Says" with words by Josh White and Warren Cuney, laments the fact that although everybody's flying, Negroes are not wanted in the Air Force. The second stanza deals with the Navy. Keynote Album 107.

1363. "Half a Million Workers." *Fortune* 23:3 (March 1941): 98, 163. [Special issue on aspects of aviation in the military, commerce, in factories, and laboratories]. The fastest growth a U.S. labor force has ever known crowds green hands around the assembly lines. This article examines the workers, stating the aircraft industry had "an almost universal prejudice against Negroes - and in the West Coast plants against Jews... you almost never see Negroes in aircraft factories... there is little concealment about the anti-Negro policy."

1364. "Hastie Challenges Truth of Statement by War Secretary." *Washington Tribune* (April 17, 1943).

1365. "Hastie Says 99th Squadron Will Go into Action without a Single Veteran Pilot." *Washington Tribune* (March 6, 1943). [This is the fifth article by William H. Hastie. The others were published weekly in February]. These articles were to give the public the examples of racial discrimination "as I have known them in the Army Air Forces for over two years."

1366. "How to Become an Airline Stewardess." *Sepia* 10:10 (October 1961): 67. A very brief article that gives general information, but which also addresses the fact that, "only a handful of Negro girls have been hired for these excellent positions. The National Urban League and the NAACP are tussling with the airlines to get colored girls on planes."

1367. Lambert, Bruce. "Delos Wilson Rentzel Dies at 81; Helped Develop Airline Industry." *New York Times* (September 8, 1991): 44. Rentzel "provoked contoversy in 1948 by ordering an end to segregation at Washington' National Airport, where blacks were barred from the main restaurant and coffee shop. The concessionaire, citing the racial laws of Virginia, at first refused to comply."

1368. "Lawsuit Settled Between Blacks, Braniff Airlines." *Jet* 60:9 (May 14, 1981): 42. Blacks who were rejected for flight attendant jobs from 1973-75 will be awarded $1,000 each as part of an out-of-court settlement. The suit was filed in 1977.

1369. Lazo, Rodrigo. "2 Civilians Accuse George AFB of Racial Discrimination." *Air Force Times* (August 3, 1992): 18. Two black workers charge they were passed up for promotions and harassed by their supervisors at George AFB in California. Each has asked $300, 000 in damages. They are Darlene Boswell, a supply clerk, and Fred McCreary, a branch superintendent.

1370. "Limit Negro Air Jobs." *Kansas City Star* (March 17, 1941). J.H. Kindelberger, president of North American Aviation, told the press that in a new plant he is building, Negroes will only be hired as janitors or in other maintenance work. More than 10,000 employees will work in the new plant at Kansas City.

1371. MacGregor, Morris J., and Bernard C. Nalty. *Blacks in the United States Armed Forces: Basic Documents.* Wilmington, DE: Scholarly Resources, 1977. [13 volumes]. Vol. 4, Segregation entrenched, 1917-1940; Vol. 5, Black soldiers in World War II, and all further volumes deal with aspects of segregation and equal treatment. This is an extraordinary collection.

1372. McGuire, Phillip. *Taps for a Jim Crow Army: Letters from Black Soldiers in World War II.* Santa Barbara, CA: ABC-Clio, 1983. Some of the letters are from men in aviation squadrons. They are, for the most part, letters sent to newspapers to complain of discrimination.

1373. "Michigan Highway Pilot." *Ebony* (February 1958): 4. Marlon D. Green is the only full-time pilot ever hired by the Michigan State Highway Department. Green had been a captain in the Air Force for nine years, but was unable to find employment in commercial aviation.

1374. "Missouri Air School Advertises for 'White U.S. Citizens' Only." *Kansas City Call* (May 24, 1940). The Missouri Aviation Institute, operating under the approval of the U.S. Civil Aeronautics Authority, wants to train only white citizens.

1375. "Montgomery Plans to Close Facilities." *New York Times* (January 5, 1962). Seats will be removed from the waiting rooms at Montgomery's municipal airport, rather than comply with an integration order. Toilets will be locked and water fountains plugged. The restaurant will remain open for now, but will close if "a concerted effort" is made to integrate it.

1376. "NAACP Protests Airforce Aid to Jimcrow Travel." *Daily Worker* (December 1, 1953). "The NAACP appealed to Air Force brass to halt reprimands and suspensions handed Negro personnel who demand their constitutional rights in opposing jimcrow seating in interstate travel." Lt. Thomas Williams was suspended for refusing to sit in the back of the bus in Florida. Three officials of the Air force are quoted.

1377. Nalty, Bernard C., and Morris J. MacGregor. *Blacks in the Military: Essential Documents*. Wilmington: Scholarly Resources, 1981. A one-volume work, using documents or selections which show how the racial policies of the armed forces evolved from discrimination to impartial treatment. Eleven chapters, from slavery to the early 1970s, use military orders, letters, memoranda, reports, articles in periodicals, and other documents to trace this development. There is no separate chapter on the Air Force, but the index has many citations.

1378. "Negro Air Officer 'Forced' to Resign." *New York Times* (November 25, 1956). Lt. Titus A. Saunders Jr., at Lockbourne AFB, Ohio, claims he is being forced to resign his commission because of Sen. Stennis of Mississippi. Saunders was in an auto accident in Mississippi, but a companion was driving. Police asked him to drive the car to the curb, and then arrested him for drunken driving.

1379. "Negro Flyers Find Bias at Soo Locks." *New York Times* (August 30, 1953). Negro airmen assigned to guard the Sault Ste. Marie canals in Michigan find that barber shops, restaurants, and taverns refuse to serve them. They are welcomed in Canada less than a mile away. The troops are pleased with the base, but once off base, there is nothing to do and they encounter hostility.

1380. "Negro Graduate Refused Job by Aircraft Company." *California Voice* (September 13, 1940). William A. Dickinson Jr., who completed a training course at Bakersfield (California) Junior College in aircraft metal, was told by San Diego Consolidated Aircraft Company that no Negroes would be accepted.

1381. "Negro Leader Tells of Airport Threat." *New York Times* (September 25, 1960). Gloster B. Current was denied service at the airport restaurant in Charleston, SC. Current, director of branches for the NAACP, was in town for the group's annual convention. He threatened legal action.

1382. "Negro Officers Held in Air Force Dispute." *St. Louis Post-Dispatch* (April 12, 1945). Charges are being filed against three Negro officers for "jostling" a provost marshall on duty at Freeman Field Army Air Base, Indiana. The officers are: Marsden A. Thompson, Shirley R. Clinton, and Roger C. Terry. They protested discrimination and they may face court martial proceedings. This largely reports a story in the *New York Post*.

1383. "Negro Pilots." *Crisis* 70 (March 1963): 156-157. Industry discrimination in general, and the case of Marlon Green in particular.

1384. "New Yorker Refused in Army Air Corps." *Crisis* 47 (November 1940): 359. [Roy Wilkins was the editor and may have been the writer]. Lt. Thomas Dale Davis was refused further training as a pilot because "there are no units composed of colored men."

1385. "North American Aviation Figures Show Minority Discrimination is True." *News & Letters* (1966). [Schomburg Center for Research in Black Culture, New York Public Library, Fiche-Airlines-Employment]. Statistics released by NAA show that while they do hire minorities "by the droves," it is only for the lowest-paying jobs. Reference to an article in the *Los Angeles Times*, October 17, 1966.

1386. Norwood, William R. "A Guiding Brotherhood." *Air Line Pilot* 58:2 (February 1989): 26-28. Norwood, a pilot for United Air Lines, and president of the Organization of Black Airline Pilots, gives the history of the group. Its purpose is to assist black pilots, to help increase black participation in aviation, and to motivate young people.

1387. Osur, Alan M. *Blacks in the Army Air Forces during World War II: The Problem of Race Relations.* Washington, D.C.: Office of Air Force History, 1977. Based on the author's Ph.D. dissertation, this work examines racial attitudes of the War Department and the black community before, during and after the war. It describes the protests and riots which discrimination provoked. He also describes the role of black pilots in the Mediterranean Theater against the Axis power. Bibliography, pp. 207-217.

1388. "Panel Faults Airlines on Hiring of Blacks." *New York Times* (August 1, 1988): D10. A House of Representatives committee charged that airlines had failed to hire enough blacks as pilots or in other professional positions. The report notes that little progress has been made, and that some airlines have regressed. The following statistics are given: blacks make up 30 percent of unskilled workers and less than two percent of professionals; no more than 200 of the industry's 45,000 pilots are black.

1389. Peck, Jim. "As Jim Crow Flies." *Independent* (February 1958). Peck, himself a pilot, writes about the color bar in aviation. He is struck by the contrast between the antiquated employment policies of the airlines with their being at the forefront of the most modern means of transportation. There is mention of the current group seeking to cross the barrier: Ruth Carol Taylor, Perry H. Young, and Dorothy Franklin.

1390. "Personnel: The Race Problem." *Time* (February 8, 1943): 58. "The smoldering bitterness of U.S. Negroes against segregation in the services flared into flame again last week." The occasion was the resignation of William H. Hastie as the Negro Civilian Aide to the Secretary of War. Hastie resigned because the Army continued segregation. Article concludes, "Judge Hastie's airing did his cause no harm."

1391. Phillips, Don. "Study Finds Few Black Airline Pilots." *Washington Post* (August 1, 1988): A4. A report on a study done by the House Government Operations Committee. The report states that fewer than 200 of the country's 45,000 airline pilots are black, and that airlines have done little to promote blacks to other professional and managerial jobs. The study focussed on the largest airlines: United, TWA, and American. Some factors are beyond the control of the industry, but a large part of the blame must be laid to the "old-boy network." Other statistics quoted are from EEOC studies in 1986 that blacks are 30.5 per cent of unskilled airline workers (19.5 per cent in other industries) and 1.6 per cent of airline professionals (4.7 per cent in other industries.) The study was aided by the Organization of Black Airline Pilots, who submitted 47 letters from black pilots telling of numerous job rejections.

1392. Price, Jo-ann. "T.W.A. to Hire Negro Air Hostess." *New York Herald Tribune* (February 10, 1958). T.W.A. will be the first American international commercial airline to hire a Negro girl as a flight hostess in 90 days. The announcement came the day before the result was due from the hearing against T.W.A., which was brought by Dorothy Franklin. Franklin may not be the one selected.

1393. "Reneging on Bias Laid to Airlines." *New York Times* (July 3, 1957). The Urban League of Greater New York charged that sixteen of eighteen airlines had failed to abide by their agreement, made nine months ago, to hire qualified Negroes in flight service jobs. The two airlines employing Negroes are New York Airways, a helicopter service, and Seabord and Western, a cargo carrier.

1394. Rorty, James. "The First Colored Air Hostess." *Crisis* 65:6 (June/July 1958): 339-342. In December 1958 Ruth Coral Taylor became the first black hostess, for Mohawk Airlines, New York. She was assisted by the New York State Commission Against Discrimination (SCAD). Most of the article is about SCAD's work. At press time Margaret Grant became the first black hostess on an international airline, TWA.

1395. "SCLC Plans Boycott of Delta Air Lines." *Washington Post* (September 3, 1970): A2. The Southern Christian Leadership Conference in Atlanta has planned a boycott of Delta Air Lines, based in that city. SCLC contends that there aren't enough Negroes employed in professional jobs, they are employed as maintenance workers only. Delta denies this. Statistics.

1396. "Screen Segregation Banned at Airport." *New York Times* (January 7, 1960). A Federal District Court has banned the practice of putting Negroes behind a screen when they eat at the airport restaurant in Atlanta, Georgia.

1397. "Seek Negro Applicants for Airlines Jobs." *Daily Worker* (July 23, 1954). The New York Urban League has held meetings with various airline companies in the effort to open up non-menial jobs to Negroes.

1398. "Select Two Race Colleges for Civil Aviation Courses." *Pittsburgh Courier* (September 16, 1939): 2. The Civilian Aviation Authority (CAA) named Agriculture and Technical College at Greensboro, North Carolina and West Virginia State College at Institute, West Virginia, as centers for the civilian pilot training program. Only these two, out of 166 colleges, are for Negroes. The newspaper mentions its campaign, started twenty months ago, to blot out discrimination in the armed forces.

1399. "Southerner Protests Use of Negro Flyers." *St. Louis Post-Dispatch* (December 19, 1944). The father of a white pilot killed in a crash with a plane piloted by a Negro says Negroes are not yet qualified. He blames the government for moving too fast, not the Negro pilot, who was also killed, along with eleven others.

1400. Spivack, Robert G. "Into the Wild Blue Segregated Yonder." *New York Post* (September 6, 1958). Recounts the passing back and forth of responsibility between the Department of Defense and the U.S. Office of Education on the case of the Little Rock Air Force Base school.

1401. Spivack, Robert G. "A Jim Crow School? AF 'Still Working on It'."
New York Post (August 26, 1958). [The paper had an editorial "Surrender" on August 24, 1958 on this subject]. Air Force officals bowed last week to an Arkansas demand that a school built for Air Force personnel with federal funds be restricted to white students. It is just outside the base, and so is subject to state laws. There were indications that this would not be allowed to stand.

1402. "Stimson Aide Quits; Charges Army With Race Bias." *New York Post* (February 1, 1943). William H. Hastie cited his reason for resigning was to protest "discriminatory practices of the Army Air Forces in matters affecting Negroes."

1403. "Suits Accuse Airline of Anti-Negro Bias." *New York Times* (March 30, 1950). Elmer W. Henderson and John E. Myles Jr. have filed separate actions against American Airlines and Sky Chefs. They were refused service in an airport restaurant in Covington, Kentucky.

1404. "Too Dark for Army Air Corps." *Crisis* 47 (September 1940): 279. [Roy Wilkins was the editor]. This editorial tells of a young Negro student at the University of Minnesota who was rejected for further training by the U.S. Army Air Corps, because "there is no place for Negroes." The student was later accepted in Canada for Great Britain's Royal Air Force. The editorial comments that if bombs were to be dropped in Boston or New York they'd have room for anyone who could stay in the air for thirty minutes.

1405. "T.W.A. Chooses Negro to Fill Executive Job in Office Here." *New York Times* (August 28, 1957). James O. Plinton was appointed executive assistant to the director of personnel and industrial relations. Both President Nixon and the Urban League hailed this appointment. The NAACP, although pleased, remarked that this in no way changes the fact that Trans World Airlines practiced discrimination.

1406. "T.W.A. Hires a Negro Student to Become Flight Stewardess." *New York Times* (May 12, 1958). [An editorial appeared the following day]. Margaret Grant, a psychology major at Hunter College, became the third person to break the ban on Negroes on the airlines. It is the first hiring connected to an anti-discrimination suit. Dorothy Franklin, who brought the suit, dropped it when Grant was hired.

1407. "$2 Million Settlement Ends Air Force Race-Bias Case." *New York Times* (January 14, 1981). After a class action suit, the Air Force has to establish a $2 million fund, and Eglin AFB has to hire 100 black workers for their civilian labor force. They also have to promote immediately twenty civilians who are already employed.

1408. Twombley, Mark R. "Pilots: Lang J. Stanley." *Pilot (Airplane Owners & Pilots Association)* (June 1989): 130. Lang J. Stanley is based in Los Angeles, and flies a Cessna 182. He is a counselor to veterans. Article recounts roadblocks put in his way because he is black.

1409. "U.S. to Pay $2 Million to Blacks in Bias Case at Florida Air Base." *New York Times* (March 8, 1981). Hundreds of black workers and job applicants will begin receiving payments as a result of a class action suit.

1410. "USAir Settles Suit of 2 Black Pilots Charging Bias." *New York Times* (June 13, 1991): 27. USAir agreed to discontinue a hiring practice that gave preference to relatives of employees. The lawsuit was brought against the airline by Philip A. Garland and Larry C. Taylor, who both work for USAir, but who are entitled to back pay. The airline must also recruit black pilots and issue a statement it will not tolerate harassment of employees because of race.

1411. Wechsler, James A. "Anti-Negro Bias Charged." *PM (New York)* (February 1, 1943). Article reprints William H. Hastie's letter of resignation, containing specific charges of discrimination in the Air Force.

1412. "Whites and Negroes Battle at Air Base." *New York Times* (March 24, 1960). Racial violence, including a cross burning, broke out at an integrated radar station in Albuquerque, New Mexico. The violence occured after a dance. Those involved face courts-martial.

1413. "Wild White Yonder." *Saturday Review* (January 18, 1958). Notes Ruth Carol Taylor is the first Negro stewardess ever to fly on regularly scheduled American plane. She will fly for Mohawk Airlines, after having been rejected by Trans World Airlines for "intangible reasons."

1414. "Williams to Study Bias Charge at Soo." *New York Times* (September 3, 1953). Governor Williams acknowledged that some businesses in Sault Ste. Marie have violated the Michigan Civil Rights Statute. They have refused to serve black airmen stationed there to guard the locks. Gov. Williams intends to talk to community leaders to work out the problem.

1415. Witkin, Richard. "Aviation: Stewardess." *New York Times* (December 24, 1957). [Articles on Taylor also appeared in *Time* and *Newsweek* on January 6, 1958]. Biographical information on Ruth Carol Taylor, as well as an analysis of discrimination by airlines.

History

1416. "The Baggy Pants of Black Paratroopers." *Eagle & Swan* 1:2 (March 1978): 48-49. In 1944, 16 blacks arrived at Ft. Bennington, Georgia, to be trained as paratroopers. Despite taunts and lack of faith that they would succeed, they trained harder than was required. They became the nucleus of the 555th Parachute Company, also known as the Triple Nickles [*sic*]. Today there are 4,000 black paratroopers.

1417. Barbour, George Edward. "Early Black Flyers of Western Pennsylvania, 1906-1945." *Western Pennsylvania Historical Magazine* 69:2 (April 1986): 95-119. Barbour, himself a pilot, gives a historical survey of pilots in Pennsylvania. He also mentions pilots from other states. Barbour identifies Charles Wesley Peters as the first black pilot, 1911. There is biographical information on: Eugene Bullard, James L. H. Peck, Charles Vincent Proctor, George Allen, Raymond Jackson, Abram P. Jackson, Joseph D. Ellison, Charles Asa Ross, Lawrence E. Anderson Jr., Charles Foxx, James T. Wiley, William O. Thompson, Marshall Fields, William H. Edwards, Mary L. Parker, Clarence Jamison, Rose Rolls, and Art Barnes.

1418. Biggs, Bradley. *Gavin*. Hamden, CT: Archon Books, an imprint of Shoe String Press, 1980. [Black author, *The Triple Nickles*]. Biography of Gen. James M. Gavin, a combat leader and airborne commander, who later headed a research company and was ambassador to France. Biggs knew Gavin when he tried to ease racial restrictions for the 555th Parachute Infantry Battalion, the Triple Nickles [*sic*].

1419. Biggs, Bradley. *The Triple Nickles [sic]: America's First All-Black Paratroop Unit*. Hamden, Ct: Archon Books, imprint of the Shoe String Press, 1986. Captain Biggs narrates the history of the 555th Parachute

Infantry Battalion, the first all-black parachute unit in the world, and the first army unit to be integrated into the Army Strategic Reserve.

1420. "Black Americans in Flight." *American Visions* 5:6 (December 1990): 10-11. A mural, 51 feet long and titled "Black Americans in Flight," has been placed on permanent display at Lambert International Airport in St. Louis.The mural depicts 75 African-American aviators and was painted by Spencer Taylor. The drive to complete and install the mural was spearheaded by Vesta Pruitt, daughter of Wendell Pruitt, one of the aviators depicted.

1421. "Black Aviation Mural Unveiled at Lambert St. Louis International Airport." *South Carolina Black Media Group* (August 30 - September 5, 1990): 3A. A mural by Spencer Taylor was unveiled August 13 before a capacity crowd. The five-panel 51-foot-long mural is called Black Americans in Flight.

1422. *Black Aviators and Astronauts.* New York: Black Achievers Project, 1990. This set of posters depicts eight African Americans who played a role in aerospace. Each 17-by-22 poster includes a black and white photograph and a brief biography. The subjects are Guion S. Bluford, Willa B. Brown, Eugene J. Bullard, Bessie Coleman, Frederick D. Gregory, Mae C. Jemison, Ronald E. McNair, and the Tuskegee Airmen. They are distributed by Black Books Plus, 702 Amsterdam Avenue, New York, NY 10025.

1423. *Black Pilots of New York: 25th Anniversary Celebration.* New York, 1992. This souvenir journal marks the 25th anniversary of the Black Pilots of New York, a chapter of Negro Airmen International (NAI). It was held at the Family Life Center, 172-17 Linden Blvd., St. Albans, NY, on November 1, 1992. There is full-page information on the following pilots: Edward A. Gibbs, the founder of NAI, Melva Jackman, the current chapter president, C. Alfred Anderson, Leslie A. Morris, W. Anthony Manswell, Roscoe C. Brown Jr., Eddie Raynord Hadden, Alfred Porter, David Strachan, Ronald Sadler, Anthony Samuel, Ruby L. Bostic, John Dunham, Joyce C. Ware, Joseph H. Haynes, Richard Rock, Cecil S. Hueston Jr., Augustus L. Barnes, George Gay Daniel, and Levere D.L. Deane. Many other flyers are mentioned as well, making this publication an important source of information.

1424. "'Black Wings' Exhibit." *Western Queens Gazette* (September 14-20, 1983). The Smithsonian exhibition opened September 13, at the International Arrivals Building at JFK Airport. The exhibition has a new feature, "New York Black Wings," which tells the story of regional blacks in aviation.

1425. "Black Wings: The American Black in Aviation." *Ebony Jr!* 10:8 (February 1983): 29. Information about the Smithsonian Institution's exhibition: hours, organization.

1426. Brown, Tony. "The Triple Nickles: America's First all-Black Paratrooper Unit." *New York Times Book Review* (June 29, 1986). [Book review]. Brown does not really review the book, but reminds us there were two wars going on in World War II. Segregated black paratroops "never lost faith in a country that had little faith in them." And it "tells the story of how pride overcame ignorance and racism."

1427. Drew-Holland, Carol. "People & Places." *New York Voice* (October 1, 1983): 11. Descriptive biographical article about Joe Haynes, a pilot, an engineer, a railroad safety specialist, and a member of Negro Airmen International. Haynes is an aviation historian and he assisted with the exhibition, "Black Wings: The American Black in Aviation." In September he was one of the recipients of the annual awards given by the National Black Coalition of Federal Aviation Employees. Also included is an excerpt from a report of the Department of Commerce, September 1940, giving the numbers of Negroes holding various kinds of licenses during the years 1935-1940.

1428. Duggan, Dennis. "Blacks Who Soared Above the Bias." *Newsday* (June 6, 1983). Review of "Black Wings: The American Black in Aviation" when it opened at the American Museum of Natural History. The exhibition points out history that is largely unknown, because blacks received no notice even when their achievements were remarkable. Stories are told by pilots Clarence D. Lester, Charles Smith, and John W. Greene.

1429. Duvall, Henry. "Black Military Experience Captured." *New York Amsterdam News* (April 27, 1985): 10. The Moorland-Spingarn Research Center of Howard University recently added to its collection transcripts and oral history tapes of interviews with black service men in World War

II. The Black Military Oral History Project was launched in 1981. The Air Force member cited in the article is Col. Dudley Wardell Stevenson.

1430. "First Monument Recognizing Black Aviators is Unveiled." *Jet* 78:21 (September 3, 1990): 34. A 51-foot long mural depicting black Americans in aviation has been unveiled at the St. Louis Lambert International Airport. The artist is Spencer Taylor, and he depicts 75 aviators from 1917 to the present.

1431. Gropman, Alan L. *The Air Force Integrates*. Washington, D.C.: Office of Air Force History, 1978. Based on the author's dissertation, the book chronicles the Air Force's evolutionary development away from segregation and towards equal opportunity. Statistical appendices and documents; bibliography pp. 353-365.

1432. Hardesty, Von, and Dominick Pisano. *Black Wings: The American Black in Aviation*. Washington, D.C.: National Air and Space Museum, Smithsonian Institution, 1983. Exhibition catalog of photographs, text, and documents. This landmark exhibition created great interest in the subject, and is now on permanent display at the Museum.

1433. Hunton, Benjamin L. "Aviation and the Negro." (May 13, 1939). [I was not able to locate the periodical, although the article is from the Claude A. Barnett Papers, Chicago Historical Society. This is "a series of articles on the Colored man in civilization's least known-about industry."]. This is a lengthy article about Howard University's efforts to make it one of the centers for aviation courses. An interview with Dr. James M. Nabritt Jr., executive assistant to the president of the University.

1434. "Johnson Approves Air Force Plan to Distribute Negroes Among Units." *New York Times* (May 12, 1949): 54. The Secretary of Defense, Louis Johnson, approved Air Force proposals for integration.

1435. Kriz, Marjorie. "They Had Another Dream: Blacks Took to the Air Early." *FAA World* 10:2 (February 1980): 2-6. A brief history of blacks in aviation which manages to cover many events and people, and is illustrated with twelve photographs.

1436. Low, W. Augustus, and Virgil A. Clift. *Encyclopedia of Black America*. New York: McGraw-Hill, 1981. Entry on Aviation, pp. 145-146, further references.

1437. Matheus, John F. "'All God's Chillun Gittin' Wings'." *Opportunity*
19:10 (October, 1941): 299-301, 316. Brief history of the government's
decision to establish centers of "training in flying at the several land-
grant colleges, including at least one Negro school." Gives the names of
ten colleges that have programs and mentions Willa B. Brown, James C.
Evans, Mac Ross, L.D. Davis, Ralph Jackson, Edward Wilson, Marshall
Fields, Rose Agnes Rolls, Wilson Eagleson, Hector Strong, Lloyd Hathcock, Charles D. Minor, George Dananche, Troy W. Newkirke, and Max
Bondurant. Notes that *Contact*, the official bulletin of the National Airmen's Association appeared in May 1941.

1438. Mattison, E. G. "Integrating the Work Force in Southern Industry."
147-154. [This article is in Herbert R. Northrop and Richard L. Rowan,
eds. *The Negro and Employment Opportunity*, Ann Arbor, MI: Bureau of
Industrial Relations, University of Michigan, 1965]. Lockheed's policy
on segregation and integration in the forties and fifties.

1439. Messiha, Khalil. "African Experimental Aeronautics: A 2,000-Year-Old
Model Glider." *Journal of African Civilizations* 5 (April/ November
1983): 92-99. [Also published as *Blacks in Science Ancient and Modern*,
edited by Ivan Van Sertima, New Brunswick, NJ: Transaction Books,
1983]. Egyptians were experimenting with flying machines as early as
the 4th or 3rd century B.C. Messiha describes a wooden model in the
Egyptian Museum in Cairo, which was discovered in Sakkara in 1898.
Photos and diagrams are included.

1440. Northrup, Herbert R. *The Negro in the Aerospace Industry*. Philadelphia:
University of Pennsylvania, Wharton School of Finance and Commerce,
1968. [Report No. 2 of the Racial Policies of American Industry].

1441. Northrup, Herbert R., Armand J. Thieblot Jr., and William N. Chernish.
The Negro in the Air Transport Industry. Philadelphia: University of
Pennsylvania, The Wharton School of Finance and Commerce, 1971.
[Report No. 23 of The Racial Policies of American Industry].

1442. Peters, Raymond, and Clinton M. Arnold. *Black Americans in Aviation*.
San Diego: Neyenesch Printers, Inc., 1975. "This is a chronicle of the
very limited progress that the black man had made, and is making, in an
effort to become part of a single...phase of endeavour. It is a true, but by
no means all encompassing, outline." Section I, pp. 3-21, is a history

from 1903 to 1974; Section II, pp. 23-74, includes biographical information and photographs; Section III, pp. 76-80, provides a list of the members of the Negro Airmen International.

1443. Reynolds, Pamela. "The Black Aviators." *Boston Globe* (February 10, 1986): 11, 13. Philip S. Hart, professor at the University of Massachusetts, is digging up information about early black flyers.

1444. Rowe, Billy. "Flight History Jets into 20th Century." *New York Amsterdam News* (October 16, 1982): 13. Rowe gives a fine review of the Smithsonian's exhibition, "Black Wings: The American Black in Aviation." He recaps the history from 1917 to 1939, and promises the rest in a future column.

1445. Schlitz, William P. "Blacks in U.S. Aviation: The Pioneers." *Air Force Magazine* (January 1983): 68-72. A historical sketch up to 1941. "Since the beginning of powered flight, black Americans have been steadfast in their determination to overcome barriers of racial discrimination and economic privation to share in the wonders of flying." There is a box describing the exhibition "Black Wings" at the National Air and Space Museum.

1446. Schlitz, William P. "Blacks in Aviation: From Tuskegee to Space." *Air Force Magazine* (February 1983): 74-79. "While social equality is far from a reality in America, over the past 40 years major progress has been made. Nowhere is this more evident in the efforts of black Americans to pursue careers in aviation." The information in this two-part series comes from NASA's exhibition, "Black Wings."

1447. "West Virginia State College First To Be Approved For Air Pilots." *Pittsburgh Courier* (July 1940): [I was not able to locate this article for date and pagination]. On September 11, 1939 the West Virginia State College was approved by the Civil Aeronautics Authority as the first training site for Negroes. Newly certified pilots are Hector Strong, Marshall Fields, Vashon Eagleson, Rose Agnes Rolls, Edward Wilson, L.D. Davis, Lloyd Hathcock, Dorothy A. Layne, Andrew Hester, Mac Ross, Alfonso Dowell, Charles Brown, and Robert Lee Robinson. Nine other students who are completing requirements for a pilot's certificate are listed.

Women

1448. "Advertisement." *Ebony* (December 1964). Clyde Sumpter made up her mind to become an airline stewardess the day her dog had puppies. She has been with American Airlines for five years.

1449. "Advertisement." *People* (September 8, 1980): 1. Charlotte Smith is a reservation sales agent for Delta Airlines. She has been with the company for eight years.

1450. "Advertisement." *Ebony* (November 1980): 1. Myrna Anderson is responsible for the management of eleven flight attendant supervisors. They guide nearly 1,000 flight attendants for Eastern Airlines.

1451. "Advertisement." *Essence* 13:12 (April 1983): 130. Gwendolyn Williams, a reservations sales agent for Delta Airlines, is featured.

1452. "Aerodynamics Research Engineer." *Ebony* (January 1985): 7. Christine Mann Darden is a senior projects engineer at Langley Research Center for NASA. Named Hampton's outstanding 20-year alumnus [*sic*].

1453. "Aerospace Professor." *Ebony* (June 1983): 7. 1st Lieut. Sandra Myers teaches aerospace studies for the ROTC program at Boston University.

1454. "African Girls Take Wings." *Sepia* 13:1 (January 1964): 40-43. First African girls to train as stewardesses for East African Airways have just completed their course at Nairobi. Recruitment for African girls began in 1961; on the last course seven of 22 girls were African. Qualifications are given, only one of 20 is accepted. Those shown are Lucy Semakula of Uganda, a stewardess, and three receptionists: Grace Awori, Francisca Peter, and Elma Hilton.

1455. "Air Force Gets 1st Black Female Non-Medical Col." *Jet* 65:13 (December 5, 1983): 13. Lt. Col. Rosetta Armour-Lightner is one of fewer than 25 women in the Air Force who are colonels or higher. She is head of Air Force ROTC at Grambling State University.

1456. "Air Force Graduates First Black Woman Pilot." *Ebony* (January 1983): 46, 48. The first black woman pilot for the U.S. Air Force is 2nd Lt. Theresa Claiborne, at Laughlin AFB, Texas.

1457. "Air Force's Education Expert." *Ebony* (November 1969): 88-91. Col. Ruth Lucas is the highest ranking black woman in the Air Force. She organizes programs to raise the educational level of personnel. Of the 45,000 men who enter the military annually, almost all read below 5th grade, and 30 per cent of these are black. Biographical information about Col. Lucas, who has been in the military 27 years.

1458. "Air Pair." *Ebony* (April 1987): 36, 38, 40. Howard and Barbara Williams are an air traffic couple who keep planes and their marriage on course in Cleveland. Of 14,000 air controllers, 1,153 are black.

1459. "Air Route Controller." *Ebony* (February 1977): 6. Barbara A. Williams is an air traffic controller specialist with the Federal Aviation Administration in Cleveland. Her husband is also an air traffic controller.

1460. "Air Traffic Agent." *Ebony* (December 1961): 7. Joan E. Wiltshire is a traffic agent for Lufthansa German Airlines at New York's International Airport.

1461. "Air Traffic Manager." *Ebony* (November 1988): 6. Barbara Gardner-Martin is an air traffic manager at the Detroit City Airport. She is a member of the Negro Airmen International.

1462. "Aircraft Training Scheduler." *Ebony* (February 1992): 8. Karen E. Davenport is a scheduler and planner at Boeing Co. in Seattle.

1463. "Airline General Manager." *Ebony* (May 1985): 6. Joyce M. Coleman is general manager of inflight services for Trans World Airlines at St. Louis, the airline's largest domestic terminal.

1464. "Airline Promotion Manager." *Ebony* (June 1979): 6. Carrie J. Surratt has worked for Pan American Airlines in Washington, D.C. for 11 years. She is an ordained minister.

1465. "Airlines Clerk." *Ebony* (October 1955): 5. Patricia Yates is the first Negro airlines clerk employed by American Airlines in Chicago.

1466. Airports Authority of Trinidad & Tobago. *The History of Aviation in Trinidad & Tobago, 1913-1962*. Newton, Port-of-Spain: Paria Pub. Co., 1987. From the photographs it appears most of the people involved were white. The exceptions are Ulric Cross, now a judge, but who fought over Germany with the RAF, p.92, and Pearl Marshall Beard, the first black BWIA air hostess (1956), and the first to fly on international flights, pp.110-111.

1467. Allen, Zita. "'Take-Off From a Forced Landing' is Powerful, Exciting." *New York Amsterdam News* (June 30, 1984). An enthusiastic review of Dianne McIntyre's new dance about her mother who was a pilot, Dorothy L. McIntyre. Allen comments that "one of the most powerful elements ... are the revealing reminiscences of Mrs. McIntyre whose spirit soared in spite of racist restrictions ... as she watched her children take flight not instead of her, but because of her."

1468. Allsup, Dan. "Quest for the Gold." *Airman* (January 1985): 37-42. Second Lt. Alonzo Babers won two gold medals at the 1984 Olympic Games for track. He is the first Air Force Academy graduate to win an Olympic gold medal. His sister Teresa is also a second lieutenant in the Air Force.

1469. "Antonia Martin Receives Stewardess Wings." *Sun-Reporter [Miami]* (December 9, 1967): 15. Photograph shows Antonia Cottrell Martin during graduation ceremonies in October at Pan Am International Stewardess College in Miami.

1470. Aquilante, Daniel. "High-Flying Dancers at Joyce." *New York Post* (June 22, 1984). Brief notice of Dianne McIntyre's "Take-Off From a Forced Landing," the story of her mother, Dorothy Layne McIntyre, a pilot.

1471. "Arizona Stewardess Gets Wings." *Sepia* 12:10 (October 1963): 8-13. [Cover story]. Joan Dorsey, in the top ten per cent of her class is a stewardess for American Airlines. She may be the first at American, but since they keep no records by race, it is hard to tell. Dorsey describes her rigorous training, and there is biographical information.

1472. "Armed Forces Employ Top Negro Civilians." *Ebony* (May 1958): 20-22, 24, 26. Photos and brief descriptions of work done by twenty-seven Negro scientists, both civilian and military, in government research. There is also a list of companies not providing information for *Ebony*. Some of the scientists mentioned are: C. M. Davenport, Edward L. Harris, U.S. Taylor, Elmore Kennedy, Jesse J. Mayes, Milton H.Hopkins Jr., John W. Lee, Elmer D. Jones, Ambrose M. Nutt, Frank A. Crossley, Charles E. Stewart, John W. Blanton, William Brooks, Oliver L. Harris, Boyd Hall Jr., Arthur R. Blackwell, William H. Ramsey, Jewel Rich, Cynthia Cannaday, and Archie D.Lytle.

1473. "Army's First Black Woman Pilot Finds Challenge Exciting." *Birmingham News* (November 26, 1979). Lt. Marcella A. Hayes graduates from the Army Aviation School at Ft. Rucker, Alabama. She flies helicopters and has a paratrooper's badge. Biographical information and course description.

1474. "Army's First Black Woman Pilot." *New York Amsterdam News* (December 8, 1979). Information about Marcella A. Hayes, who will pilot helicopters.

1475. "Aviation." *Opportunity* 14:6 (June 1936): 188. The Division of Negro Affairs, Bureau of Foreign and Domestic Commerce, reveals that at least 55 Negroes, two of them women, hold licenses from the Bureau of Air Commerce. Other statistics as well.

1476. "Aviation's Pied Piper." *Ebony* (November 1978): 106-108, 110. Ida Van Smith, a licensed private pilot and ground instructor, runs eleven flight clubs for youngsters in New York, Texas, North Carolina, and St. Lucia. Biographical information.

1477. "Aviation School's Branch Instituted." *New York Amsterdam News* (May 7, 1930). The American Aviation School, 736 Lexington Ave., opened a branch in Harlem at 222 W. 135th St. Mr. and Mrs. William Daughtry are in charge. He is the manager, and Mary, a parachute jumper for the last ten years, is an instructor.

1478. Baker, Rob. "Dianne McIntyre Takes Off in Dance." *New York Daily News* (June 19, 1984). Information about Dorothy Layne McIntyre, a pilot and the subject of her daughter's dance, "Take-Off from a Forced Landing."

1479. "A Beauty Learns to Fly." *Ebony* (June 1956): 55-58. Bonnie Collins, a black model and pilot, and Bob Garrity, a white disk jockey, are planning to marry. They fell in love while Garrity taught Collins to fly in New York.

1480. Bennett, Lerone. "Integration in the Air Force Abroad." *Ebony* (March 1960): 27-30, 32, 34-35. [Benjamin O. Davis Jr. is on the cover]. Report of a 9,000 mile trip by the author and a photographer, G. Marshall Wilson. The author notes that while integration in the United States is still unacceptable in many areas, it is no longer a major problem in the U. S. Air Force. It works best in foreign countries where there is no tradition of discrimination. Germany is the location.Biographical information on Benjamin O. Davis, pp.28-30. Those mentioned, with photographs and brief information are: Lee A. Archer, Nelson S. Brooks, Lonnie King, Sybil Evans, Eddice C. Joplin, Annie V. Williams, Jordan Johnson, Thomas B. Smith, Sylvia Crooks, Delia Frances Greer, and Isaiah Johnson.

1481. "'Bird' Colonel at War College." *Ebony* (March 1985): 94, 96, 98. Rosetta Armour-Lightner sets a precedent with Air Force line rank. She was chosen to attend Air War College at Air University, Maxwell AFB, Montgomery. Only the Air Forces top 10 per cent are invited to enrol. Biographical information.

1482. "Black Coed at Armed Forces College." *Ebony* (November 1970): 108-110, 112. Air Force Major Bernice McGhee is the first black woman to attend Armed Forces Staff College at Norfolk, VA. In the Air force since 1954, she has served in Spain.

1483. "Black Fashion Designers." *Black Enterprise* 3:5 (December 1972): 46-47. Gail Fox, former airline stewardess and dressmaker, teamed up with Ric Daniels to form Foxey World.

1484. "'Black Pilots of NY' Back Again for Mas'." *Sunday Guardian (Trinidad and Tobago)* (February 25, 1990). Fifteen black pilots, representing Negro Airmen International, flew to Trinidad on a commemorative trip. There were four women pilots in the group. The purpose was to celebrate Black History Month and to mark the first Goodwill Flight made by C. Alfred Anderson and the late Dr. Albert Forsythe in 1934. The pilots were led by the association's president, Melva Jackman. "Mas'" refers to Carnival in Trinidad.

1485. "Black Woman Heads Gary's Second Largest Airport." *Jet* 40 (September 2, 1971): 15. Jan Tate is probably the first woman to manage an airport in the U.S., and probably the only black woman to do so.

1486. "Black Woman Named AF Brigadier General." *Los Angeles Times* (January 11, 1990). Col. Marcelite J. Harris is the first black woman to hold this rank in the Air Force. A 1964 graduate of Spelman College, Harris was the Air Force's first black aircraft maintenance officer.

1487. "Black Woman Pilot: Flying the Friendly Skies." *Ebony* (April 1991): 62, 64, 66. Biographical sketch of Shirley Tyus, first black woman pilot at United Airlines. There are three other black women among the more than 7,000 pilots.

1488. "Breaking the Sex Barrier: Women in Non-Traditional Jobs." *Ebony* (December 1987): 100. Marie Heaney, after 11 years as secretary at United Airlines in California, became a mechanic at the company.

1489. "Brenda Robinson: Flying High." *Eagle & Swan* 3:6 (December 1980): 25-26. Robinson is the first and only black woman aviator in the U.S. Navy. Biographical information about Robinson, although she shuns interviews and downplays her achievements. Technical information about the planes she flies, and about planes she may not fly.

1490. "Brig. Gen. Marcelite J. Harris: The Air Force's First Black Female General." *Ebony* (December 1992): 62, 64, 66. Harris is now the vice commander of the Oklahoma City Air Logistics Center at Tinker AFB, and she has over 27 years of service. Biographical information as well as a description of her duties.

1491. Burgen, Michelle. "Flying High: Careers in Aviation." *Essence* 10:8 (December 1979): 28, 30, 34. Burgen, herself a pilot, describes three women who took off in new career directions. They are: Brenda Thomas, who was a teacher, but is now an air traffic controller; Pat Graham, an aircraft mechanic; and Jill Brown, a pilot. Includes statistics and information on where to write for brochures.

1492. Burgen, Michelle. "Winging it at 25,000 Feet." *Ebony* 33 (August 1978): 58-60, 62. Burgen, herself a pilot, profiles Jill Brown, the first and only black woman pilot for a major commercial airline. Brown, a former teacher, flies for Texas International Airlines. She once flew for Wheeler Airlines. Statistics.

1493. "BWIA Hostess Finds Herself Unlikely Heroine." *New York Amsterdam News* (July 20, 1985): 31-32. Pearl Marshall Beard arrived at New York's Idlewild Airport twenty-nine years ago to find herself the center of attention, because she was the first black hostess ever to fly in the United States. She is a native of Trinidad and she is now the manager of public relations/sales at the Holiday Inn in Port-of-Spain. She is also a member of the board of directors of BWIA there, the only woman, and the only one to have been employed by the airline.

1494. "Californians Take Lead in Aviation." *Chicago Defender* (May 23, 1936): 20. Photographs show William J. Powell, head of the Craftsmen of Black Wings. This California organization consists of 75 members, of whom six are white and two are Mexican. Those named, besides Powell, are: Gwendolyn Morton, Bridget Walton, Latinia Myatt, Marie Dickerson, Ann Jefferson, Willie Mae Sims, and Zola Benjamin.

1495. "Career Women 1976." *Essence* 6:11 (March 1976): 40. Leona Norman is an air traffic controller at Raleigh, North Carolina.

1496. "Celesta J. Wiley." *Jet* (February 17, 1977): 26. Wiley is the manager of material administration for the Aerospace Shuttle Program of Rockwell International Corporation. She is the highest ranking black woman in the California company.

1497. "Chicago Crows Air-Minded - Women Join Men in Learning Flying." (May). [This is an ANP (Associated Negro Press) release, dateline May 14. Claude A. Barnett Papers, Chicago Historical Society]. Aviation is attracting the attention of more and more of Chicago's colored people.

1498. "Chopper Cop." *Ebony* (October 1980): 44-46. Ann Scott of Washington, D.C.'s Metropolitan Police Department, is the first black woman to fly as an observer in a helicopter, but her ambition is to be a pilot.

1499. "Civilian Pilot Training under the C.A.A. at West Virginia State." *Opportunity* 19:7 (July 1941): 218. The number of civilian pilot trainees enrolled here will reach 80. This flight unit was organized in 1939 with Prof. James Evans as the head, the first in a Negro college. Other firsts at this unit include Rose Agnes Rolls, the first Negro girl to fly under the C.A.A. and Mary L. Parker, the first colored girl to solo in a seaplane. A photo shows John Frazier, William Edwards, Mary Parker, Melvin Bentley, George Oliver, and Lindsey Gore.

1500. Collins, Lisa. "Is Hollywood Really Spoiling Lynne Moody?" *Black Stars* 6:7 (May 1977): 60-65. Lynne Gatlin Moody was a stewardess for Northwestern Airlines before she became an actress.

1501. Cox, Dan. "Flying into New York with Dianne McIntyre Dance." *Dancemagazine* (June 1984). "Take-Off from a Forced Landing" will premiere in New York on June 19, 1984. It is based on the experiences of her mother Dorothy Layne McIntyre, a pilot. The dance "incorporates dance, drama, and more of a narrative line than McIntyre has ever used before." She said she used flying as a metaphor for individuals trying to reach their dreams.

1502. Crump, Robert A. "Girl Aviator to Fly From Detroit to Joe Louis Camp." (June 11, 1938). [ANP press release, Claude A. Barnett Papers, Chicago Historical Society]. Dorothy Darby, "the only Negro woman aviatrix in the country with a pilot's license," will fly to Louis' camp in Pompton Lakes, where he is preparing to fight Max Schmelling in New York on June 22. Darby is carrying more than 50, 000 signatures wishing victory. Darby parachuted over his camp in 1935,and this flight will give her the chance to fly solo across several states.

1503. DeWitt, Karen. "Black Women in Business." *Black Enterprise* 5:1 (August 1974): 18. Winifred E. Gittens is an employment representative for American Airlines.

1504. "Disability Washes Out Negro as Air Hostess." *New York Post* (July 1, 1958). Margaret Grant has a rare disability. It is not infectious, but would be aggravated by flight duty. With her departure and that of Ruth Carol Taylor, who married last week, Perry H. Young is the only Negro now flying in commercial aviation.

1505. "Dr. Irene Long: A Pioneer in Aerospace Medicine." *Ebony* (September 1984): 61-62, 64. A lifetime dream of mixing medicine and aviation has come true for the chief of biomedical research at the Kennedy Space Center.

1506. Drew, Carol. "People & Places." *New York Voice* (March 1985). [After March 6, 1985]. Drew discusses the flight of Melva Jackman, a teacher, and Ruby Bostic, a social worker. They are the first black women to fly a single engine plane from New York to Trinidad. The flight started on February 10; both women were taught to fly by Joseph H. Haynes. All are members of Negro Airmen International. Biographical information about the women.

1507. Drew, Robin. "2nd Lt. Marcella A. Hayes, Army's First Black Female Aviator." *Eagle & Swan* 3:2 (May 1980): 34-35. Lt. Hayes describes her vigorous training and provides biographical information.

1508. Dunning, Jennifer. "Dance: Dianne McIntyre's Sounds in Motion." *New York Times* (June 20, 1984). Review of "Take-Off From a Forced Landing." Dunning calls it haunting, praises all aspects of the piece, and gives some biographical information on Dorothy L. McIntyre, the inspiration for the dance. "Its script is strong, created from Mrs. McIntyre's no-nonsense memories and crisp flight instructions."

1509. Dunning, Jennifer. "A Dance Troupe Takes Flig..t." *New York Times* (June 17, 1984): [Section 2, Arts and Leisure]. Background information on "Take-Off from a Forced Landing," a full-evening work by Dianne McIntyre. It tells the story of her mother, Dorothy Layne McIntyre, a black woman who learned to fly in 1939 and got her license in 1940. "And people didn't always believe us when we talked about our mother being a pilot."

1510. Dupree, Adolph. "Wings of the Wind: Kraig Kenney, Aircraft Pilot." *about ... time* 17:9 (September 1989): 14-17. [Cover story]. Kraig Kenney is a pilot for Xerox Corporation. There is much information on Xerox, as well as biographical information on Kenney, and technical information on his training and the planes he flies. His father Wilfred A. Kenney is an aerospace engineer. Another black pilot at Xerox is Rosemary Dean.

1511. Elder, Charles. "Flight Attendant to Pilot's Seat." *Washington Post* (March 9, 1989): 1, 11. Shirley Tyus became a flight attendant for United Airlines in 1971, now she is a pilot for the same airline. She is the first black woman pilot flying for United. Along the way she married and had three children. She credits her success to being single-minded and focussed on her goals.

1512. "Ethel Carter." *Essence* 7:11 (March 1977): 88-89. Ethel Carter, who works at the maintenance operations center for United Airlines, at San Francisco, discusses women working in a male environment.

1513. Evans, Linda N. "Air Force Neurologist: Dr. Venus Jones." *Black Collegian* 11 (April-May 1981): 99, 101-102. Dr. Venus Jones is chief of the neurological unit at Andrews AFB in Maryland, one of only a few such units in the Air Force.

1514. "Evelyn Washington." *Essence* (September 1983): 108. Washington has two jobs in Houston, Texas. She is an air traffic controller and an interior designer.

1515. "FAA Academy Section Chief." *Ebony* (May 1982): 7. Georgetta James is chief of the Methodology & Standards section of the Federal Aviation Administration Academy in Oklahoma city.

1516. "FAA Flight Manager." *Ebony* (June 1984): 7. Paulette Barnes is the only black woman to manage an air traffic station in the FAA's eight-state great lakes region. She is at Capitol City Airport in Lansing, Michigan.

1517. "Faculty Win NU Grants: Manning, Freydberg, Graham and Scott." *Afro-Chronicles: African-American Studies at Northeastern University* (Spring 1991): 21-22. Elizabeth Hadley Freydberg received a $5,000 grant from the Faculty Development Fund to conduct interviews with African-American women pioneers in aviation. The women are: Janet Harmon Bragg [see also "Waterford" in the index] in Arizona, Mary Oglesby in Indiana, and Ida Van Smith in New York.

1518. Farrar, G. W. "Military Women: First Black Female Navy Aviator, Brenda Robinson." *Black Collegian* 11 (April-May 1981): 94-95. Biographical information.

1519. "Fifteen Girls Get Air Course." *Atlantic World* (October 26, 1939). [ANP release, Claude A. Barnett Papers, Chicago Historical Society]. Ten percent of the places in the training program of the Civil Aeronautic

Authority will be for women of color. The reporter then refers to them as querulous, garrulous girls who will torment males. He also says they will be armed with parachutes and powderpuffs and will shriek.

1520. "First Black Woman Gets Military Aviator's Wings." *Columbus Enquirer* (November 27, 1979). Marcella A. Hayes.

1521. "First Black Woman Pilot Likes 'Exciting Challenge'." *Jet* 57: 15 (December 27, 1979): 47. Marcella A. Hayes was named last month the first black woman pilot in armed forces history. Lt. Hayes is a helicopter pilot at Ft. Rucker, Alabama.

1522. "First Negro Hired as Stewardess." *New York Times* (December 23, 1957). Ruth Carol Taylor, Mohawk Airlines.

1523. "First Negro Stewardess." *Sunday News (New York)* (May 4, 1958): 34-35. [Magazine section]. Article is largely composed of photos of Ruth Carol, here called Carol, Taylor.

1524. "Flight Attendants: Cashing in on Time Off." *Ebony* (July 1982): 60-62, 64, 66. Their on-the-ground moonlighting ranges from modeling to the ministry. Thirteen flight attendants and eight airlines are mentioned.

1525. Flowers, Sandra H. *Women in Aviation and Space*. Ozark, Alabama: Alabama Aviation & Technical College; U. Department of Transportation, Federal Aviation Administration, n.d. [The address of the college is P.O. Box 1209, Ozark, Al 36361-1209]. Full page of information on Mae C. Jemison, p.15 and on Ida Van Smith, p. 18. Brief information on Willa B. Brown, p.15.

1526. "Flying Sisters." *Ebony* 20 (November 1964): 81-82, 84-86. Sisters are stewardesses for Northwest Airlines. Eugenia Catlin won her wings in June 1963. She persuaded her sister Naomi to join in December 1963. Other Negro stewardesses with the line are Rosalyn Ingersol and Claudia Goodman.

1527. "Gail Benjamin and Vaughn Benjamin." *Staten Island Advance* (May 25, 1980). The Benjamins are the first brother and sister to be graduated from any of the country's service academies, in this case, the Air Force Academy. This class is the first to include women cadets.

1528. "Ghana's Control Tower Girl." *Ebony* (September 1967): 115-116, 118-119. Dinah Eva Kweiki Steiner is "probably the only girl in Africa to work in a control tower. ...Dinah's persistence helped her beat anti-female bias." Steiner works in Accra. Her German last name is the result of a disappearing custom where Africans took European names when they entered school.

1529. Gilbert, David. "$5,000 to Stewardess Fired for Afro Hairdo." *Chicago Tribune* (September 3, 1970): 18. United Air Lines also offered Deborah Renwick reinstatement in her old job with full seniority and benefits. Renwick refused. She was fired a year ago for not altering her hairdo.

1530. "Girl Flyer is Injured as She Leaps from Plane." *Chicago Defender* (October 15, 1932): 1. Dorothy Dorby [probably Darby] broke both ankles and suffered internal injuries after a bad parachute landing in an exhibition at Curtis Field in Chicago. Miss Darby is a native of Cleveland, Ohio.

1531. "Girl Operates Realty Office, Flies as a Hobby." [*New York Amsterdam News*?] (December 18, 1937). [Gumby Collection, Columbia University, Scrapbook 1]. Lola Jackson, a real estate operator in Jamaica, is the only Negro woman flier in the East. She is the only woman member of the National Flying Club, of which 25 of its 29 members are Negroes.

1532. "Going Down." *Headlines and Pictures* 2 (October 1945): 33. Rachael Babcock is first Negro girl to take a parachute training jump under Army Air Force auspices. She is 15 years old, trained by Lt. Earsley Taylor, a squadron commander of the Civilian Air Patrol in Detroit.

1533. "Grooming Consultant." *Ebony* (February 1973): 6. Jeanne-Marie Allen, a grooming consultant for Eastern Airlines at Kennedy Airport, instructs 1,000 flight attendants on personal appearance.

1534. "Guinea Airline Hostesses Train in Canada." *Ebony* (February 1963): 71-72, 74, 76. Guinea, independent for three years, has sent 20 young women to the Canada Air Career School in Toronto to train as stewardesses for Air Guinea. Only Dalanda Diallo is featured.

1535. Haynes, Eleanor. "Leslie-Graham Nuptials in Atlanta." *New York Voice* (March 25-31, 1993): 23. Jonathan Lyle Graham married Veronica Lee Leslie. He is a pilot for Delta Airlines, and was a captain in the Air

Force. They will live in Chicago. The bride's sister, Pamela, is a flight attendant for Delta.

1536. Heister, Mike. "Capt. Pamela Howard: An Air Force Midwife." *Eagle & Swan* 2:6 (December 1979): 39. Capt. Howard is stationed at Eglin AFB, Florida since June 1979. Capt. Howard, in the Air Force since 1974, is preparing to become a pilot.

1537. "Her Career Ended in Crash." *Journal & Guide (Norfolk, Va.)* (November 16, 1940): 15. Theodosia Fraser, a student pilot at Virginia State College, was killed in a crash at Hopewell Airport. It was her second solo flight in the flight course established by the Civilian Aviation Authority.

1538. "High Flying Hostess." *Ebony* (May 1960): 43-48. Airman Loretta Cecilia Johnson, Bronx born, is a member of the Women's Air Force and serves as an airline hostess for the Military Air Transport Service. Biographical information.

1539. Hine, Darlene Clark, ed. *Black Women in America: An Historical Encyclopedia*. Brooklyn, NY: Carlson Publishing Inc., 1993. [Two volumes. Associate editors are Elsa Barkley Brown and Rosalyn Terborg-Penn]. Janet Harmon Waterford Bragg by Elizabeth Hadley Freydberg (EHF), pp. 159-161; Willa Beatrice Brown by EHF, pp. 184-186; Bessie Coleman by EHF, pp. 262-263; Marcelite Jordan Harris by Linda Rochelle Lane, pp. 538-539; Mae C. Jemison by Christine A. Lunardini (CAL), pp. 633-635; Lattimer, Agnes D. by CAL, pp. 698-699; Mary Oglesby by EHF, pp. 901-902; Smith, Ida Van by EHF, pp. 1079-1080.

1540. Holden, Henry M. *Ladybirds: The Untold Story of Women Pilots in America*. Mt. Freedom, NJ: Black Hawk Publishing Co., 1991. [With Captain Lori Griffith]. Four black women are included: Bessie Coleman, pp.41-45; Willa B. Brown, p.45; Marcella A. Hayes, p.136; and Mae C. Jemison, pp.148-150.

1541. "Howard Grad Stewardess with Northwest Airline." *Jet* 25 (January 16, 1964): 18. Naomi Catlin of Wilmerding, PA, is assigned to Northwest Orient Airlines in Minneapolis-St. Paul. Catlin studied oral hygiene at Howard.

1542. "International Airport Flight Announcer." *Ebony* (December 1954): 5. Esther N. Harris is a flight announcer at Philadelphia International Airport. A member of the field's flying club for employees Mrs. Harris averages a flight a week.

1543. James, Curtia. "Essence Women: Theresa Deborah Newsome." *Essence* 12 (April 1982): 22-23. Newsome was a flight attendant for Delta Airlines, and is now an in-flight service coordinator. She holds five different flying licenses, the most treasured is one for certified flight instructor, achieved November 1981. Her hope is to become a commercial pilot, now a white, male domain.

1544. "Janet H. Bragg, Pioneer Black Aviatrix, Succumbs at Age 86." *Jet* (May 10, 1993): 36. Obituary reports Bragg's death in St. Francis Hospital in the Chicago suburb of Blue Island. No date or cause of death is given. Only one relative is mentioned, her cousin Frances Moore, widow of Dr. Fred Moore, who will keep her ashes.

1545. "Jealousy: How the Wives of Famous Men Handle it." *Ebony* (January 1979): 44. Tina Marie Graham is a former airline stewardess, now married to Larry Graham of Graham Central Station.

1546. Jeffries, Georgia Thomas. "Essence Women." *Essence* 5:12 (April 1975): 21. Maria Broom, head of WJZ-TV Public Defender Unit in Baltimore, had been a stewardess for Pan American Airways. She is also a dancer who has received a Fulbright scholarship.

1547. Jenkins, Walter. "Views and Comments on Kim Hamilton." *Black Stars* 4:5 (March 1975): 6-11. An actress in film, television, and theater, Hamilton is also a licensed pilot. She says piloting a plane is one of the most exciting things she's done.

1548. "Jill Brown May be First Black Woman Navy Pilot." *Jet* 47:5 (October 24, 1974): 19. Jill Brown has been sworn into a program which may result in her becoming the first black woman to be a military pilot. Biographical information.

1549. "A Job Well Done." *New York Amsterdam News* (May 17, 1958). Editorial about the hiring of Margaret Grant by Trans World Airlines.

1550. Johnson, Jesse J. *Black Women in the Armed Forces, 1942-1974: A Pictorial History*. Hampton, VA: Hampton Institute, 1974. [Chapter 3, "Black Women in the Air Force," pp.23-32]. Biographical sketches of Jeanne M. Holm, Billie Marie Bobbitt, Willa Brown (Mrs. J.H. Chappell), Rosetta A. Armour, Sylvia I. Parker, Bettye Whitehurst, and Terri Reynolds.

1551. Jones-Miller, Alice. "Essence Women." *Essence* (February 1981): 31-32. Carolyn Shelton, a flight attendant for Continental Air Lines, is also a career and self-improvement counselor for young black people, especially women. Since 1976 she has been teaching the art of self presentation, and she counts McDonald's among her clients. Biographical information.

1552. Jones-Miller, Alice. "Readers' Resolutions." *Essence* (January 1981): 30. Christine Knighton is a second lieutenant on her way to Germany to be a test pilot and participate in the maintenance of helicopters. She will be there for three years, and she wants to go as far as she can in aviation maintenance. She plans to be involved in the Tuskegee Airmen, Inc., as well as with other associations.

1553. Kleiner, Richard A. "Loving Mother and Air Force Member." *Eagle and Swan* 3:4 (September 1980): 32-34. Profiles two couples with children and a single parent who are in the Air Force, stationed at Vance AFB, Oklahoma. They are Pearl and Forrest Tucker, Linda F. and Sidney W. Rivers, and Gwendolyn Perkins. The Air Force provides prenatal and child care, maternity uniforms, and there is support from the base community.

1554. "Kool Kalani from Hawaii." *Sepia* (August 1979): 32-34. Pin-up pictures of Kalani Mickle, a former airline hostess, now a journalist and accountant.

1555. "Lady Plane Mechanic." *Ebony* 3 (January 1948): 28-31. Harlem mother is the only Negro in American Airlines shops. Louise Williams is an ex-school teacher, and she has invented an ignition harness gadget which has saved the company hundreds of dollars a year.

1556. "Legless Pilot." *Ebony* (May 1951): 43-44, 47-48. Neal V. Loving operates with C. Earsly [*sic*] Taylor the Wayne School of Aeronautics at Detroit City Airport. They have both been flying since 1939. Loving is the first amputee and the first black to belong to the Professional Racing Pilots Association. Other biographical information.

1557. "Life in Africa: A Study in Contrasts." *Ebony* (August 1976): 120. Elaine Keita quit an airline job and departed for Senegal, where she married Souleyman Keita, an artist.

1558. "Mail Service Director." *Ebony* (February 1970): 6. James L. Gibbs directs mail services for Mohawk Airlines, after having been a flight crew scheduler. He claims to have recommended the first black stewardess [Ruth Taylor] on a U.S. airline, whom Mohawk Airlines hired in 1958.

1559. Marsh, Antoinette. "Hollywood Black Secretaries Help Make the Stars Shine." *Black Stars* 5:9 (August 1976): 33. Arlene Jones, personal secretary to Sidney Poitier for twelve years, is a travel agent for United Airlines when Poitier is out of town.

1560. Martinez, Manny. "Ensign Brenda E. Robinson: Aviator, A Navy First." *Eagle & Swan* 3:5 (November 1980): 28-29. Robinson won her wings on June 6, 1980, one of 42 women to earn wings in the Navy. She had a private pilot's license before joining the Navy.

1561. "The Master Recruiter Is a Lady." *Eagle & Swan* 3:5 (November 1980): 32. Sgt. Christina Glasco, Willingboro, New Jersey, received the Master Recruiting Badge, the highest award. She is the only woman to receive this honor, outproducing fifty-five other recruiters. Her husband, not named in the article, is also a sergeant in the Air Force, at McGuire AFB. The previous issue, September, shows a photograph of Glasco, p. 52.

1562. Montgomery, Patricia. "Their Favorite Vacation Spots." *Black Enterprise* (April 1974): 24, 26-27, 29. Black airline pilots and stewardesses recommend trips on three continents.They are Judith Henriquez, William S. Todd, Geraldine Flowers, Fred Pitcher, Carolyn Todd, John Gordon, and Loreena Strickland.

1563. Moore, Marjorie Wyatt. "Essence Woman: Michele Freeman." *Essence* 3:3 (June 1972): 24. Biographical information on Michele Freeman, at American Airlines, who has been a stewardess, instructor, and writer/analyst.

1564. Morris, Rachel. "Essencewomen." *Essence* 7:12 (April 1977): 6. Profile of Jeannie Wilson, a flight attendant at American Airlines for the last eight years.

1565. Murray, Joan. *The News.* New York: McGraw-Hill, 1968. [pp.92-105]. Murray, the first accredited black woman television news correspondent (WCBS), describes how she learned to fly, which she did for a documentary she made in 1965. The following year she entered the 20th annual Women's Transcontinental Air Race (Powder Puff Derby), the first "woman of color" to do so.

1566. "Names in the News." *Black Enterprise* 6:2 (September 1975): 8. Sara Hurst Smith, a trainer of customer service personnel at Pan American Airlines from 1965-1973, now works for Con Edison.

1567. Narine, Dalton. "Have Plane, Will Travel." *Ebony* (December 1988): 118, 120, 122, 124. [Twenty people, with brief biographical information, are named]. Hundreds of blacks, in all walks of life, are flying their own aircraft for fun and profit. The Negro Airmen International has 550 members.

1568. "NASA P.R. Officer." *Ebony* (November 1984): 6. Weida Tucker Brewington is a public affairs officer at the Kennedy Space Center, who writes, edits, and broadcasts.

1569. "Navy Trains First Black Woman Pilot." *Jet* (November 28, 1974): 20-24. [Cover story]. Biographical information on Jill Brown, as well as information on Spann Watson, retired colonel of the Air Force.

1570. "A New Star in the TV Heavens." *Ebony* (January 1967): 70-72, 74, 76. Nichelle Nichols plays a spaceship crewman on *Star Trek*. She plays Lieut. Uhura, and according to present-day earth records, the first Negro astronaut, a triumph of modern-day television over modern-day NASA. It is the year 2166. Biographical information.

1571. "Nichelle Nichols and the Possible Dream." *Encore* (January 15, 1979): 23-24. [Cover Story]. Discusses Nichols' involvement with recruitment programs at NASA, and her firm, Women in Motion. Biographical information, including her forthcoming novel *The Uhura Connection*, to be published by Bantam.

1572. "Northern Black Women, Southern Black Women: How Different are They?" *Ebony* (January 1979): 116. Clarinda Gipson, a stewardess for United Airlines, comments.

1573. "Open Skies for Negro Girls." *Ebony* 18 (June 1963): 43-46, 48, 50. Describes the career of Veronica Gonzalez, born in Seattle, Washington. She works for United Airlines, now that "major airlines have begun to straighten up and fly right and welcome Negro applicants."

1574. Perry, Regenia A. *Free Within Ourselves: African-American Artists in the Collection of the National Museum of American Art*. Washington, D.C.: Smithsonian Institution, 1992. *Jesus is My Airplane* is the title of a painting by Sister Gertrude Morgan, a visionary artist. It is shown on pp. 142-143. A poem by the artist with the same title is on p. 145.

1575. "Queen Christina of the Nigerian Airways." *Sepia* 8 (November 1960): 48-50. Christina Tugele is the first Nigerian girl to represent the national airline as a stewardess on flights between London and West Africa. Biographical information on Tugele, who graduated with honors in 1958.

1576. "Race Girl Hostess on Air Line." *California Voice* (March 1, 1940). Fay Tull was one of thirty young women to serve as hostesses on American Air Lines. No colored person has previously been admitted. Tull is now a graduate student in Home Economics at Columbia University. She is a graduate of Lincoln University in Jefferson City, Mo.

1577. Randall, Alice. "Washington's Other Elite." *The Washingtonian* (May 1982). Stacey Mobley, a lawyer in charge of monitoring environmental legislation for DuPont, is a glider pilot.

1578. "Reaching New Heights." *Chicago Sun Times* (April 20, 1978). Photograph of Jill E. Brown, the first black woman pilot for a major U. S. airline, Texas International Airlines.

1579. "Rites Set For Bragg; Nurse, Pilot." *Chicago Defender* (April 15, 1993): 26. Obituary for Janet Harmon Bragg who died April 11, at the age of 86. Bragg was a pilot in the thirties in the Chicago area. She eventually owned three planes, and she continued flying during the seventies. Funeral services were held today at St. Edmund Episcopal Church, 6105 So. Michigan Ave. Biographical information.

1580. Robeson, Robert B. "3 Times a Lady." *Sepia* (July 1981): 20-22, 24. Biographical article on Carolyn Shelton, a flight attendant with Continental Air Lines since 1969, and who flies on routes to Asia. She has her own organization to raise the self esteem of young black girls and women. She has produced programs for television in Houston, and she has worked with the schools. Her husband, now dead, was James Shelton of the Air Force.

1581. Robinson, Nancy. "Black Wings Made to Fly." *Sepia* 30:6 (June 1981): 56-57. A brief history of blacks in aviation, giving statistics and mentioning well-known and lesser-known names. Some of the latter are Victor King of Chappara Airlines and Lottie Theodore.

1582. Schuyler, George [pseud. Samuel I. Brooks]. *Black Empire*. Boston: Northeastern University Press, 1991. [Edited,with an Afterword by Robert A. Hill & R. Kent Rasmussen]. Comprising two novellas from Schuyler's columns in the *Pittsburgh Courier* (1936-1938). *Black Empire* tells the story of black, wicked men and women conquering the world. Chapter 10, "Carl Slater Learns Patricia Givens is Head of Air Force" introduces this beautiful capable woman who tells him "Our airport and airplane factory in Westchester County has trained five hundred colored pilots, men and women, and manufactured one hundred pursuit planes and fifty bombing planes." Later Carl wonders, " Would she be interested in love - this beauty who superintended an aircraft factory, piloted planes across country and talked of conditioning the masses, world revolution and such things."

1583. Scott, Gil. "Evelyn Gibson's Flying Colors." *Eagle & Swan* 1:2 (March 1978): 38. A Senior Airman at McGuire AFB in New Jersey, Evelyn Gibson is a weather observer. She joined the Air Force three years ago.

1584. "Senior Airman Carla Nix-Taylor." *Eagle & Swan* 3:5 (November 1980): 44. Only nineteen, Carla Nix-Taylor has earned the following honors: Airman of the Month, Airman of the Quarter, and Outstanding Airman of the Quarter. She works in a non-traditional area, but the article does not explain further. She appears to be working on equipment in the accompanying photograph.

1585. "She Flies Through the Air." *Pittsburgh Courier* (July 13, 1940): 5. A photograph shows Leah Foster, one of Chicago's most ardent aviatrices.

She spends her spare time at Harlem Airport working on engines and flying. Some biographical information.

1586. "She's United with United." *Sepia* (December 1967): 39-43. Lynn Scott is one of fifty-eight Negro stewardesses employed by United Airlines. The first black stewardess was hired in 1963. The article is mainly about United's policies, training programs, and statistics on the employment of blacks. Scott is Canadian; other women mentioned are Sylvia Banks and Betty Patterson.

1587. "'Show Me State' Girl Shows the Way." *Ebony* (April 1980): 101-102, 104. Second Lt. Marcella Hayes became the first black woman pilot in the entire U.S. Armed Forces last November. Her instructor "wanted to find out whether a woman had any business in the cockpit." He "wasn't too sure a woman could handle being a pilot." Biographical information and statistics.

1588. Simmons, Rose. "Learning to Fly." *Essence* 23:4 (August 1992): 76, 78, 120, 122. [Winner of magazine's fiction contest]. A black woman, Cleo, is taught to fly by a white woman. She keeps the lessons secret from her husband. When he finds out he asks her to choose between him and learning to fly, because he wants her to stay at home to help with his new business.

1589. "Sisters-in-Arms: Marching into Their Brothers' Territory." *Ebony* (August 1982): 90-92. Women in the Air Force are: Willadean Brooks, Donna Hamilton, Rita Mahome, Brenda Robinson, and Cynthia Shelton.

1590. *Sixty and Counting: The 60th Anniversary Commemorative Collection.* Oklahoma City: The Ninety-Nines, Inc., 1989. The Ninety-Nines are a group of women pilots who organized at Curtiss Field in Valley Stream, New York in 1929. Ida Van Smith, a member since 1977, appears to be the only African American pictured.

1591. Smith, Daniel L. "Brenda Newberry: Competition Serves to Help Us Grow and Develop." *Eagle & Swan* 1:4 (1978): 50-51. Staff Sgt. Brenda Newberry was selected as one of the twelve Outstanding Airmen of 1978. Her husband Maurice is also a staff sergeant. Biographical information about this couple who joined the Air Force in Chicago and have served in Spain.

1592. Smith, Elizabeth Simpson. *Breakthrough: Women in Aviation*. New York: Walker and Company, 1981. Of the nine chapters, one is devoted to Jill Elaine Brown, cargo pilot, pp. 38-51. Her unpleasant time in the Navy is discussed, as well as other jobs, both successful and unsuccessful. She worked for Wheeler Airlines, and she now works for Zantop International Airlines, the world's largest commercial all-cargo carrier.

1593. Smith, Ida Van. *Fly With Me Coloring Book (A True Story)*. Rochdale Village, NY: Keith Publishers, Inc., 1988. A young girl is taken by her father to an airport to see stunts, and she decides to become a pilot herself. The young girl is the author.

1594. Smith, Jessie Carney. *Notable Black American Women*. Detroit, MI: Gale Research Inc., 1992. Bessie Coleman by Penelope Bullock, pp. 202-203; Marcelite J. Harris by Jessie Carney Smith (JCS), pp. 467-468; Mae C. Jemison by JCS, p.571-573; Joan Murray by Dhyana Ziegler, pp. 782-783.

1595. "Space Center Engineer." *Ebony* (January 1974): 6. Linda G. Mobley is the first woman to ever "power up" the spacecraft launching apparatus. Mobley is operations engineer for Chrysler Corporation Space Division at Cape Canaveral, FL.

1596. Speedy, Nettie George. "Sepia Air Pilots Thrill World's Fair Visitors." *Pittsburgh Courier* (July 22, 1933): 3. [Second section]. At the Century of Progress Exhibition in Chicago, students and instructors of the Aeronautical University built planes and gave flying exhibitions. Members of the Challenger Air Pilots Association use an airport they had to build themselves at the all-Negro town of Robbins, Illinois. Biographical information on Janet Harmon Waterford, Doris Murphy Tanner, Ellen Gray, Dorothy Weaver, Grover C. Nash, Dale L. White, John C. Robinson, Harold Hurd, and A.B. Porter.

1597. Stein, Ruthe. "Lifestyle: Dr. Shirley Ann Hoskins - Scholar and Adventuress." *Ebony* (March 1982): 67-68, 70, 72, 74. Dr. Hoskins is a mountain climber, skier, pilot, scientist, and dean. She rents and flies a plane at San Carlos, California.

1598. "Stewardess Hired by TWA after Delta Fired Her." *Jet* (March 19, 1970): 26. Delta fired Carolyn Todd because she would not resign when she and two roommates were asked to, when miniature Delta liquor bottles were found in their room. Trans World Airlines then hired her, believing in her innocence.

1599. Tapley, Mel. "Choreographer Dianne McIntyre Has 'Flying' in Her Blood." *New York Amsterdam News* (June 30, 1984). Biographical material about Dianne McIntyre and her pilot mother, Dorothy L. McIntyre. Mrs. McIntyre remarks, "People who have always been on the ground would be surprised at what they don't know."

1600. Taub, Eric. "Footnotes." *Ballet News* 6:1 (July 1984). Biographical information on Dianne McIntyre, who created a dance, "Take-Off From a Forced Landing," based on the life of her mother, Dorothy Layne McIntyre. "I portray my mother. I show her dream of flying. I see parallels between us. My dancing is my way of flying - it grew out of her flying."

1601. Taylor, Len. "Traveling Bag: High-Flying Girls." *Essence* 1:10 (February 1971): 14. Profiles of Lorane Vaughn and Donna Wright, stewardesses for Pan American Airlines.

1602. "Then... ...and Now." *99 News* 9:10 (December 1982). Cover features a photograph of the Long Island Chapter members recreating the photograph of the charter meeting in 1929. The Ninety-Nines is an organization of women pilots. Two black women are on the cover: Ruby Bostic and Ida Van Smith.

1603. "They Build New Plants." *Ebony* (September 1950): 18. Mamie B. Johnson, a mathematician, does restricted work on airplane flight research for Cornell Aeronautical Laboratory in Buffalo, New York.

1604. "They Welcomed Col. Robinson." *Chicago Defender* (May 30, 1936): 7. Photograph of five women members of the Challenger Air Pilots Association, in aviation dress and carrying flowers: Doris K. Murphy, Janet Waterford, Billie Renfroe, Willa B. Brown, amd Mrs. James.

1605. "TWA Hires First Negro Air Hostess." *Ebony* (July 1959): 37-38, 40. [Cover Story]. Mary E. Tiller has become the first Negro to represent a major airline as a hostess.

1606. Washington, Iris L. "Women in the Armed Forces." *Essence* 9:12 (April 1979): 26. Deirdre Gill is one of four women profiled, the only one in the Air Force. She was trained as air operations/systems management specialist, but stayed only one year. She wanted to be trained in other specialties, and she didn't like dormitory life or the food. But she may re-enlist.

1607. Waterford, Janet. "First Race Airport was Destroyed in a Big Storm." *Chicago Defender* (May 2, 1936): 12. Waterford, herself a pilot, descibes the destruction of Robbins Airport and planes during a freak winter storm. Mentions Johnny [Robinson], Grover Nash, and [Cornelius] Coffey.

1608. "When is a "99" a "49 1/2 ?" When He's a Male!" *Civil Rights Review* 2:6 (January 1980): 23. Biographical information on Rufus A. Hunt, the first black man to participate in the Illi-Nines Air Derby. This is the Illinois chapter of the 99s, a women's aviation organization founded by Amelia Earhart. Hunt was the co-pilot for Michelle Burgen in the 1979 race. In 1978, her co-pilot was Yvonne Warren. They were the first black women to fly in the derby.

1609. Whitaker, Charles. "Cook County's Top Doctor." *Ebony* (September 1986): 44, 46, 48. Dr. Agnes Lattimer, a pediatrician, is the director of the Cook County Hospital, Chicago. She is also a pilot.

1610. "Who's Who." *Playbill* (June 1984): [19-20]. [Joyce Theater (N.Y.) edition]. A lengthy biographical article on Dorothy Arline Layne McIntyre, a pilot who obtained her private pilot's license on February 23, 1940, at West Virginia State College. The occasion is the New York premiere of "Take-Off From a Forced Landing," a dance choreographed and danced by Dianne McIntyre and her company, Sounds in Motion. There is other information about mother and daughter, the company, and aviation throughout the magazine.

1611. "Winging It at 25,000 Feet." *Ebony* (August 1978): 58-60, 62. Jill Brown, former teacher of home economics in Anne Arundel County, Maryland, becomes the first black woman pilot to fly for a major U.S. commercial airline, Texas International Airlines.

1612. Witherspoon, Roger. "Wings: America's Black Flying Clubs." *Black Enterprise* 13 (March 1983): 75, 77. A report on the growing number of black men and women who are flying for fun and profit. The groups mentioned are Atlanta Negro Airmen Flying Corporation, Ravens Flying

Club (New Jersey), and Negro Airmen International. Some flyers are: Pat Key, Bravelle Nesbitt, Yolanda Booker, Ruby Bostic, and Gilbert Cargill.

1613. "Woman Navigator Spans the Globe for U.S. Air Force." *Ebony* (December 1978): 85-86, 90, 92. Capt. Betty Payne is the first black woman to guide huge C-141 aircraft on world-wide missions. She is stationed at Travis AFB, California.

1614. "Woman Pilot to Teach Class in Aircraft." *Baltimore Afro-American* (1942-43). [I was unable to locate this article for date and pagination]. Mrs. Dorothy L. McIntyre, one of the first colored women to receive a pilot's license, will teach a class in aircraft at War Production Training School No. 453, 775 Waesche Street. The course will cover aircraft structure, rigging, engines, theory of flight, and regulations. The course is free and is calculated to interest women who want to work in the aircraft industry now and after the war. Mrs. McIntyre is a secretary in the industrial department of the Baltimore Urban League.

1615. Young, A. S. (Doc). "She's 'Mother' to Ethiopians." *[Chicago Defender]* (n.d.). [Young was a syndicated columnist whose work appeared in the *Chicago Defender*. Bragg moved to Arizona in 1972, so this article is earlier]. A biographical article about Janet Waterford Bragg, who maintains warm relations with Ethiopian students who come to the United States. She began helping students at the request of her former instructor, John C. Robinson, who later fought for Ethiopia. When Emperor Haile Selassie visted the United States in 1954 he presented Bragg with a medal.

List of Pilots

Adams, Paul
Allen, Clarence
Allen, George
Allen, Thomas C.
Anderson, C. Alfred
Anderson, John C.
Anderson, Lawrence E.
Anderson, Paul T.
Archer, Lee A.
Armstead, Joseph E.
Ashby, Robert
Ashe, Charles
Ashley, Willie

Bailey, Charles P.
Bailey, George
Bailey, James
Bailey, S. David
Baker, Ann
Baker, Bill
Baker, Cecil
Banning, J. Herman
Barbour, George E.
Barnes, Art
Barnes, Augustus L.
Barnett, William
Barrow, Errol W.
Barton, Don
Baugh, Howard L.
Bennett, J. Bruce

Bentley, Melvin
Biffle, Richard
Black, Pickens
Bluford, Guion S.
Bolden, Charles F.
Bolling, George R.
Bonner, Michael
Booker, Yolanda
Bostic, Ruby L.
Bragg, Janet H.
Brame, Jim
Branch, Walt
Briggs, Eugene
Briggs, John
Broadwater, William F.
Brooks, Sidney P.
Brothers, James E.
Brown, Charles
Brown, Charles D.
Brown, Charles L.
Brown, Drew T.
Brown, Harry
Brown, Jesse L.
Brown, Jill E.
Brown, Luther J.
Brown, Phillip
Brown, Raymond
Brown, Roscoe C.
Brown, Theodore E.
Brown, W. L.

Brown, Willa B.
Brown, William E.
Browne, Ernest
Bruce, Samuel L.
Bryant, Joseph
Buckner, William A.
Bulkley, Alfred H.
Bullard, Eugene J.
Bumpus, William M.
Burgen, Michelle
Burke, Vernon W.
Burns, Rusty

Cable, Theodore
Campbell, Frank
Campbell, Franklyn D.
Campbell, William
Carey, Carl E.
Cargill, Gilbert A.
Carroll, Julius
Carroll, Lawrence W.
Carter, Earl L.
Carter, Herbert
Carter, J.Y.
Carter, Rachel
Cates, Solomon H.
Celestin, Phillippe
Chambers, Charlie
Chandler, Marvin
Charles, Norris A.

Green, Marlon D.
Greene, John W.
Gregory, Frederick D.

Hadden, Eddie R.
Hall, Charles B.
Hamilton, Kim
Hanson, Jesse M.
Harmon, Janet
Harp, Solomon
Harris, David E.
Harris, Greg
Harrison, Alvin E.
Harrison, Jim
Hart, Christopher A.
Harvey, James F.
Hathcock, Lloyd
Hawkins, 'Ace'
Hayes, Harold C.
Hayes, Marcella A.
Haygood, Juan C.
Haynes, Joseph H.
Haynes, Lloyd
Haywood, W.
Heath, Percy
Henderson, Bill
Henderson, Eugene R.
Hennagan, Thomas L.
Henriquez, Joseph S.
Henry, Connie
Hester, Andrew
Hill, Charles
Hill, Charles A.
Hobson, Julius W.
Holsclaw, Jack D.
Hoskins, Shirley A.
Howard, Joseph
Hueston, Cecil
Hunt, Rufus A.
Hurd, Harold

Hutcherson, Fred
Hutchins, Fred E.
Hutchison, Fred

Isabelle, Leonard W.

Jackman, Melva
Jackson, Abram P.
Jackson, Leonard M.
Jackson, Lewis A.
Jackson, Lola
Jackson, Raymond L.
Jackson, Raymond
James, Charles E.
James, Daniel III
James, Daniel
Jamison, Clarence C.
Jefferson, Alexander
Jefferson, Howard
Jennings, Richard
Johnson, Carl
Johnson, Charles
Johnson, Conrad A.
Johnson, Hayden C.
Johnson, James
Johnson, Joey
Johnson, L. E.
Johnson, Leonard W.
Johnson, William
Jones, Johnny L.
Jones, Lola
Jones, M. Perry
Jones, Reginald
Julian, Hubert F.

Kennedy, Elmore M.
Kenney, Kraig H.
Key, Pat
Keys, Leonard F.
Knighten, James B.

Knighton, Christine
Knox, George L.

Lambert, Alexander
Lattimer, Agnes D.
Lawrence, Edwin B.
Lawrence, Robert H.
Lawson, Herman A.
Layne, Dorothy A.
Lee, Frank
Lee, Philip F.
Lester, Clarence D.
Levister, Wendell W.
Levy, James E.
Lewis, Roosevelt
Long, James
Lopez, Henry
Loving, Neal V.
Lynch, Lewis

Macon, Richard
Mann, Frank
Manswell, W. Anthony
Marchbanks, Vance H.
Mareno, W.C.
Martin, George H. O.
Mauney, Cornell A.
Maxwell, Robert L.
McClenick, William
McClurkin, Fred E.
McCoy, Leslie J.
McCreary, Walter
McCullin, James L.
McDaniel, Armour G.
McDaniel, Norman
McDaniel, R. C.
McDonald, Harvey
McEnheimer, I.L.
McGee, Charles
McIntyre, Dorothy L.

Strong, Hector
Sullins, Palmer
Sutton, Percy
Swanigan, Lovell
Sylvain, August
Syphax, William T.

Tanner, Doris M.
Tate, Ralph M.
Taylor, Earsley
Taylor, George
Taylor, Larry C.
Terry, Roger C.
Terry, Wladimir
Theodore, Lottie
Thomas, Benjamin
Thomas, Harold
Thompson, Paul D.
Thompson, William O.
Thompson, William R.
Tilmon, James A.
Todd, William S.
Toppins, Edward

Tresville, Robert B.
Turner, Allen H.
Tyus, Shirley

Walker, Leo
Walker, Robert
Ward, Alonzo S.
Ware, Joyce C.
Warren, John
Warren, Yvonne
Warrender, Albert
Waterford, Clark
Waterford, Herman L.
Waterford, Janet H.
Waters, Carroll M.
Watkins, Charles
Watson, Spann
Weaver, Dorothy
Wells, Irvin E.
Wheeler, Warren
White, Charles
White, Dale L.
White, Eugene

White, Jepheth
White, Sherman W.
Whitehead, John L.
Wiley, James T.
Wilks, Robert C.
Williams, Archie
Williams, Charles T.
Williams, Lewis R.
Williams, Louis A.
Williams, Paul E.
Williams, Roderick C.
Williams, William F.
Wilson, Bertram
Wilson, Edward
Witts, Thomas
Woods, Jim
Wright, Linwood C.

Young, Coleman
Young, Otis B.
Young, Perry H.

Index

About the Compiler

BETTY KAPLAN GUBERT was head of the General Research and Reference Division of the Schomburg Center for Research in Black Culture, New York Public Library, for twenty-one years, and retired in 1991. She is the editor of *Early Black Bibliographies, 1863-1918* (1982) and of numerous articles in the field of black studies. She is currently the art editor of *MultiCultural Review* and consults on various publishing projects.